REA

3·7·80

CHAUCER AND OVID

The two poets whose affinity this book explores shared a skeptical view of human understanding that they expressed most clearly in their subversion of Dante and Vergil. Both Chaucer and Ovid turn repeatedly to a basic epistemological problem: the extent to which the artist, or indeed any human being, is capable of setting up structures of perception and understanding that are true or at least sufficiently trustworthy to permit effective action in the world.

Each poet answers this problem by leaving it unresolved. Their works are full of juxtapositions and oppositions. We repeatedly find thesis and antithesis, with no synthesis. We encounter elaborate systems that collapse as soon as they are built, playing off order against energy, stasis against flux. We come to expect palinodes; the conflicting and unresolved claims of authorities, and of authority and experience; and, as a basic metonymy of the human condition, the uncertain results and paradoxical nature of love. The effect of this irresolution is to revise our understanding of the fallible narrators whom Chaucer and Ovid use. We do not, finally, stand with the poet in ironic superiority to his narrator. Rather, we come to see that his infirmity and failures of understanding are our own.

After an introductory discussion of Ovid's elegiac poems and his influence on later medieval poetry, John Fyler offers in this book new readings of Chaucer's major works, from an Ovidian perspective, with special emphasis on the dream visions—the *Book of the Duchess*, the *House of Fame*, and the *Legend of Good Women*.

CHAUCER
AND OVID

JOHN M. FYLER

NEW HAVEN AND LONDON
YALE UNIVERSITY PRESS
1979

Designed by Sally Harris
and set in IBM Press Roman type.
Printed in the United States of America by
Vail Ballou Press, Binghamton, N.Y.

Published in Great Britain, Europe, Africa, and Asia (except Japan) by Yale
University Press, Ltd., London. Distributed in Australia and New Zealand by
Book & Film Services, Artarmon, N.S.W., Australia; and in Japan by Harper
& Row, Publishers, Tokyo Office.

Library of Congress Cataloging in Publication Data
Fyler, John M
  Chaucer and Ovid.
  Bibliography: p.
  Includes index.
  1. Chaucer, Geoffrey, d. 1400–Sources. 2. Chaucer, Geoffrey, d. 1400–
Criticism and interpretation. 3. Ovidius Naso, Publius–Influence–Chaucer.
I. Title.
PR1912.093F9   821'.1   78-10369
ISBN 0-300-02280-8

For my parents

CONTENTS

ACKNOWLEDGMENTS

I owe thanks to a great many people, of whom several groups ought especially to be singled out. I have been lucky in my teachers: William R. Crawford, W. R. Johnson, Richard A. Lanham; and, above all, Phillip Damon and Charles Muscatine, the director of my dissertation. I have been equally lucky in my students at Tufts University: they have helped me to clarify my ideas. I also owe a lot to several friends, for a great many conversations over the years and for occasional, timely editorial advice: Fredric V. Bogel, William C. Dowling, Julia A. Genster, Florence V. Goldstine, and H. Marshall Leicester, Jr. I am grateful to Robert W. Hanning and John Leyerle, for their useful comments on earlier versions of the manuscript; and I have benefited from the expertise of my editors, Ellen Graham and Jean Toll. The most immediate debt I have, and it is a substantial one, is to the American Council of Learned Societies, for a fellowship that gave me the time to finish this book; I am also grateful to the National Endowment for the Humanities, for the earlier help of a summer stipend.

Parts of two chapters have been published previously, in *Classical Journal* 66 (1971), 196-203, and in *Speculum* 52 (1977), 314-28; and they appear in their present form with the kind permission of the editors of those journals. I read part of the chapter on the *Legend of Good Women* to a seminar at the 1973 convention of the American Philological Association; and I am grateful to Mary-Kay Gamel Orlandi for the opportunity to have done so.

For the sake of simplicity and clarity, I have tried to keep annotation to a severe minimum, acknowledging only my most obvious, pressing, and recent debts to the work of other critics. By so doing, I may have risked slighting some even deeper obligations—including several that go back to my first readings of Chaucer—to critics who have provided the very terms from which all recent Chaucerian criticism develops. To redress a possible imbalance, I have appended a list of the works that have most influenced, stimulated, or—occasionally—provoked me in the long preparation for writing this book.

I have used Robert K. Root's edition of *Troilus and Criseyde* (1926; rpt. Princeton: Princeton University Press, 1952). Quotations from the rest of Chaucer come from F. N. Robinson's edition of the *Works* (2d ed., Boston: Houghton Mifflin, 1957).

1

OVID AND CHAUCER

Is there any certainty in human sight and hearing, or is it
true, as the poets are always dinning into our ears, that
we neither hear nor see anything accurately?
                                          Plato, *Phaedo*

A way of seeing is also a way of not seeing.
           Kenneth Burke, *Permanence and Change*

The affinity of Ovid and Chaucer has long been recognized. In John
Dryden's words, "both of them were well-bred, well-natured,
amorous, and libertine, at least in their writings, it may be also in
their lives."[1] Their similarities derive in part from the fact that
Chaucer, like most later medieval and Renaissance poets, owes more
to Ovid than to any other classical author. It is, indeed, hard to over-
estimate Ovid's importance to later writers as a source of material.
The *Metamorphoses* offers a particularly handy collection of stories
and the most wide-ranging if not most systematic compendium of
information about the gods and heroes. Its central concern, the
pathos and comedy of love, is the avowed topic of the elegiac
poems. Through them Ovid becomes the Freud of the Middle Ages:
the *Ars Amatoria, Remedia Amoris, Amores,* and *Heroides* provide
the most elaborate and memorable terminology for describing the
uncertain stability of the lover's mind.

Nonetheless, as Dryden's choice of adjectives suggests, the relation
of Ovid and Chaucer is not simply that of source and legatee; and
Dryden is not the only critic to have noticed the remarkable sympa-

1

thy between them. One measure of their sympathy, in fact, has been
the sort of critical response their works have often provoked. Not so
long ago, it was fashionable to weigh Ovid and Chaucer to the
measure of Vergil and Dante, and to find them wanting—usually because of frivolity or, in Matthew Arnold's words, a lack of that "high
and excellent seriousness, which Aristotle assigns as one of the grand
virtues of poetry."[2] It would be hard nowadays to find a critic of
English literature who would deny seriousness to Chaucer; and
Ovid's reputation, though still in the shadow of Vergil's, has risen a
great deal in the past ten or twenty years. Yet the comparison with
Vergil and Dante is even now, for different reasons, a useful one; it
lucidly defines opposing poetic stances. In fact, Ovid and Chaucer
invite the contest, not only by historical proximity to their com-
petitors, but by their own insistence on alluding to and counter-
pointing the *Aeneid* and the *Commedia*. Chaucer's use of Dante is of
central importance in the *House of Fame*. The Ovidian response to
Vergil will serve here as a prelude to some more general comments
about Ovid's legacy and his relationship to one of his most dis-
tinguished heirs.

I

In *Aeneid* VI the Cumaean Sibyl warns the hero of the arduous
ascent back from the land of the dead: "hoc opus, hic labor est"
[this is the labor, this the task].[3] Ovid steals the phrase to describe
an equally difficult task—seducing a woman without spending
money on her (*Ars* I.453).[4] The imagery and vocabulary of the
Georgics, those great expositions of Roman piety toward agriculture,
reappear in Ovid's didactic poems; but pastoral pursuits take on
comic, bawdy connotations in an urban and worldly context.[5] The
epic heroism of Aeneas's pious band sinks to bathos in the last four
books of the *Metamorphoses.* Even the language of epic debases itself
in the doddering hexameters of brutal old Nestor, who remembers the
carnage at Hippodamia's wedding by the mnemonic thumpety-
thump of poetry:

Quinque neci Caeneus dederat Styphelumque Bromumque
Antimachumque Elymumque securiferumque Pyracmon:
vulnera non memini, numerum nomenque notavi.
[XII.459-61]

[Caeneus had handed over five men to death: Styphelus and
Bromus and Antimachus and Elymus and axe-bearing Pyracmos.
I don't remember their wounds, but I marked down name and
number.]

Dido loses out to the milder Lavinia in Vergil's epic; Ovid gives the
heroine a chance to present her side of things in *Heroides* VII, and
she shows Aeneas up for the sneak and gadabout that he is.

As these opposites suggest, Ovid chooses Vergil as an exemplar of
the classical ideal, and uses him to subvert and parody its blueprint
of human life. By exposing the limitations of genre as an ordering
principle, his attack goes to the heart of classicism. Horace's *Ars
Poetica,* for example, gives "normative value" to genre and "its
companion principle decorum."[6] There may be some question
"whether the notion of *decorum* entertained by him refers to something intrinsic to the nature of things or to something established by
human convention."[7] But as often as not, the classicist argues that
nature as well as art comprises a stable hierarchy of categories. Indeed, the vehement defenses even of literary stability may be at-
tributed to a threatened world view: in a classical universe, mixed
genres mean chaos, not simply the abuse of conventional proprieties.
For Alexander Pope, lapses of decorum are "anti-natural" and
promise only the unwelcome "complete body of modern *Ethics and
Morality.*"[8]

Such an attitude toward genre and decorum appears in the peculiarly Augustan blend of utopian wish-fulfillment and propaganda.
The *Aeneid* incorporates the tenets of the classical poetic hierarchy,
in which epic has preeminence, elegy a subsidiary position. Public
responsibilities outweigh private passions, the epic hero's exploits
count for more than the lover's. As Brooks Otis has argued, the irrational *furor* of Dido, Juno, and Carthage succumbs to the higher
claims of Aeneas's *pietas* and the rational order of Jupiter and

Rome.[9] The tone of Vergil's epic is more complex than this simple scheme might suggest; and Ovid chooses for his own purposes to misrepresent Vergil's message. Aeneas's victory is not an easy one, and its achievement necessitates *labor* and tragic human suffering.[10] Nonetheless, the *Aeneid* does herald the Golden Age of the fourth *Eclogue*, the final triumph of reason and order over the disruptive tendencies in man's nature.[11] Vergil's moral vision, reviving a serious treatment of the gods and appealing to the myth of noble Roman primitivism, poetically approaches that triumph and suggests— beyond mere flattery—that under Augustus's guidance it can occur in reality.

The *Metamorphòses* is best understood in this Vergilian context. Its hexameters give Ovid's poem at least the pretense of being an epic; but in every other respect it opposes, and often parodies, the *Aeneid*. Ovid's theme is not the establishment of rational order, but continuing causeless flux. No teleological scheme patterns the changes described in the poem. The gods are Hellenistic jokes, not the cosmic forces of the *Aeneid;* their motives for causing metamorphoses are almost always comic or petty.[12] And it is impossible to take seriously the last three books, fustian dressed up as solemn Roman history.[13] Ovid's hilarious description of Caesar's apotheosis (XV.745-851) cannot be confused with Vergil's vision of a new Golden Age. Recent criticism has made much of Ovid's introductory description of the poem as a *carmen perpetuum* (I.4), which is to "go from the world's origin to his own times without a break."[14] Yet chronological progression by itself offers only the barest of structures. In fact, Ovid's emphasis of avoided anachronisms is usually disingenuous. "Nondum laurus erat, longoque decentia crine / tempora cingebat de qualibet arbore Phoebus" (I.450-51) [there was not yet a laurel tree, and Phoebus made a wreath for his temples, comely with long hair, from any tree around], he informs us; the next line begins the story of Daphne's timely metamorphosis.

The *Metamorphoses* is a fifteen-book exercise in mixed genre. Ovid typically portrays a character belatedly trying to adapt to the demands of his new external form. Io's half-comic plight (I.635-38) is typical:

> illa etiam supplex Argo cum bracchia vellet
> tendere, non habuit, quae bracchia tenderet Argo,
> et conata queri mugitus edidit ore
> pertimuitque sonos propriaque exterrita voce est.

[and when as a suppliant she wanted to stretch out her arms to Argus, she did not have arms which she could stretch out to Argus. Mooing proclaimed her efforts to bemoan; she panicked at the sounds, and was terrified by her own voice.]

Human beings are always outwitted by time in the Pythagorean world of the poem, where formal structures inevitably collapse (XV.165-261). Unstable by nature, such a world makes decorum impossible. Change and decay rule without contest.

Formal structures fare as badly in Ovid's love poetry. The *Amores* opens with a disingenuous apology to decorum:

> arma graui numero uiolentaque bella parabam
> edere, materia conueniente modis.
> par erat inferior uersus; risisse Cupido
> dicitur atque unum surripuisse pedem.
>
> [I.i.1-4]

[I was getting ready to proclaim wars and violent struggles in a dignified meter, with subject-matter befitting the measure. The second line was equal; Cupid is said to have laughed and stolen away a foot.]

These lines imply that Ovid's poetry is of necessity trivial. The limitations imposed by the hierarchy of genres make elegy unsuitable for serious subjects: "quid volui demens elegis imponere tantum / ponderis? heroi res erat ista pedis" (*Fasti* II.125-26) [why did I, senseless, want to put so great a burden on elegiac verses? That was a theme for the epic measure]. And the asymmetrical lines of the elegiac couplet suggest a comically hobbled genre. Elegy personified has one foot longer than the other (*Amores* III.i.8), and Thalia rides a lopsided chariot (*Ars* I.264-65). Indeed, it is likely that the epigraph to the *Amores*, which notes a change from five *libelli* to three, is more than a foreword to a revised edition; it announces a structural analogue to Ovid's self-proclaimed insufficiency.

Yet the opening lines of the *Amores* establish a serious thematic concern as well as an easy, self-deprecating apology. Ovid playfully maintains that an amorous version of the vatic madness has overwhelmed him. Cupid's control of subject and meter threatens poetic decorum: "quis tibi, saeue puer, dedit hoc in carmina iuris? / Pieridum uates, non tua, turba sumus" (I.i.5-6) [who gave you, cruel boy, this right over poetry? We bards are the Muses', not your crowd]. What would happen, Ovid complains (7-12), if the other gods were to reverse their roles? Apollo would have to learn to carry a spear, Mars a lyre (11-12). Universal disruption would replace rational order. And, in fact, the complaint has some justification. Cupid's breach of poetic decorum starts a consistent pattern of incongruity. The "arma . . . uiolentaque bella"—as if by a comic, unconscious resistance to Cupid's dictating power—soon impinge upon elegiac purity. Fresh captives and shouts of "io triumphe!" accompany the triumphal chariot of victorious Love (I.ii), a military hero worthy of Caesar, his distant cousin on Aeneas's side of the family (51), and of his stepfather Mars (24). In *Amores* I.ix the neoteric poets' juxtaposition of love and war has its fullest expression, in a comic point-by-point comparison. The analogy of the two becomes equality: the poem constructs an outrageous proof that love is a heroic activity.

The general strategy of Ovid's love poetry is to puncture the integrity of such generic categories by the use of ironic incongruity. This device, which pervades *Amores* I.ix, appears as zeugma in the most local of contexts. Ovid repeatedly combines incongruous objects in a coordinate series, invariably with an ironic result. "Et color et Theseus et uox" [color and Theseus and voice] desert Ariadne (*Ars* I.551). Decorum ("hoc decet"), "leges duxque pudorque iubent" [the laws and our ruler and modesty command] that "nupta uirum timeat, rata sit custodia nuptae" (*Ars* III.613-14) [the bride fear her husband, that the guarding of the bride be secured]; decorum and *pudor*, we infer, easily would be overcome were it not for the *dux* and his *leges*.[15] In the funniest example, Ovid's presentation of his lover's credentials, a list of comically incongruous gods and unexceptionable but rather banally stated virtues, ends with a bawdy ambiguity (*Amores* I.iii.11-14):

> at Phoebus comitesque nouem uitisque repertor
>   hac faciunt et me qui tibi donat Amor
> et nulli cessura fides, sine crimine mores,
>   nudaque simplicitas purpureusque pudor.[16]

[but Phoebus and his nine companions and the discoverer of the vine support me; and Love, he who gives me to you; and also fidelity that will yield to no one, morals without a fault, and naked simplicity and blushing modesty.]

Indecorous linkages are usual in Ovid's treatment of the gods and heroes. In Vergil's serious context the gods, if not understood literally, are to be considered the symbolic representation of benign and malevolent cosmic forces. So used, myth—like aetiologies, proverbs, and exempla from experience—appeals to authority and places the poet's specific interest in a larger, confirming framework of meaning. In other words, it subordinates the instance to its genre. Ovid, on the other hand, deprives the gods of their symbolic stature and the epic heroes of their grandeur.[17] They are treated with decorum only in his ironic apologies:

> Callimachi numeris non est dicendus Achilles;
>   Cydippe non est oris, Homere, tui.
> quis ferat Andromaches peragentem Thaida partes?
>   peccet, in Andromache Thaida quisquis agat.
> Thais in arte mea est: lasciuia libera nostra est;
>   nil mihi cum uitta; Thais in arte mea est.
>   [*Remedia* 381-86]

[Achilles is not to be spoken of in the meters of Callimachus; Cydippe is not for your voice, Homer. Who would bear Thais playing Andromache's part? Whoever would play Thais in the guise of Andromache would err. Thais belongs to my art; my wanton playfulness is unrestrained; I have nothing to do with the fillet; Thais belongs to my art.]

Ovid's procedure is to set up a generic category which can contain

mythical exemplum and magisterial advice only by making them
both trivial. The lover should endure rainy nights on his mistress's
hard doorstep because Apollo himself once herded Admetus's cattle:
"quod Phoebum decuit, quem non decet?" (Ars II.241) [if it was
seemly for Phoebus, for whom is it not seemly?]. If Hercules could
spin Omphale's wool, the lover should not be ashamed to be servile:
"i nunc et dubita ferre quod ille tulit" (Ars II.222) [go ahead, hesi-
tate to endure what he endured]. A healing ex-lover should burn old
letters: "Thestias absentem succendit stipite natum: / tu timide
flammae perfida uerba dabis?" (Remedia 721-22) [Althaea set fire
to her absent son by burning a log: will you only timidly give treacherous words to the flame?]. The authority for forgetting one love by
taking another is not Ovid himself (Remedia 465-66). Agamemnon
has set the proper example, by stealing Briseis from Achilles: "ergo
adsume nouas auctore Agamemnone flammas, / ut tuus in biuio
distineatur amor" (485-86) [therefore, take on new passions, with
Agamemnon as your precedent, and your love will be divided in two
directions].

   Having reduced heroic figures to the status of amorous exemplars,
Ovid can make fun of them for their crudeness and epic solemnity
(Ars III.517-24):

> odimus et maestas; Tecmessam diligat Aiax,
>   nos, hilarem populum, femina laeta capit.
> numquam ego te, Andromache, nec te, Tecmessa, rogarem,
>   ut mea de uobis altera amica foret;
> credere uix uideor, cum cogar credere partu,
>   uos ego cum uestris concubuisse uiris.
> scilicet Aiaci mulier maestissima dixit
>   "lux mea" quaeque solent uerba iuuare uiros!

[We hate sad women too: let Ajax love Tecmessa; a cheerful
woman captivates our fun-loving crowd. I would never ask
either one of you—you, Andromache, or you, Tecmessa—to be
my mistress. I can scarcely seem to believe, though I am forced
to by your offspring, that you ever had intercourse with your
husbands. Can you imagine that saddest of women saying to
Ajax "my light" and the kind of words that delight men?]

And it is an easy step from here to turn the tables completely by applying the rules of the *Ars* to epic situations and mythical characters. As Ovid tells a famous group of deceived and abandoned heroines, "quid uos perdiderit, dicam: nescistis amare; / defuit ars uobis: arte perennat amor" (*Ars* III.41-42) [I'll tell you what ruined you all: you didn't know how to love; you lacked art; with art love lasts for many years]. The implication here, that he could have given Dido and the others the necessary art, is made explicit at the beginning of the *Remedia.* Ovid claims that he could have prevented— among other tragedies—the rape of Philomela, and the Trojan War: "redde Parin nobis, Helenen Menelaus habebit / nec manibus Danais Pergama uicta cadent" (65-66) [give Paris to me, and Menelaus will keep Helen, nor will conquered Pergamon be destroyed by Danaan hands].

The ironic juxtaposition in these passages of an artless past and sophisticated present is characteristic. Elegy, we are told, decorously fits its subject by being a sophisticated pimp for Venus: "rustica sit sine me lasciui mater Amoris: / huic ego proueni lena comesque deae" (*Amores* III.i.43-44) [the mother of playful Love would be countrified without me: I came on stage as a bawd and companion for this goddess]. But the sharpest examples of the juxtaposition appear in Ovid's references to primitivistic myth. The Golden Age and its equivalent, Romulus's Rome, have as much importance in Ovid's poetry as they do in Vergil's. Ovid deflates the pretenses of Augustan primitivism by making a hyperbole of Vergil's comparison of Romulus and Augustus. "Romule, concedes" (*Fasti* II.133) [you must give in], orders the narrator: your rape of the Sabine women pales beside Augustus's marriage laws (139); moreover, "caelestem fecit te pater, ille patrem" (144) [your father made you a god, he made his father one].[18] Augustus does indeed rule "aurea Roma" (*Ars* III.113); but greed, not Astraea, has returned to announce a literally golden age. "Aurea sunt uere nunc saecula: plurimus auro / uenit honos, auro conciliatur amor" (*Ars* II.277-78) [now is truly the golden age: many an honor comes by means of gold, with gold love is procured]. Ovid celebrates the present (*Ars* III.122) for precisely the reasons that would be most abhorrent to Augustus: not because of gold-mining (123) or the Augustan building program (125-26), "sed quia cultus adest nec nostros mansit in annos / rusticitas priscis illa superstes auis" (127-28) [but because refinement is now here and rusticity, which survived until our old-fashioned grandfathers, has not lasted to our time]. Vergil's pastoral idyll is no longer possible. Amaryllis now wants expensive presents, not chestnuts (*Ars* II.268). Ovid's sole concession to Augustan atavism is his praise of older women as mistresses: "mihi fundat auitum / consulibus priscis condita testa merum" (*Ars* II.695-96) [for me let a jug put down under ancient consuls pour out its well-aged wine].

By thus portraying Golden Age sincerity as barbaric rudeness, the *Ars* abolishes passion, subordinates past to present, and celebrates modern sophisticated game-playing. The replacement of simplicity by *cultus* both arises from and makes necessary strategy, art, and cunning deception. *Simplicitas* survives only in the drunk (*Ars* I.241-42), as a basis for effective amorous action only in the naturally beautiful woman (*Remedia* 349; *Ars* III.250-54) and the rich man:

> non ego diuitibus uenio praeceptor amandi;
>   nil opus est illi, qui dabit, arte mea.
> secum habet ingenium qui, cum libet, "accipe" dicit;
>   cedimus, inuentis plus placet ille meis.
> pauperibus uates ego sum, quia pauper amaui;
>   cum dare non possem munera, uerba dabam.
> [*Ars* II.161-66]

[I do not come as the preceptor of loving for rich men; he who will give has no need of my art. He has enough wit about him who, whenever he wants to, says "take"; I give up, he pleases more than my stratagems do. I am the bard for poor men, because as a poor man I loved; since I could not give presents, I gave words.]

Ars is necessary if one has to give words—ambiguously poetry and, following the idiom, deception—instead of gifts; and *cultus* is required by the majority of women, to whom only *cura* will give beauty (*Ars* III.105).

Yet the teacher of this *ars* is a pedantic fool; we err greatly if we identify him with Ovid or take his self-characterization seriously. The game of the *Ars* and the *Remedia* is to set up an inherently comic system. The narrator applies epic gravity to a subject that is by Augustan standards ridiculous.[19] Ovid poses as a pedagogue: we find intrusive textbook outlines (*Ars* I.35-40), comic aetiologies (I.101ff.), pedantic digressions (I.287-88), and questions posed in anticipation of an implied student (I.375). The *magister* has a stake in modernity, on which after all his livelihood depends. In the *Amores* Ovid had ironically advocated a sophisticated resignation to the way of the world: "rusticus est nimium, quem laedit adultera coniunx, / et notos mores non satis Vrbis habet" (III.iv.37-38) [he is too countrified, whom an adulterous wife vexes, and he does not know sufficiently well the customary ways of the City]. Here the mock-epic vow to sing great things (*Ars* II.536) and the exhortation "ardua molimur, sed nulla, nisi ardua, uirtus" (537) [I labor at difficult matters, but virtue is nothing if not difficult], build up to comically civilized advice: "riualem patienter habe" (539) [bear a rival patiently]. Such sophistication is difficult to achieve, we are warned. Something of the rustic survives even in the expert teacher: "hac ego, confiteor, non sum perfectus in arte; / quid faciam? monitis sum minor ipse meis" (547-48) [in this art, I confess, I am not perfect. What should I do? I am myself inferior to my warnings]. Lamentably, "barbaria noster abundat amor" (552) [my love abounds in uncouthness].

It becomes apparent that successful suppression of such outmoded *rusticitas* requires not only cunning manipulation of others, but constant self-deception. We are told to follow the Delphic admonition *nosce teipsum*, but only in the adoption of favorable, self-flattering positions (*Ars* II.497ff.; III.771). The *Ars* advocates self-deceptions that assist the libido, while the *Remedia* prescribes

self-deceptions to resist a passion gone out of control; their comic
opposition is made obvious in directly contradictory teachings (*Ars*
II.657ff.; *Remedia* 315ff.).

To this extent, Robert Durling is right in saying that "the fun
depends on our keeping clearly in mind the distinction between
genuine human passion and its metamorphosis into shallow pleasure-
seeking. If we mistake the Poet's Phaedra for a real Phaedra, or this
pretended world for the real world, we lose the effect of the wit."[20] If
the system is to work, passion must be replaced by detached, cold
strategy. It is necessary to treat people as objects, the *quod* of the
Ars (I.35) or the *materia* of *Amores* I.iii. But the whole point of
these poems is that the *ars* is ineffective. There is no reason for us to
accept the *magister*'s premises; indeed, it soon becomes clear that we
misunderstand. Ovid if we do so. He pretends to have imposed a
rational framework on the irrational impetus of love: "quod nunc
ratio est, inpetus ante fuit" (*Remedia* 10) [what was violent impulse
before is now a system]. His *ratio* requires the reduction of passion
to triviality. Yet even the *magister* himself cannot wholeheartedly
wish for the complete triumph of cold, rational strategy. It would
save one from passion, but also deny pleasure; its comically horrifying sexual result would be a Roman matron:

> odi, quae praebet, quia sit praebere necesse,
>   siccaque de lana cogitat ipsa sua;
> quae datur officio, non est mihi grata uoluptas:
>   officium faciat nulla puella mihi.
>
>   [*Ars* II.685-88]

> [I hate a woman who offers herself because she has to, and
> who, herself sober, thinks about her wool-spinning; pleasure
> that is given as a duty is not pleasing to me: let no girl do her
> duty on my behalf.]

A little passion, to be carefully controlled, is thus necessary. But
once admitted, the rustic *barbaria* of the libido causes the pretense
of systematic strategy to collapse. It refuses to remain bound by its
framework, and overwhelms the generic propriety of other cate-

gories. The lawyer, for example, becomes a lover: "qui modo patronus, nunc cupit esse cliens" (*Ars* I.88) [he who was a patron of clients, now desires to be a client]. More important, it resists the efficacy of the *magister*'s own ordering scheme. His *ars* is ironically simple and unimpressive; yet, even so, it fails precisely when it is most needed (*Remedia* 119-20) and fails even the *magister* himself: "curabar propriis aeger Podalirius herbis / (et, fateor, medicus turpiter aeger eram)" (*Remedia* 313-14) [I, a sick Podalirius, was being cured by my own herbs; and, I confess, I was a shamefully sick physician].

The comic result appears in the *Amores*, which can be considered a presentation of the diploma-carrying lover in action. He in fact becomes a study in illogicality. Ovid forecasts with comic querulousness a banquet to which Corinna will come with her husband: "ante ueni quam uir; nec quid, si ueneris ante, / possit agi uideo, sed tamen ante ueni" (I.iv.13-14; see also 41-46) [arrive before your husband; and yet, if you do arrive before, I don't see what can be done, but nonetheless arrive before him]. The teacher of the *Ars* admits that the wise lover will be a protean adapter to experience (I.759ff.), using different rules as different situations require. Yet the *Amores* shows with splendid wit that in some instances, recalcitrant human nature makes all strategies useless. In *Amores* III.iv the husband simply cannot win; as in the brilliant II.xix, caution arouses would-be lovers all the more, but the "beneficial" effects of leniency are ironically apparent in the poem's conclusion:

> si sapis, indulge dominae uultusque seueros
>   exue nec rigidi iura tuere uiri
> et cole quos dederit (multos dabit) uxor amicos:
>   gratia sic minimo magna labore uenit;
> sic poteris iuuenum conuiuia semper inire
>   et, quae non dederis, multa uidere domi.
>
> [43-48]

[If you are wise, indulge your mistress, take off your stern expression, and do not guard the rights of a rigid husband. Cultivate the friends whom your wife will bestow—she will

bestow many. Thus great esteem comes with the tiniest effort;
thus you will always be able to go to the banquets of the
young, and to see many gifts at home that you won't have
given.]

Thus love becomes, for Ovid as for Vergil, a metonymy for the
irrational impulses in the human mind. It would be a serious error to
consider Ovid the first courtly-love poet. But it is also a mistake to
regard him as merely a witty writer of light verse about a trivial
subject.[21] His comic irony has a serious point. Ovid shows the per-
sistence of passion in the human temperament; and he views
skeptically the possibility of controlling passion by encompassing it
in a rational framework.

This tension between passion and the generic framework designed
to restrain it occurs at the deepest levels of Ovid's poetic technique,
in a structural confirmation of his thematic concerns. Vergil's serious
use of the vatic narrator simplifies the artistic difficulties of presenting the triumph of rational order, because the pretense of vatic
powers allows the illusion of truth. Vergil's distanced *vates*—the
vehicle for the utterances of fate—can avoid admitting the limitations of human understanding. Ovid, on the other hand, repeatedly
rejects the vatic pose by accepting it with comic irony. In the *Fasti*,
for example, he pungently transforms the *magister* of the *Ars* into a
rather stupid student (e.g., IV.936ff.), the man whom Janus
addresses as "vates operose dierum" (I.101) [laborious singer of the
days].[22] The sources of his vatic numen appear to him in visions that
he claims are real. But their authority is fallible, as the hilarious
conflicting etymologies of the names April, May, and June so neatly
show. The narrator's emphasis on his attention to verifiable fact, in
the midst of explanatory chaos, becomes a recurrent comic device.
Wavering between an identification of Taurus as Io or as the bull
that carried off Europa, he laments: "vacca sit an taurus, non est
cognoscere promptum: / pars prior apparet, posteriora latent"
(IV.717-18) [it is not easy to know whether it is a cow or a bull: the
fore part is visible, the rear parts are hidden].

Thus, like the opening lines of the *Amores*, the *Fasti* uses the
vatic pose as a comic suggestion that Ovid's poetry is out of his

control. This suggestion frequently appears in the *Ars* and the *Remedia*, in the narrator's complaints that he has said too much: "quo feror insanus?" (*Ars* III.667) [where am I being carried in my madness?]. Such loss of control is especially comic when Ovid exploits the traditional figure of the didactic poem as a ship.[23] The narrator so defends inconsistent teachings: "nec leuitas culpanda mea est: non semper eodem / impositos uento panda carina uehit" (*Ars* II.429-30) [nor is my inconsistency to be censured: not always by the same wind does the curved ship carry its passengers]. He will discuss trivialities before the furor of a strong wind impels him to greater themes (III.99-100). Narrative control is especially precarious after his vision of Cupid in the *Remedia*. He admits that the vision was probably illusory, having nonetheless reported the subject of Cupid's interruption (555-56); yet he then adds:

> plura loquebatur; placidum puerilis·imago
> destituit somnum, si modo somnus erat.
> quid faciam? media nauem Palinurus in unda
> deserit: ignotas cogor inire uias.

> [575-78]

[He was saying more; the boyish image deserted my quiet sleep, if it was merely sleep. What am I to do? Palinurus abandons ship in mid-sea: I am compelled to enter upon unknown ways.]

Robert Durling argues that "the effect of such pretenses of doubt and lack of control is obviously a function of the general pose of absolute control."[24] His argument is partially confirmed by the comic elements of this last example, Cupid as Palinurus. Yet the place of the image in the total context of Ovid's poetry connotes a serious purpose. Vergil's *Georgics* uses the ship, and the similar image of the charioteer, to embody a moral: "man at best is a rower going upstream against a violent current: only the fiercest *labor* can keep him on his course; if he once relaxes and loses control he will be carried headlong to destruction. But man is also a charioteer who can no longer guide his *own* course and is consequently involved in

moral chaos."[25] The elements of Ovid's metaphor are similar. The
image is particularly apt for the *Ars* and the *Remedia* because it
combines *impetus* (wind, horses) and *ratio* (navigation, reins). It is
often used for low comedy: sexual intercourse can be compared to a
chariot race (*Ars* II.725, 731); the happy lover sails on "suo uento"
(*Remedia* 14) [under his own wind]. But other uses are more
comprehensive and suggestive. Both the poet-teacher and his "student" lovers can be described as sailors: "me duce damnosas,
homines, conpescite curas, / rectaque cum sociis me duce nauis eat"
(*Remedia* 69-70) [with me as your leader, men, curb your ruinous
love-anxieties, and with me as your leader let the ship and its crew
run in a straight line]. What in Vergil is threatened loss of control
becomes the comic reality in Ovid:

> mollior es neque abire potes uinctusque teneris
> et tua saeuus Amor sub pede colla premit:
> desine luctari; referant tua carbasa uenti,
> quaque uocant fluctus, hac tibi remus eat.
>
> [*Remedia* 529-32]

[Are you weaker and unable to depart and, though overcome,
do you persist; and does cruel Love press your neck beneath
his foot? Stop struggling: let the winds carry your sails back,
and whatever way the waves summon you, there let your oar
go.]

These nautical images link together the poetic art and the art of
love, both of which are like ships sailing out of control, both of
which construct systems that are inevitably undermined. At the
beginning of chapter 5, I will discuss the most striking analogy
between the two arts, Ovid's comparison of himself as poet and
magister with Daedalus the supreme artificer (*Ars* II.21ff.), both of
them craftsmen whose artifices collapse under the pressure of youthful impatience and intractable human nature. Ovid's poetics, as all
these instances suggest, confirms the lesson of his treatment of experience. Poetry itself shows the taint of its human maker, and has
difficulty in setting up structures that are permanent and stable.

Accordingly, Ovid's poetry directly opposes Vergil's. Both poets explore the means by which art and experience can be ordered; each sets up frameworks of perception and understanding in a search for a coherent rationale of human action. They also share an awareness of the ways in which experience and art resist such ordering. In Vergil such resistance can be overcome. Ovid, on the other hand, is not simply "keenly aware of the gap between Augustan words and Augustan deeds."[26] Comedy and pathos result from his refusal, and subtly emphasized inability, to impose a normative generic hierarchy on experience.

II

To assess Ovid's influence on Chaucer, I have found it useful to concentrate on the *Ars, Remedia,* and *Amores,* even though the major evidence of direct borrowing is from the *Metamorphoses.*[27] From that work Chaucer takes stories, from the love poems he adopts a cast of mind. The *Metamorphoses* presented a special problem to the Middle Ages: as a bible of the pagan gods,[28] it provoked Christian apologetics, euhemerism, and attempts to account for the similarities between Ovid's narrative of the Creation and Flood and the biblical one. Moreover, medieval commentators usually felt some compulsion to deal with the disturbing theological implications of metamorphosis itself.[29] Chaucer is oblivious to these issues: he does use the *Ovide Moralisé,* but only as a handy translation to help him in construing Ovid's Latin.[30] By omitting the metamorphoses at the ends of Ovid's stories, he avoids the problems that require moralization.[31] Indeed, the omissions indicate his lack of interest in what for us seem the dominant qualities of the poem: its exploration of psychopathology and the supernatural; its attendant vividness and, often, grotesqueness of imagery.[32]

Chaucer's deeper affinities are with the poet whom he honors as "Venus clerk, Ovide, / That hath ysowen wonder wide / The grete god of Loves name" (*House of Fame* 1487-89). As a love poet Ovid influences Chaucer directly, and also indirectly through the per-

vasively Ovidian filter of later medieval poetry. Much of that poetry
is so steeped in Ovid's vocabulary of paradox and juxtaposition[33]
that it inhabits an Ovidian ambiance with remarkable comfort and
ease. In his translation of the *Ars Amatoria*, Maître Élie—whose title
itself translates *magister* Ovid's—carefully replaces details of Roman
topography with those of thirteenth-century Paris: if you want to
pick up women, he advises his audience, try the area around
St.-Germain-des-Pres, or the miracle plays in the parvis of the
cathedral.[34] Élie also shows himself to be aware of the ironic subtleties of Ovid's meaning: he catches the important play on words in
the idiom *verba dare* (*Ars* II.166), and glosses it for his readers.[35]
Such Ovidian language and wordplay saturate the notorious comedy
Pamphilus, in which art, deception, and worldly sophistication
combine.[36] They set the tone of a number of other poems as well—
even when, as often happens, Ovid becomes the butt of his own
joke. The *Ars Amatoria,* in such cases, becomes the rulebook that
the fool follows to the letter, when he should be keeping pace with
the shifting social realities that the rules try to fix and codify.[37] Yet
another comic allusion is one that Ovid himself would have ap-
preciated. Dipsas, the drunken bawd of *Amores* I.viii, advises her
young charge to fall for rich men, not poor poets: "qui dabit, ille
tibi magno sit maior Homero" (61) [let the man who will give be
greater for you than great Homer] ; and the *Ars Amatoria* echoes her
warning: "ipse licet uenias Musis comitatus, Homere, / si nihil
attuleris, ibis, Homere, foras" (II.279-80) [even if you yourself,
Homer, should come accompanied by the Muses, if you bring
nothing, Homer, out you will go]. Her descendant, La Vieille of
Jean de Meun's *Roman de la Rose*, repeats the advice with one
addition, an affectionate glance at the master:

> D'amer povre home ne li chaille,
> qu'il n'est riens que povre home vaille;
> se c'iert Ovides ou Homers,
> ne vaudroit il pas .II. gomers.
>
> [13587-90][38]

[It would not be worth it for her to love a poor man, for a poor man isn't worth anything; even if it is Ovid or Homer, he won't be worth two goblets.]

Of all Ovid's legacies to later medieval poetry, probably the most important is his self-conscious, obtrusive narrator, who refuses to be a clear medium for the poem he recites. It is no doubt significant, in this regard, that Ovid's influence on medieval poetry became predominant in the late eleventh and twelfth centuries, exactly the time of what R. W. Southern has described as "the emergence of the individual from his communal background."[39] There is a clear, new emphasis on the narrator's personality in the poetry of Marbod of Rennes, Hildebert of Lavardin, and Baudri of Bourgueil.[40] There is, moreover, a forecast of later medieval love poetry in Baudri's exact imitations of the *Heroides.* In his letters *Paris to Helen* and *Helen to Paris* the narrator is not only obtrusive but untrustworthy, a lover who unconsciously shows us the extent of his rationalizing self-deception. Helen persuades herself that betraying Menelaus will not be a sin because it was ordained by the gods; and the gods, after all, themselves commit crimes for the sake of love.[41]

Chaucer's medieval Ovidian models are later: the idiosyncratic narrator of Guillaume de Machaut,[42] and especially the freewheeling, oblivious Amant of Jean de Meun's *Roman de la Rose.* Yet Jean at least to some degree fuses Ovid with another source of the naive narrator, Boethius's *Consolation of Philosophy;* and an accurate description of Chaucer's method must avoid blurring the two traditions.[43] The Boethian model depends for its effect on an authoritative voice, implied or real, against which we can measure the narrator's failures of understanding and gradual spiritual progress. When Lady Philosophy instructs Boethius, when Virgil and Beatrice teach Dante, when Pearl explains her lofty rank in Heaven to the *Pearl* poet, the narrator's literal-mindedness has provoked explanations that can lead to knowledge. But except in the *General Prologue,* where traditional social and moral hierarchies in part obtain, Chaucer does not consistently set up an absolute standard against which we can measure much of anything.[44] Authorities and authority figures in Chaucer's poetry, as in Ovid's, turn out not to be authoritative.

This meeting point implies the rest: Chaucer develops more fully than any other medieval poet the complex of attitudes behind Ovid's untrustworthy narrator. As I have argued, Ovid attacks the principle of a rational hierarchy, which is at the heart of the classical definition of self and society. Fittingly, his own favorite among his verses, according to the elder Seneca, was the outrageous description of the Minotaur: "semibouemque uirum semiuirumque bouem" (*Ars* II.24) [the half-bull man and half-man bull].[45] For the phrase epitomizes the central, pervasive sense in Ovid's work of the instability of forms and categories. In the *Metamorphoses* reality itself is adrift in such instability; elsewhere in his poetry it becomes an attribute of mind, as generic confusion blurs the outlines of every category of thought and perception—including the generic boundaries of poetry itself. Chaucer is most Ovidian when he shows his interest in such problems of knowledge. Part of his closeness to Ovid no doubt derives from a similar skepticism in temperament; it is also well attuned to the major developments in fourteenth-century philosophy and to "late Gothic" attitudes toward human experience and thought.[46] Chaucer, as a medieval Christian, does not follow Ovid in his attack on rational hierarchy. He does repeatedly—as do Duns Scotus and William of Ockham—suggest man's inability to understand God's order or to decide, from an earthly perspective, where truth resides.

Yet if Ovid's specific concerns are not Chaucer's, the poetic expressions of their skeptical viewpoints are conspicuously alike. Each turns repeatedly to a basic epistemological problem: the extent to which the artist, or indeed any human being, is capable of setting up structures of perception and understanding that are true, or at least sufficiently trustworthy to permit effective action in the world. Each answers the problem by leaving it unresolved.[47] Their works are full of juxtapositions and oppositions. We repeatedly find thesis and antithesis, with no synthesis. We encounter elaborate systems that collapse as soon as they are built, playing off order against

energy, stasis against flux. We come to expect palinodes; the conflicting—and unresolved—claims of authorities, and of authority and
experience; and, as a basic metonymy of the human condition, the
uncertain results and paradoxical nature of love. The effect of this
irresolution is to revise our understanding of the fallible narrators
whom Chaucer and Ovid use. We do not, finally, stand with the poet
in ironic superiority to his narrator. Rather, we come to see that his
infirmity and failures of understanding are our own.

The fullest expression of this view of human limitation is in the
myth of the Golden Age and declining world; and the myth itself
expressly appears in the *Metamorphoses,* the *Ars Amatoria,* and—as I
shall argue—in Chaucer's first major poem, the *Book of the Duchess.*
The narrators of both poets are inhabitants of a fallen world; and
their failures of vision are in part a consequence of that fall. In
neither poet, however, does the myth receive a simple treatment.
The *Metamorphoses* describes a world that gets worse and worse. In
the *Ars* the notion of decline is more complicated: Ovid celebrates
the modernity of civilized decadent Rome, but in terms that disguise
beneath their anti-Augustanism and love of artifice a certain
nostalgia for lost innocence and simplicity. The moral dimensions of
the myth are, obviously, readily adaptable to medieval Christian
purposes, but Chaucer on the whole leaves latent the theologian's
strict view of sin and possible redemption. Instead, he uses elements
of the myth in an Ovidian manner, as a way of contrasting the world
ruled by natural law with the special complications added by human
consciousness and will. In the *Book of the Duchess* the historical
dimensions of the myth fully appear. In his later works chronology
is collapsed: the simplicity and unconscious purposiveness of Nature
set off by contrast the complexity and potential for chaos in human
motives and action. As in Ovid, the theme leads in two directions at
once: to an implicit moral on natural law and the effects of its
impairment; but also to a sheer delight in the vitality and exuberance
of human possibility.

This is the crucial point at which Matthew Arnold and his suc-
cessors misunderstand, and undervalue, Chaucer and Ovid; and here

the comparison with Vergil and Dante, with which this chapter
began, is especially instructive. What distinguishes the narrators of
Ovid and Chaucer from those of Vergil and Dante is their emphatically human position. Each is, to use Ovid's terminology, a
poeta and only by comic indirection a *vates*. The difference is important: the *vates* can present truths he could not normally discern,
because he is speaking for a numinous power that allows him to
escape human limitations; the *poeta,* on the other hand, is self-
consciously trapped by those limitations. The effect is comic irony,
but an irony that at once points to the frailty and celebrates the
fragile nobility of the human condition. Ovid explores the psychology of how emotion inevitably frustrates rational control.
Chaucer generalizes this exploration to a view of the limitations of
human reason and knowledge. His concerns are Ovidian; the rest of
this book will show his deep understanding of Ovid, and his skill at
adapting Ovidian techniques of style and structure to fit the demands of his own temperament and historical situation.

2

CHAUCER'S FAULTY VISION:
THE HOUSE OF FAME

> But how many a man, that was ful noble in his tyme,
> hath the wrecchid and nedy foryetynge of writeris put
> out of mynde and doon awey; al be it so that, certes,
> thilke wrytynges profiten litel, the whiche writynges
> long and dirk eelde doth awey, bothe hem and ek hir
> auctours!
>
> *Boece* II.pr.7,84–90

From the beginning Chaucer's poetry examines the two ways we have of learning about the world. Books, which preserve the wisdom of the past, constitute the first; confronting that written authority is the evidence of one's own experience. As I suggested in the first chapter, Chaucer no doubt learned from Ovid how to generate irony by opposing the two; for both poets, in any case, books and life prove to be equally suspect as sources of truth. Experience is partial and tendentious, and its meaning is fully apparent, if ever, only after the present has firmly become the past. Authorities disagree, and the distant past is not always clearly relevant to present needs. When the Ovidian narrator tries to mediate between the two, he succeeds only in revealing his own uncertainty or bias. Ovid's narrator is an amatory expert who still makes the mistakes of a novice; Chaucer's completely lacks experience in love, even though it dominates his dreams and poetry. But these extremes, sophisticate and innocent, enfold a common theme: the imperfections of authority, experience, and the human mind that attempts by balancing them to make sense of things.

These issues appear in an already highly developed form in the *House of Fame*, Chaucer's second major poem. The *Book of the Duchess*, his first, is less representative of his usual practice, largely because of the panegyric requirements of elegy, which dictate that there be at least poetic truth in his reading and his dream. Even so, this elegy does herald the concerns of Chaucer's later works; and their similarities in structure and theme are more important than their differences. The dreamer who tries to console John of Gaunt is a lover whose perceptions are distorted by a private obsession; Chaucer's later narrators make claims of objectivity and detachment that lead to no greater certainty. In the *Book of the Duchess* the conflict between authority and experience has its meeting place, and partial resolution, in a dream. Beginning with the *House of Fame,* Chaucer uses the dream—notoriously open to misinterpretation and of uncertain causes, effects, and veracity—as an emblem of fallible experience. The effect is heightened by the fact that his dreams are about love, since, for Chaucer as for Ovid, love is in some sense the epitome of experience, and it exactly replicates the dream's qualities of ambiguity and paradox.

The *House of Fame* outlines, in other ways as well, the central concerns in Chaucer's later poetry. It is no doubt Chaucer's most confusing poem, largely because it explores something equivalent to the Ovidian conflict of *ratio* and *impetus*, that is to say in poetic terms, of the structuring impulse, and the forces in the self and the world that work to subvert its efforts. Teetering on the brink of formless energy and flux, the *House of Fame* is the closest of Chaucer's poems to the *Metamorphoses.* For once Ovid's epic starts with the Creation, harmonizing the four elements out of chaos, poem and world begin to move in time and to subject themselves to process: the *carmen perpetuum* the poet promises is hard put to it to keep up with the ceaseless shape-changing and degeneration of man and of man's surroundings. The narrator keeps his own balance by some tricky footwork in the transitions from one story to the next. But only by an artificially imposed stasis—Ovid's favorite device is to freeze his characters into tableaux, at the very instant of their metamorphosis—can order be pretended. The energy of blind flux immediately takes over again.

Similarly, Chaucer in the *House of Fame* repeatedly builds systems only to undermine them, and his poem moves in a diastolic / systolic rhythm of expansion and collapse. Such tensions between stasis and flux have been explained as the result of Gothic ornamentation or "inorganic structure."[1] They can be described at least as well in Ovidian terms. For Chaucer's primary, unifying purpose, like Ovid's, is to explore the limits of human understanding, as the mind confronts its sources of knowledge and its natural surroundings. Conveniently, the traditional editorial divisions of the poem mark out four expositions of Chaucer's favorite themes. The Proem constitutes his fullest statement on the nature of dreams and the problems of dream interpretation. Book One explores the difficulties written authorities raise, especially when they deal with love. Book Two examines the claims of experiential knowledge. And the jumble of Book Three more or less recapitulates what has gone before, though it ends in anticlimax, not resolution or synthesis.

The Proem

Chaucer's catalogue of dream types is the first instance in the poem of order gone haywire. Its confusion may in part come from the complications of medieval dream theory. But Chaucer's narrator is also a good deal more confused than the facts of medieval dream theory require him to be—even as they are construed by his wordiest source, the goddess Nature's oration in the *Roman de la Rose:*

> Ne ne revueill dire des songes
> s'il sunt voirs ou s'il sunt mançonges,
> se l'an les doit du tout ellire
> ou s'il font du tout a despire,
> por quoi li un sunt plus horrible,
> plus bel li autre et plus pesible,
> selonc leur apparicions
> en diverses complexions,

et selonc les divers courages
des meurs divers e des aages;
ou se Dex par tex visions
anvoie revelacions,
ou li malignes esperiz
por metre les genz es periz:
de tout ce ne m'antremetrai,
mes a mon propos me retrai.

[18469-84]

[I do not wish in turn to pronounce on dreams: if they are true or if they are lies; if one should elect all of them or if they are all to be disdained; why some are more horrible, others more beautiful and peaceful, according to their manifestations in various temperaments, and according to the various hearts in men of different manners and different ages; or if God by such visions sends revelations, or if evil spirits do, to put people in peril. I will not meddle in all this, but will return to my theme.]

Nature is as much a chatterbox as ever here (see 18269-70), but compared with the opening of the *House of Fame,* her statement is at least a model of clarity. The oppositions she sets up are simply stated and easy to follow; in fact, her either / or syntax almost makes them seem to be variations of a single antithesis. Chaucer's catalogue, on the other hand, becomes a muddle: he gives us so many particulars of dream theory, in a long list of alternative possibilities, that it is impossible to keep everything in mind at once. Confusion results, paradoxically, from excessive precision. The narrator asks

Why that is an avisioun
And this a revelacioun,
Why this a drem, why that a sweven,
And noght to every man lyche even.

[7-10]

But "there does not seem to be any regularly recognized distinction between *drem* and *sweven*";[2] and the difference between an *avisioun* and a *revelacioun* is not easy to remember without a dream guide handy.[3] Hair-splitting distinctions between terms with closely related or uncertain meanings lead to chaos, unless definitions follow. By their omission Chaucer creates a feeling of breathlessness and confusion, which collapses into prayer as the end of the Proem (57-58) restates the pious hope of the beginning: "God turne us every dreṁ to goode!" (1).

Both the comic desperation of this prayer and its phrasing are reminiscent of the opening of the *Parliament of Fowls*: " 'God save swich a lord!'—I can na moore" (14). In the *Parliament* Chaucer points back at a confused mass with the indeterminacy of "Al this mene I by Love" (4); at the end of the Proem he asks for an unearned reprieve from his jumbled recital of the "causes" and "distaunce of tymes" of dreams, and the "gendres" of "hir signifiaunce." The ambiguities of dreams and the paradoxes of love are, evidently, more easily named than disentangled. Rational system breaks down, and the narrator cannot win through to meaning. But the two failures are in effect one; and the balance of Chaucer's emphasis rests on the limits of human understanding. For the comic despair of the Proem does not come primarily from the lists themselves: the different opinions about dreams are not really at variance with one another, despite the impression that the narrator's syntax gives. They are all traditionally recognized dream categories, which describe different kinds of dreams. The problem is that Chaucer is going to recount a particular dream; and as medieval dream theory emphasizes, one cannot say anything authoritative from the perspective of a dream itself about its causes, effects, and truth value. The system, like Ovid's *ars amatoria*, fails when it confronts the quandaries of a particular instance.

Its failure is more noticeable because of the way Chaucer defines his own place in the poem. The narrator of the *Parliament* can claim at least some objectivity because he is not a lover; the narrator of the *House of Fame* is, unfortunately, a dreamer, and he exhibits all the distortions and complications of perspective that arise from describing an experience from the inside. His efforts to categorize his dream (52-58) produce a comic tension between bias and objectivity, and between Chauntecleerian pretensions and Pertelotish common sense. Chaucer's request to Morpheus the god of sleep, appropriate after the hesitations of the Proem, is simply that he be able to "telle" his dream "aryght" (79); its evaluation, one assumes, will be left to the "grete clerkys" who are expert in such dark matters. But, in a quick about-face, proprietary rights assert themselves: we learn that any attack on the dream will be taken for an attack on its dreamer. The narrator's defensive posture is understandable, if the cause of his dream turns out to have been indigestion or an emotional disorder. Yet the Invocation thus erases most of the categories so extensively listed by the Proem. If we debunk the narrator's vision, we will be cursed by a "nursery rhyme" anathema[4] for our "malicious entencion" (93) and be told about King Croesus, who refused to heed his prophetic dreams (99-108). Self-respect demands that Chaucer's dream too possibly be an *avision*; and the machinery of the poem proceeds to back up self-respect, by establishing an astronomical configuration that will give the dream an elevated status. December 10, the day it supposedly occurred (111), falls near the end of Sagittarius; and Sagittarius is the sign that "was, among other things, the house of dreams, tidings, and travels," and "is the night domicile of Jupiter, the most benevolent of the planets." Moreover, in December the Sun "approaches close to *Aquila,* the constellation of the eagle."[5] But despite such pointers, the evidence is not all in favor of Chaucer as a prophet. The bookishness of his dream suggests that it may simply be a mirror of his reading. Indeed, the eagle's later account of Chaucer's studiousness, "daswed . . . look," and eremitic life (652-59) recalls one of the less elevated sources of dreams, even as his embonpoint—" 'thyn abstynence ys lyte' " (660)—discounts the possibility of another:

> Or ellys thus, as other sayn,
> For to gret feblenesse of her brayn,
> By abstinence, or by seknesse,
> Prison, stewe, or gret distresse,

> Or ellys by dysordynaunce
> Of naturel acustumaunce,
> That som man is to curious
> In studye, or melancolyous.
>
> [23-30]

The correct category for Chaucer's dream is never proved decisively, though its details imply either that it results from too much study, or that *avisions* are not what they used to be. Chaucer does not, as it turns out, learn much of real value or see anything, however marvelous, that is very lofty. Accordingly, he does not share the absolute confidence of Guillaume de Lorris (*Roman de la Rose* 1-30) that his dream is a true one. He follows instead the lead of Jean de Meun's Nature; and the Proem reproduces the inconsistencies of her discourse. She admits, in the passage I have quoted, that some dreams are oracular, but her grudging admission comes only after two hundred verses poking fun at man's credulous belief in delusory dreams. Her reluctance does not warm into advocacy; as befits her natural perspective, the goddess refuses to pronounce on supernatural matters, and instead moves on to a discussion of clouds, comets, and the natural equality of men.

We may infer that Nature is as much the presiding spirit of the *House of Fame* as she is of the *Book of the Duchess* and the *Parliament of Fowls*. The action of the poem entirely takes place within her sublunary realm, and within the limitations of her earthbound perspective. By copying the hesitations of Jean de Meun's goddess, the opening of the *House of Fame* presents in brief compass the problems that the rest of the poem will take up. The most obvious of these is the narrator's inability to know what he knows, expressed by Chaucer's usual opposition of authority and experience. The confusion of traditional dream categories intensifies the dreamer's bafflement when he tries to make distinctions among them; and the opposing pressures of objectivity and subjectivity frustrate even further his efforts to decide the truth and value of this particular dream. For a dream is at once an experience to be interpreted and classified, and the mysterious product of one person's mind. Some dreams are sent from heaven, though our "flessh" is too weak to understand them (43-51); but others are simply distorted reflections of the dreamer's own waking experience, filtered through the complexities of his imagination. In such a morass it is difficult enough to keep one's bearings, let alone decide questions of truth and falsehood or cause and effect.

Book One

The first part of Chaucer's dream takes place within Venus's temple of glass. It recounts the history of her son Aeneas, which is pictured on the temple walls. To be exact, it recounts a book about that history, as we realize when the dreamer begins his narrative with a translation of *arma virumque cano* (143-48). Yet even if our knowledge of the *Book of the Duchess* and the *Parliament* prepares us for Chaucer's having so bookish a dream, the relevance of Venus and Vergil to the palace of Fame must be at first glance rather murky. If John Keats's example may allow us to speak of love and fame in the same breath, it does not lead us to see what Vergil has in common with dreams, eagles, and whirling wicker houses—beyond the fact that he mentions swift Fama in *Aeneid* IV (173-90).

The best way to bring the relationship into focus is to put three brief descriptions—of dreams, of Fame, and of Vergil—side by side. Chaucer may or may not have had in mind Statius's description of the god of sleep, but it sums up with epigrammatic brevity the theme of the Proem: "adsunt innumero circum vaga Somnia vultu, / vera simul falsis permixta. . . ." [vague dreams of countless shapes stand round about him, true mixed with false].[6] He did have in mind the *Anticlaudianus* of Alanus de Insulis, which the *House of Fame* mentions by title (986). Chaucer's description of Fame's ·tidings as "of fals and soth compouned" (1029) translates almost exactly Alanus's portrait of the goddess in action: "Nuncia Fama uolat et ueris falsa maritans" (VIII.305)[7] [the herald Rumor flies, marrying false things to true]. More surprisingly, Alanus uses identical terms to describe Vergil's poetry: "Virgilii musa mendacia multa colorat / Et facie ueri contexit pallia falso" (I.142-43) [Vergil's poetry colors many lies, and interweaves his mantles of falsehood with the appearance of truth]. In this shadowland of poetry, dreams, and rumor, Vergil becomes something unexpected: half historian, half liar.

Any surprise one has at such a statement is a modern reaction. The sentiment is one that medieval commentators often apply to classical authors; and it lies behind the frequent use of "St. Augustine's formula of 'spoiling the Egyptians' " to justify the reading of pagan literature.[8] It has special force when it applies to those who record historical events, for example the squabbling authorities who bear up the fame of Troy:

> But yet I gan ful wel espie,
> Betwex hem was a litil envye.
> Oon seyde that Omer made lyes,
> Feynynge in hys poetries,
> And was to Grekes favorable;
> Therfor held he hyt but fable.
>
> [1475-80]

These lines allude to a dispute of some importance in medieval literary tradition. Its terms are set by the late antique forgeries of Dares the Phrygian and Dictys the Cretan, whose narratives provide Benoit de Sainte-Maure and his Latin translator Guido delle Colonne with their accounts of the Trojan War. Benoit insists that Dares told the truth dispassionately, even though he fought on the Trojan side; Homer, on the other hand, was not an eyewitness, but lived a century later.[9] Guido assures us that Dictys and Dares actually took part in the war "et horum que uiderunt fuerunt fidelissimi relatores" [and were extremely reliable reporters of the things they saw]. The epigone Homer shows his Greek bias by extravagantly praising Achilles, the treacherous, cowardly murderer of Hector and Troilus. Vergil, according to Guido, is a more reliable source for the truth about Troy. Even so, he and Ovid join Homer as poets who mix fact with fiction, and whose narratives require pruning.[10]

Another version of this dispute raises more complicated issues of psychology and aesthetics, and its ultimate origin is the *Aeneid* itself. When Aeneas looks at pictorial representations of the Trojan War (I.453ff.), Vergil achieves a delicate balance between the emotions of a participant—his description of the paintings is emphatically subjective—and the detached coldness of artistic form: "animum pictura pascit inani" (I.464) [he feeds his soul on an empty picture]. Bernardus Silvestris coarsens Aeneas's subjectivity: in *Aeneid* II the hero "mixes true and false in all that he says" when he recounts his history to Dido "(for Dares tells us that Aeneas, describing the fall of Troy, put his people in a favorable light)."[11] Chaucer shows a more sophisticated awareness of the kinds of ambiguities that Vergil's hero exemplifies, as both tale-teller and audience. The distinction between a participant and a detached reporter matches Chaucer's opposition of lover and non-lover, which he describes by the image of a wrestling match and its spectators (*Parliament* 162-66); it also parallels the conflict of bias and objectivity in the interpretation of dreams. An eyewitness has the virtues of immediacy and involvement, but these virtues also create partisanship. A later writer can at least start from a disinterested position, though anyone's experience with the Troy story shows how hard it is never to choose sides; but he has no way of verifying the truth of past events. If authorities disagree, their conflict must remain unresolved, unless the mind can find reasons for rejecting one authority or the other. Even worse, the mind cannot always trust its reasons. When we read about the distant past, the initial detachment of our response may change to involvement, as interest quickens; and growing involvement changes objectivity to bias. If we must distrust the poets who record history, we must also be suspicious of ourselves as their readers.

Such problems are magnified as the past recedes further and further, and a writer is forced to rely on authorities who themselves lived long after the events they describe. He has no other recourse: books are indeed the key of remembrance, as Robert O. Payne has reminded us, 'and Chaucer's skeptical comment on eschatology extends to history as well:

> . . . ther nis noon dwellyng in this contree,
> That eyther hath in hevene or helle ybe,
> Ne may of hit noon other weyes witen,
> But as he hath herd seyd, or founde it writen;
> For by assay ther may no man it preve.
>
> [*Legend of Good Women* F 5-9]

Yet one is impossibly distanced from the whole truth, even at the simplest level of what his authorities have thought important enough to repeat or trivial enough to omit. The narrator of *Troilus* excuses himself for not rehearsing "every word, or look, or sonde, or cheere" (III.492) of his hero:

> For sothe, I have nat herd it don or this,
> In story non, ne no man here I wene;
> And though I wolde, I koude nat, ywys;
> For ther was som epistel hem bitwene,
> That wolde, as seyth myn auctour, wel contene
> An hondred vers, of which hym liste nat write;
> How sholde I thanne a lyne of it endite?
>
> [III.498-504]

In Venus's temple of glass the story of Aeneas begins very much as Vergil's account of events—and of events that are unrecoverable except through books about them. Chaucer cannot know how Creusa died (183-84) because Vergil does not say.

Chaucer makes Vergil himself question the possibility of poetic truth, when he attaches an absolutely un-Vergilian sentiment to the first line of the *Aeneid*: " 'I wol now singen, yif I kan, / The armes, and also the man' " (143-44). If the phrase "yif I kan" implies in general terms the uncertain ability of art to be true to the facts, it also points to the specific episode in Vergil's poem that Chaucer— like so many other readers, medieval and modern—makes the center of his attention. Ovid heads the list of those who maintain that, at least in Book Four, Vergil has chosen the wrong hero to write an epic about. In *Heroides* VII, an Alexandrian inversion of heroic pretense, he wittily takes a swipe at the *Aeneid* by seeing Aeneas's departure for Italy entirely from Dido's point of view; and he stacks the cards in her favor by letting her claim that she is pregnant (133-38). Chaucer's narrator also attacks seducer Aeneas, as do Jean de Meun, Machaut, and Chrétien de Troyes.[12] There are harsher charges against Vergil elsewhere: he is guilty not only of bias, but of "feynynge in hys poetries." "The chaste Queen Dido did never see Aeneas in her life,"[13] and Vergil's Queen of Carthage is a total fabrication. According to the Oxford Franciscan John Ridevall[14] and to Ranulf Higden's *Polychronicon*, "Aeneas could not have seen Dido, because Aeneas died more than 300 years before the foundation of Carthage."[15] Petrarch agrees,[16] and follows St. Jerome in arguing that Dido killed herself in order to preserve her chaste fidelity to her husband, not for love of Aeneas.[17] Such a defense anticipates the one made by Boccaccio, whose account of Dido in *De Mulieribus Claris* entirely ignores the *Aeneid* in its attempt to set the record straight.[18] Knowing the facts about the historical Dido might simply serve to prove that poets are liars. Boccaccio argues the other side, and manages to defend the poet while saving Dido's reputation. Vergil "was well aware that Dido had really been a woman of exceptionally high character, who would rather die by her own hand than subdue the vow of chastity fixed deep in her heart to a second marriage. But that he might attain the proper effect of his work under the artifice of a poetic disguise, he composed a story in many respects like that of the historical Dido, according to the privilege of poets established by ancient custom."[19]

The emotional impetus for these defenses of Dido—no one has ever felt compelled to speak up in quite this manner for, say, Ariadne—is to be found in the *Aeneid* itself. "Dido, when she turns silently away from her betrayer in the underworld carries the sympathy of us all, and we hang a cloud round Aeneas till the end." Vergil "has roused sympathies which are unfavorable to his central theme."[20] One important source of such sympathies is the ambiguity in the poem about the relative importance of Dido's will and the actions of the gods in creating her tragedy: Cupid disguises himself as Ascanius, and makes her fall in love; Juno is present in the cave for the consummation of the affair; and Jupiter, aroused by Iarbas's complaint, brings about its tragic ending. Venus herself is of course not guiltless; and her contradictory roles in the *Aeneid* are disturbing, especially to someone who finds himself inside her temple. She is, on the one hand, the mother of Aeneas, who tells him to leave Troy (*House of Fame* 165); gives him comfort near Carthage and the promise of finding his companions (235-38); and helps him to achieve his "aventure" by her prayers to Jupiter (463-65), which counter Juno's malevolence (461, 198-208). On the other hand, she is the direct agent of Dido's tragedy (240-44). Chaucer takes care to sharpen the contradictions in her behavior. He alters Vergil to stress Venus's work on her son's behalf: in the *Aeneid* Neptune calms the winds that Juno and Aeolus have unleashed; in the *House of Fame* Jupiter does, at Venus's tearful request (213-20). But Chaucer also strengthens Dido's claims to injury, by carefully deleting most of the excuses Vergil provides for his hero[21] and, especially, by leaving out the most telling comment on Dido's self-delusion: "nec iam furtivum Dido meditatur amorem: / coniugium vocat; hoc praetexit nomine culpam" (IV.171-72) [nor does Dido now think about secret love: she calls it marriage, and by this name hides her fault].

What Chaucer does *not* do is to release the pressure from this disturbing ambiguity by splitting Venus in two. A good many medieval iconographers and exegetes felt the urge to do so; and the paradoxes and blurred definitions of love, in life as much as in the *Aeneid*, explain their impulse. In Bernardus Silvestris's *Commentary* on the *Aeneid,* the lawful (*legitima*) Venus represents universal harmony and natural justice; the other, the goddess of wantonness (*petulantiae dea*), "we name concupiscence of the flesh because she is the mother of all fornications."[22] Boccaccio describes one Venus "as every decent and lawful desire, as is wanting to have a wife in order to have children, and the like." The other, he says, "is the one because of whom every indecent act is desired, and who is commonly called the goddess of love."[23] Such distinctions appear in several recent readings of Chaucer. B. G. Koonce so describes the entrance to the garden in the *Parliament of Fowls*: "Whereas the gold inscription, foreshadowing the spiritual meaning of the garden, leads one 'unto the welle of grace' and a 'blysful place' where 'dedly woundes' are healed and 'grene and lusty May shal evere endure,' the other, foreshadowing the temple of Venus and echoing the inscription over the gate to Dante's Hell, leads to a desert place where 'nevere tre shal fruyt ne leves bere.' "[24] In fact, a single gate leads into the garden; the misleading clarity of Koonce's antithesis nearly succeeds in building two. When a poet desires such clarity, he can easily enough obtain it: Boccaccio's *Amorosa Visione* pictures two gates, one morally correct, the other not.[25] The *Parliament of Fowls*, on the other hand, sets out to probe a "Love" that is a paradoxical unity, undifferentiated and ambiguous; and whatever distinctions may surface in the course of the poem, there are none to help us at its start.

The *Parliament* clarifies Chaucer's meaning in Book One of the *House of Fame*, where we also see the quandary of a love poet who is not a lover (615-28), faced with the paradoxes in love's temple. Venus's contradictory aspects intensify the blurring together of opposing versions of Dido's story, and of irresolute responses to its meaning. Chaucer's recounting ends in a despair about love's contradictions, and descends to that point by a progressively more subjective response to the *Aeneid*. The narrator's failure to maintain his initially disinterested position is ironically appropriate, since Vergil's own objectivity is so much an issue to his medieval commentators; and Book One thus repeats the complexities of bias and detachment explored in the Proem. For the first fifty lines of Aeneas's story the narrator, except for an occasional "alas!" and expression of pity (157, 180, 183, 189), remains a passive observer of the narrative wall painting. The beginnings of a change occur when he directly addresses Juno and Venus (198-218). His sympathy at this point is clearly with Aeneas. The story has evoked his pity; and he steps in personally to contrast Juno's vindictiveness with the benevolence of Venus "my lady dere" (213). Yet though his awakened responses are suitable for a love poet, and for someone placed in Venus's temple, they will quickly lead him into difficulties.

They first lead to a growing self-emphasis, indicated by the shift

from the passive, often repeated "Ther saugh I" to a phrase like
"For also browke I wel myn hed" (273), and to the increasingly
personal and homely nature of his moral asides and proverbial
utterances (265-92).[26] The narrator interjects himself as a commentator, whose consciousness becomes entangled with the story he
retells, and complicates its retelling. He is no longer a clear medium
for Vergil's voice, but an active participant who reshapes his source
and alters its contours and emphasis, as he describes Venus's efforts
on her son's behalf:

> And, shortly of this thyng to pace,
> She made Eneas so in grace
> Of Dido, quene of that contree,
> That, shortly for to tellen, she
> Becam hys love, and let him doo
> Al that weddynge longeth too.
> What shulde I speke more queynte,
> Or peyne me my wordes peynte
> To speke of love? Hyt wol not be;
> I kan not of that faculte.
> And eke to telle the manere
> How they aqueynteden in fere,
> Hyt were a long proces to telle,
> And over-long for yow to dwelle.
>   Ther sawgh I grave how Eneas
> Tolde Dido every caas
> That hym was tyd upon the see.
>   And after grave was, how shee
> Made of hym shortly at oo word
> Hyr lyf, hir love, hir lust, hir lord.

[239-58]

"Ther sawgh I" reappears here with a greatly altered force, as the
last six lines of the passage repeat with cool detachment the subject
of the preceding, self-consciously obtrusive *occupatio*. But the effect
of this temporary return to his earlier method of narration is simply
to counterpoint the dreamer's increasing participation in his
experience.

His involvement reaches its peak when he is able to augment Vergil's invention with his own:

> In suche wordes gan to pleyne
> Dydo of hir grete peyne,
> As me mette redely;
> Non other auctour alegge I.
>
> [311-14]

The lament that follows, which is in fact original, confirms the narrator's empathy with Dido. Chaucer sets up an analogous scene in *Troilus,* when he promises "nat only the sentence" of the hero's first love song, all that Lollius had reported, but a word-for-word rendering, "save oure tonges difference" (I.393-98). In both episodes the narrator's moment of brave self-reliance underlines his normal dependence on books.

The narrator of the *House of Fame* quickly reminds us of the problems such dependence creates when he sends us to his sources, because they offer opposing perspectives on the affair. Ovid's defense of Dido rests on his willful refusal to grant the larger demands and context of Aeneas's destiny. Chaucer temporarily repeats that refusal. He suggests reading "Eneydos" and "the Epistle of Ovyde" to find out

> What that she wrot or that she dyde;
> And nere hyt to long to endyte,
> Be God, I wolde hyt here write.
>
> [380-82]

Yet his motive for an *occupatio* is not an immediate return to Aeneas's story, but a digression into a list of most of Ovid's *heroides*. This catalogue of betrayed women emphatically derives from written authorities, though Chaucer notes in passing the proofs of experience:

> But wel-away! the harm, the routhe,
> That hath betyd for such untrouthe,
> As men may ofte in bokes rede,

> And al day sen hyt yet in dede,
> That for to thynken hyt, a tene is.
>
> [383-87]

But the narrator's bookishness itself creates his quandary, for the mention of one book leads inevitably back to another, the one with which he began. Ariadne, he says, wished only to be Theseus's wife,

> In certeyn, as the book us tellis.
>   But to excusen Eneas
> Fullyche of al his grete trespas,
> The book seyth Mercurie, sauns fayle,
> Bad hym goo into Itayle,
> And leve Auffrikes regioun,
> And Dido and hir faire toun.
>
> [426-32]

Chaucer goes on to summarize the last eight books of the *Aeneid*, with a jarring return to his earlier passivity; "thoo sawgh I" (433, 439, 451) supplants his active moralizing intercessions on Dido's behalf. His renewed passivity marks the shock of being betrayed by his source halfway through its retelling. "But, trewely, the storie telleth us" is a phrase that appears in a similar position at the end of *Troilus* (V.1051), when the narrator defends Criseyde as best he can, despite the increasing weight of evidence against her. Indeed, Book One of the *House of Fame* acts out on a smaller scale the shifting position of the *Troilus* narrator. In both poems Chaucer responds increasingly to the emotional force of a story from the past, only to find at the crucial point that it is out of his control, moving in a direction he finds intolerable but is powerless to resist. In the *House of Fame* Chaucer's passivity reacts to a tension that is not simply between Vergil and Ovid, or between poetic truth and falsehood. Vergil seems at variance with himself; and the *Aeneid* makes unresolved and perhaps irresolvable claims on our belief and sympathy. Are we to admire Aeneas's truth to his mission, or attack his falsehood in leaving Dido? The narrator is apparently disturbed, not because he has chosen the immoral side,[27] but the one that the

Aeneid rejects and that Venus seems to have betrayed. The betrayal must be particularly distressing to someone who is a love poet (620-27); and Chaucer finishes his account of the *Aeneid* with a prayer curiously reminiscent of the one at the end of the Proem:

> . . . mawgree Juno, Eneas,
> For al hir sleight and hir compas,
> Acheved al his aventure,
> For Jupiter took of hym cure
> At the prayer of Venus,—
> The whiche I preye alwey save us,
> And us ay of oure sorwes lyghte!
>
> [461-67]

The prayer is a timely one, since Jupiter's eagle is about to transport the love poet who has "no tydynges / Of Loves folk yf they be glade" (644-45) to a place of marvels. But Chaucer is never handed an exegesis of the *Aeneid*; and if he is "saved" by Venus's prayer, the salvation is not quite on a par with the one she obtains for her son. His initial response to love, like his response to dreams, proves to be correct. Its enigmas deny the possibility of understanding and discriminating judgment. All one has left in the face of the incomprehensible is a pious hope.

A pious hope, however, cannot rid the narrator of his feeling of disorientation:

> "A, Lord!" thoughte I, "that madest us,
> Yet sawgh I never such noblesse
> Of ymages, ne such richesse,
> As I saugh graven in this chirche;
> But not wot I whoo did hem wirche,
> Ne where I am, ne in what contree."
>
> [470-75]

As in the Proem, his confusion is less moral than epistemological, despite the connotations of the barren scene in which he finds himself when he leaves Venus's temple:

> For al the feld nas but of sond
> As smal as man may se yet lye
> In the desert of Lybye.

[486-88]

To gloss these lines we no doubt must bring to bear the conventional associations of Jupiter and Venus with the Libyan desert;[28] and no doubt "the desert . . . hints retrospectively at Chaucer's disillusionment over the famous classical love-story."[29] But the question is how we are to define that disillusionment. If sand traditionally symbolizes "the decadent and the illusory,"[30] Chaucer uses its "greynes" in Book Two only to suggest an almost infinite number (691);[31] and the image at the end of Book One concentrates on the smallness of the grains (487). In the state of confusion created by dream theories and a bookish dream about love, this image fittingly connotes a world of unconnected fragments.

The narrator is indeed, as he says, in need of some "maner creature" "me to rede or wisse" (489-91). And his appeal to Christ, to be saved "fro fantome and illusion" (493), is no exaggerated response to his unsuccessful confrontation with the problems of truth and knowledge. There is, however, no epiphany: Jupiter is not God, and the Eagle does not turn out to be Christ's answer to the dreamer's despairing prayer. The irony of the *House of Fame*, as it moves from Book One to Two, is contained in the disparity between the initial awesomeness of this Eagle—described with a verbal echo of Dante's nobler bird (505-06)—and the bathos of its actuality. The promise it offers of an authoritative answer is soon subverted by its "gift" of simply a larger and more elaborate version of the same question.

Book Two

> Ou quant sunt neïs en santé,
> voit l'an de ceus a grant planté
> qui maintes foiz, sanz ordenance,

par naturele acoustumance,
de trop panser sunt curieus,
quant trop sunt melancolieus
ou pooreus outre mesure,
qui mainte diverse figure
se font parair en eus meïsmes
. . . .
et de tout ce leur samble lores
qu'il sait ainsinc por voir defores.
  Ou qui, par grant devocion,
en trop grant contemplacion,
font apparair en leur pansees
les choses qu'il ont porpansees,
et les cuident tout proprement
voair defors apertement;
et ce n'est for trufle et mançonge,
ainsinc con de l'ome qui songe,
qui voit, ce cuide, en leur presances
les esperituex sustances,
si con fist Scipion jadis;
et voit anfer et paradys
et ciel et air et mer et terre
et tout quan que l'an i peut querre.

[18313-21, 18325-40]

[Or one sees a great number of those, even when they are in health, who many times, without self-rule, by natural habit are preoccupied with thinking too much, when they are too melancholy or afraid beyond reason; who make themselves see many different apparitions inside themselves . . . and it seems to them at that time that they know for a fact that all these images are outside them.

Or those who, by great devotion in too great contemplation, make appear in their thoughts the things they have pondered, and believe they see them correctly and clearly outside themselves; and this is nothing but nonsense and lies. Thus with the man who dreams, who sees, he thinks, incorporeal substances face to face, as Scipio once did; and sees hell and

paradise, and heaven and air and sea and land and all that one
can look for there.]

Jean de Meun's Nature so dismisses visionary dreams. Her speech is
one of Chaucer's sources for Book Two;[32] and it forecasts the
meaning of his own vision. But the book begins with a grandiose
claim: Chaucer promises to recount an *avisyon* more remarkable
than the most famous ones in history, dreamed by such august
dreamers as Isaiah, Scipio, and Nebuchadnezzar (512-17). By repeated allusions, explicit or submerged, to other celestial travelers
and visionary prophets, the narrator tries to make himself one of
their company. From the start he alludes to the most recent of his
visionary predecessors, by echoing (520-28) the lofty invocation at
the beginning of Dante's supernatural journey (*Inferno* ii.7-9).[33]
Chaucer translates directly from the *Purgatorio* to describe the first
appearance of Jupiter's Eagle (505-06), and the bird brings with it all
the exalted associations of its aquiline brothers in the *Commedia*.[34]
Later on Chaucer's Eagle quotes Beatrice (992); and as the allusions
to Dante continue, they are joined by elevated reminiscences of
Macrobius, St. Paul, Alanus de Insulis, and Martianus Capella. But
the inadequacy of the bird as a second Beatrice implies a general
subversion; and all these evocations of the visionary tradition prove
to be ironic.

   Chaucer's heavenly flight becomes a sustained inversion of
Dante's vatic pretensions, and thus repeats the Ovidian jokes about
Vergil. For it becomes apparent in Book Two that the narrator is
very much an inhabitant of a fallen world, where man has lost whatever intellectual access he may once have had to the source of
meaning and normative clarity. Trapped below the moon, we are
forced to rely, when books fail us, on the evidence of sense experience. But either our experience is limited by the capacities of our
senses, or it answers questions that turn out to be trivial. Vision is
faulty; and the pretenses of the vatic voice simply hide the inescapable constraints on our knowledge.

   The first indication that Chaucer's flight will not live up to its generic claims is in the details we learn about his life. There is, in visionary circles, an equivalent to the rhetorician's notion of *ethos*: a dream should fit the character and station of its dreamer. Weighty dreams generally happen to men of high status; indeed, Macrobius takes pains to establish Scipio's rank, as a major justification for the miraculous nature of his vision.[35] It is thus rather presumptuous of a dull-witted customs official with a shrill-voiced, early rising wife (561-62) to pretend to be a prophet. Given what we know and are to learn about him, the narrator's concern " 'Wher Joves wol me stellyfye' " (586) is wonderfully misplaced; and the Eagle's reply, " 'not . . . as yet' " (599), underlines its improbability. Dante himself had doubts on this score. Because they were the fathers of the Empire and the Church, Aeneas and St. Paul justified the exercise of grace that allowed them to see Hell and Heaven (*Inferno* ii.13-30); but "Io non Enëa, io non Paulo sono" (32) [I am not Aeneas, I am not Paul], and Dante has to be convinced that he too has been given a prophetic role. A measure of its gravity, in fact, is the central position in the *Commedia* of these two visionary pathfinders; they repeatedly give notice of how extraordinary Dante's journey is. Vergil is his guide, among other reasons, because the *Aeneid* describes a heroic descent to the underworld, and so marks out a path for the *Inferno* to follow. And long after Vergil the guide has disappeared, we are once more reminded of *Aeneid* VI when Cacciaguida greets Dante with the affection of Anchises seeing his son in Elysium (*Paradiso* xv.26-27); Dante in effect has become another Aeneas. He is also a direct heir of St. Paul. When he enters the *Paradiso*, he echoes (i.70-76) Paul's expression of doubt about the corporeality of the "man in Christ" who was lifted up into the third heaven:

> Si gloriari oportet (non expedit quidem), veniam autem ad visiones et revelationes Domini. Scio hominem in Christo ante annos quatuordecim, sive in corpore nescio, sive extra corpus nescio, Deus scit, raptum huiusmodi usque ad tertium caelum. Et scio huiusmodi hominem sive in corpore nescio, sive extra corpus nescio, Deus scit: quoniam raptus est in paradisum: et

audivit arcana verba, quae non licet homini loqui. Pro
huiusmodi gloriabor; pro me autem nihil gloriabor nisi in in-
firmitatibus meis.

[2 Corinthians 12:1-5]

[If I must boast—it is not indeed expedient to do so—but I will
come to visions and revelations of the Lord. I know a man in
Christ who fourteen years ago—whether in the body I do not
know, or out of the body I do not know, God knows—such a
one was caught up to the third heaven. And I know such a
man—whether in the body or out of the body I do not know,
God knows—that he was caught up into paradise and heard
secret words that man may not repeat. Of such a man I will
boast; but of myself I will glory in nothing save in my
infirmities.] [36]

The *House of Fame* also uses Vergil and St. Paul as the backdrops
to its vision; but the result is a witty parody of the first canto of the
Paradiso. Book One offers not simply Vergil but the whole *Aeneid* as
Chaucer's guide; and his paralyzing doubt at its conclusion is
answered by a diversion, not a theodicy. Like Dante's, Chaucer's
narrator is an analogue to Aeneas. Because he has served Venus
(615-18), he too is rewarded by Jupiter. The goddess does not, it
must be confessed, intercede for him actively, as she once did for her
son. Indeed, the narrator's service has been entirely poetic, and
"withoute guerdon ever yit" (619); and he is more closely akin to
Dido than to Aeneas, as one in "the daunce" of those whom Love
"lyst not avaunce" (639-40). Unlike the Queen of Carthage, he does
at least get Jupiter's attention; but his reward is not Rome, nor "(as
it might appropriately have been) an affair with the lady next
door."[37] The tourist-class character of his celestial journey, the "som
maner thing" (670) with which he is paid, becomes clear when he in
turn quotes St. Paul:

> Tho gan y loken under me
> And beheld the ayerissh bestes,
> Cloudes, mystes, and tempestes,
> Snowes, hayles, reynes, wyndes,

And th'engendrynge in hir kyndes,
All the wey thrugh which I cam.
"O God!" quod y, "that made Adam,
Moche ys thy myght and thy noblesse!"
And thoo thoughte y upon Boece,
That writ, "A thought may flee so hye,
With fetheres of Philosophye,
To passen everych element;
And whan he hath so fer ywent,
Than may be seen, behynde hys bak,
Cloude,"—and al that y of spak.
  Thoo gan y wexen in a were,
And seyde, "Y wot wel y am here;
But wher in body or in gost
I not, ywys; but God, thou wost!"
For more clere entendement
Nas me never yit ysent.

[964-84]

Chaucer's inversion of his sources in this passage is striking and marvelously funny. The lines in Boethius's *Consolation* from which he quotes describe the soul's ability, using the wings of Philosophy, to ascend beyond the elements and reach its proper home: "the swifte thoght . . . seth the clowdes byhynde his bak, and passeth the heighte of the regioun of the fir, that eschaufeth by the swifte moevynge of the firmament, til that he areyseth hym into the houses that beren the sterres. . . . And whan the thought hath don there inogh, he schal forleten the laste hevene, and he schal pressen and wenden on the bak of the swift firmament, and he schal be makid parfit of the worschipful lyght of God" (*Boece* IV.m.1). Chaucer glaringly marks off the modest limits of his own journey by cutting Boethius off in mid-sentence. His dream does act out Boethius's metaphor: Philosophy's "fetheres" are those of the Eagle, and Chaucer himself must be the "thought." Put in this context, however, the metaphor has unfortunate ramifications. After all, the narrator might well "wexen in a were" over St. Paul's question ("sive in corpore, sive extra corpus"): the jokes earlier in Book Two about his corpulence (574, 660) raise the queasy possibility that he might be dropped or fall, a possibility set up as a comic undercurrent to the Eagle's exposition of the "kyndely enclynyng" of heavy objects downward: " 'And bere hyt never so hye on highte, / Lat goo thyn hand, hit falleth doun' " (740-41). The quotation from Paul also reminds us of its context, to which Dante openly refers (*Paradiso* i.4-9): "audivit arcana verba, quae non licet homini loqui." Paul and Dante hear the *arcana verba* of the Empyrean; the *arcana verba* Chaucer will hear in Book Three are of a rather less sublime sort.

The difference between Chaucer's use of 2 Corinthians and Dante's implies the difference in scope of their visions. Dante and Chaucer unravel two strands that are still woven together in twelfth-century vision literature. Like Dante, Bernardus Silvestris and Alanus de Insulis recount celestial journeys; but they take special care to mark out the normal limits of human understanding, in order to set off the extraordinary difficulties of transcending our earthly perspective. In Alanus's *Anticlaudianus*, Prudentia (best understood as "Knowledge") travels through the heavens on a chariot made by the seven liberal arts and pulled by the horses of the five senses. As she approaches the Empyrean the horses stop in fear (V.72ff.); and Prudentia can complete her journey only because Theologia offers to be her guide. She is henceforth accompanied by the second horse alone, the one representing hearing (V.258)–the only operative sense in the dazzling realm of Paul's *arcana verba*. In the *Cosmographia* of Bernardus Silvestris, Nature makes a similar journey, which "dramatizes the limited vision of universal reality accessible to the human mind. Nature is invigorated by the warm light of the ethereal region, and moves upward through the spheres by sure degrees, but her search is long and exhausting, and she is made to seem a somewhat alien being, from whom the secrets of the heavens are sealed."[38] In both works failing vision draws the line between the created universe and Heaven. "Ad consessum sidereum et contra iubar aetheris inaccessum retusos et coniventes oculos Natura qua poterat intendebat" (*Cosmographia* II.iii.108-09) [Nature turned her dazzled and blinking eyes as best she could toward the thronging stars, and full into the impenetrable brilliance of the ether].[39] And when Alanus's Prudentia tries to look at the heavenly palace of God, she is temporarily blinded (VI.3-5), falls into a stupor, and has to be supported by Theologia (10-11). In the end she can bear the brilliance of Heaven's light only because Fides, Theologia's sister, gives her a mirror (115-20) to diffuse its blinding force. Prudentia is then able to survive even the presence of God himself (279-83).

Chaucer has such sources in mind when he refuses the Eagle's invitation to look at the stars, because " 'they shynen here so bryghte, / Hyt shulde shenden al my syghte' " (1015-16); and he thus confirms the need for the limits Jupiter has placed on his visionary flight. But he shows himself by his refusal to be a not very promising eaglet, and risks a punishment recorded in the natural lore of the medieval bestiaries. For the eagle's distinctive quality among creatures is its ability to look directly at the sun; and it tests its fledglings by carrying them aloft and, if they refuse to face the sun's brilliance, dropping them.[40] Dante too mentions the eagle's remarkable vision (*Paradiso* xx.31-33), but in order to describe his own suddenly superhuman powers. He sees Beatrice looking at the sun—"aguglia sì non li s'affisse unquanco" (*Paradiso* i.48) [never did eagle so fix his gaze thereon] —and discovers that he can follow her example:

> così de l'atto suo, per li occhi infuso
> ne l'imagine mia, il mio si fece,
> e fissi li occhi al sole oltre nostr' uso.
>
> [52-54]

[thus of her action, infused through the eyes into my imagination, mine was made, and I fixed my eyes on the sun beyond our wont.]

The imagery of vision, a traditional sign of the poet's powers, here acts out Dante's invocation to Apollo at the beginning of the canto (i.13-36). Dante claims the authority of a prophet, though with due modesty. As he explains this passage to Can Grande, poets

not only forecast what they are about to say, as orators do, "but in
addition they make use of some sort of invocation afterward. And
this is fitting in their case, for they have need of invocation in a large
measure, inasmuch as they have to petition the superior beings for
something beyond the ordinary range of human powers, something
almost in the nature of a divine gift."[41] Vergil sets the example for
Dante's claiming a superhuman clarity of vision, though there had
been a more recent precedent as well. When Prudentia nears the
Empyrean, Alanus interrupts her flight in order to make an epic
invocation (V.265-77) and to claim a newly infused authority:
"Maiorem nunc tendo liram totumque poetam / Deponens, usurpo
michi noua uerba prophete" (268-69) [I now string a mightier lyre;
and wholly laying aside the poet, I appropriate for myself the extraordinary sayings of the prophet]. God becomes the Muse of his
poem (278).[42]

The difference between Vergil and Ovid, however, repeats itself in
their medieval heirs. For although Chaucer does make a few invocations here and there, he is no *vates*; and, significantly, the Eagle
lists among Chaucer's counterparts as celestial travelers the presumptuous ones: Daedalus, Icarus (919-20), and Phaethon (941-59).
Chaucer's quotation from Boethius and echo of St. Paul may almost
make us forget that he never gets near the Empyrean, or within
range of the sound of its heavenly music. The House of Fame is in
the air (834); and Chaucer, unlike his visionary predecessors, never
rises above the sublunary world. Air is in fact the proper element for
Fame's palace, as Chaucer's sources attest. Bernardus Silvestris
elegantly phrases a conventional antithesis, when he compares the
heavenly realm above the moon—the "quies intermina, serenum
perpetuum, tranquillitas aetheris inconcussa" (II.v.193-94) [endless
calm, perpetual quiet, the unbroken peace of the ethereal re-
gions][43]—with the sublunary world:

> Infra aëris qualitas turbidior infunditur, cuius mutabilis con-
> vertitur species, quotiens expositas passionibus materias con-
> trarietas accidentium interpellat. Unde homines quia locum

incolunt inquietum tumultus instar veteris, motus perturba-
tionum necesse est experiri.

[II.v. 200-05]

[In the regions below were disposed the more turbid
properties of the atmosphere, whose volatile appearance is
altered whenever some chance occurrence offers to its passions
the material they demand. So mankind, inhabiting this unquiet
region, the very image of the ancient chaos, must needs be
subject to the force of its upheavals.] [44]

The noisy air, which contrasts with the ether "quo cuncta silent"
(*Anticlaudianus* IV.338) [where all things are still], differs in its
inhabitants as well. Above the moon are the angels and intelligences
of the spheres, God's celestial hierarchy. But the denizens of the air
are fallen angels, demons

Qui, uelud aerio uestiti corpore, nostram
Mentiti speciem, multo phantasmate brutos
Deludunt homines, falsi uerique sophyste.

[IV.282-84]

[who, clothed as if with an airy body, counterfeiting our form,
sophists of false and true, with many an apparition delude
dull-witted men.]

As purveyors of phantasm and confusers of false and true, these
"uagantes / Aerios ciues" (IV.273-74) [wandering citizens of the
air]—which Chaucer translates as "many a citezeyn" (930)—are
fitting inhabitants of a poetic world defined by dreams, fame, and
the *Aeneid*.

Indeed, once the Eagle has pointed out these "eyryssh bestes"
(932), it is as if the contamination of their sophistry casts doubt
even on their own existence. Now that he has seen them, Chaucer
says, he can believe his books:

And than thoughte y on Marcian,
And eke on Anteclaudian,
That sooth was her descripsion

> Of alle the hevenes region,
> As fer as that y sey the preve;
> Therfore y kan hem now beleve.
>
> [985-90]

In a different poem his credulity might pass without comment, especially if his celestial journey were, like Dante's and Paul's, a waking vision, a *raptus*, and not a dream. But in the *House of Fame*, with its insistence on the uncertain truth of dreams and the effects of too much study, one must wonder if the narrator's dream simply recapitulates his reading, with no independent authority of its own. And in fact, Chaucer and the Eagle repeatedly use the dream experience to prove the truth of written fictions. The first article in the Eagle's proof of the existence of Fame is the location of her palace: " 'First shalt thou here where she duelleth, / And so thyn oune bok hyt tellith' " (711-12)—that is to say, Ovid's description (*Metamorphoses* XII.39-63) is accurate. The Eagle offers to teach Chaucer some star lore, simply so that when he reads poetry, " 'How goddes gonne stellifye / Bridd, fissh, best, or him or here' " (1002-03), he will know how to find the real " 'Raven, or eyther Bere, / Or Arionis harpe fyn' " (1004-05). Most jarringly, when the narrator sums up what he saw of the air (964ff.), he uses half a quotation from Boethius to corroborate his experience: " 'Than may be seen, behynde hys bak, / Cloude,'—and al that y of spak" (977-78).

At the beginning of their flight, the Eagle told Chaucer that he was to be recompensed for the lacunae in his life, and implied that he was guilty of two kinds of subjectivity:

> "That is, that thou hast no tydynges
> Of Loves folk yf they be glade,
> Ne of noght elles that God made."
>
> [644-46]

Too much study has kept him isolated from the world outside, and the sad story of Dido has given him only a partial picture of love. But despite the Eagle's implied promise, the dilemma of Dido is never resolved in the *House of Fame*, even when there is a flood of tidings. And the world outside mirrors the books it is supposed to supplant: its topography derives from Martianus and Alanus, and not necessarily from God. Moreover, the Eagle hardly gives his charge the opportunity to contemplate his new experience. When Chaucer does stop to praise God's "myght" and "noblesse" (971), using the words of Boethius and Paul, the Eagle's response to his rhapsody ends any remaining hope for an epiphany: " 'Lat be . . . thy fantasye!' " (992).

The Eagle's words come from Beatrice, who so rebukes Dante's ecstatic reaction to the music of the spheres, a "suono" (*Paradiso* i.82) that makes him feel a keener desire than ever before to know God:

> . . . ."Tu stesso ti fai grosso
> col falso imaginar, sì che non vedi
> ciò che vedresti se l'avessi scosso.
> Tu non se' in terra, sì come tu credi;
> ma folgore, fuggendo il proprio sito,
> non corse come tu ch'ad esso riedi."
>
> [88-93]

[You make yourself dull with false imagining, so that you do not see what you would see had you cast it off. You are not on earth, as you believe; but lightning, fleeing its proper site, never darted so fast as you are returning to yours.]

His longing, she implies, shows that his thinking is still earthbound. "Man loves because he is not in his proper place,"[45] and Dante is returning home to God so quickly that he should no longer feel the pangs of desire. Beatrice is also impatient because he asked St. Paul's question, at a time when "sive in corpore, sive extra corpus" is becoming increasingly irrelevant to the reality and meaning of his experience. Though her response frees him of his first doubt, Dante once more raises, in another of its aspects, the problem of his corporeality: " 'ma ora ammiro / com' io trascenda questi corpi levi' " (98-99) [but now I marvel how it can be that I should pass through these light bodies]. Her reply, which describes how the "kyndely enclynyng" of things makes them desire a return to their proper place (103ff.), corrects both parts of Dante's "falso imaginar":

> "Non dei più ammirar, se bene stimo,
> lo tuo salir, se non come d'un rivo
> se d'alto monte scende giuso ad imo.
> Maraviglia sarebbe in te se, privo
> d'impedimento, giù ti fossi assiso,
> com' a terra quïete in foco vivo."
>
> [136-41]

[You should not wonder more at your rising, if I deem aright, than at a stream that falls from a mountain top to the base. It would be a marvel if you, being freed from hindrance, had settled down below, even as stillness would be in living fire on earth.]

This Aristotelian principle of "kyndely enclynyng" is central in medieval physics. Furthermore, as Beatrice's discourse indicates, its teleological emphasis gives it powerful moral repercussions. The desire of things to return to their proper place manifests the ruling order of God's love in the universe. Seen in this light, everything in the world shows man the way home. In St. Augustine's words, "If we were stones, waves, wind or flame, or anything of that kind, lacking sense and life, we would still show something like a desire for our own place and order. For the specific gravity of a body is, in a manner, its love, whether a body tends downwards by reason of its heaviness or strives upwards because of its lightness. A material body is borne along by its weight in a particular direction, as a soul is by its love."[46] For inanimate objects, as for both conscious and unconscious creatures, this natural inclination expresses a desire for being, unity, and self-preservation.

The Eagle, like Beatrice, explains "kyndely enclynyng" to his charge, and translates a famous statement of its meaning and implications (*Boece* III.pr.xi). He reminds us that there is a "kyndely stede" where "every kyndely thyng" "may best . . . conserved be"

(730-32), and alludes to the instinct for life implicit in the word
conserved:

> "Thus every thing, by thys reson,
> Hath his propre mansyon,
> To which hit seketh to repaire,
> Ther-as hit shulde not apaire."
>
> [753-56][47]

But there is not one hint, anywhere in the Eagle's speech, of
Beatrice's concern to link the Boethian implications of this in-
stinctual need—"good is the fyn of alle thinges" (*Boece*
III.pr.xi)—with man's inclining toward God. He replaces Beatrice's
answer to *fantasye* with the offer of a lesson in celestial topography:
" 'Wilt thou lere of sterres aught?' " (993); the principle of "kyndely
enclynyng" answers instead the least important question of the
poem. Sound, the Eagle argues, must like everything else in the
world have a "kyndely stede." Since "soun ys noght but eyr
ybroken" (765), its "kynde place" must be in the air (834). Therefore the House of Fame, the goal and magnet of every sound in the
world, must be in the air. Q.E.D.

There is a comic corollary to this proof. Dante, as a Christian
soul, moves by natural inclination to Heaven; Chaucer moves as a
poet, though not entirely by natural inclination, to the House of
Fame. But the most remarkable quality of the argument on sound is
its irrelevance to the central issues of the poem. Whether or not one
agrees with John Leyerle that the Eagle's speech is "an elaborate
joke on flatulence,"[48] his witty reading suggests in vivid terms the
comic inadequacy of the Eagle's viewpoint. If "every speche that ys
spoken . . . in his substaunce ys but air" (766-68), the accidents of
speech are by implication such trivial matters as meaning and truth
value. "Speche," considered in physical terms, is little different from
any other "soun"; and to emphasize their proximity, the Eagle repeatedly pairs the two words (783, 819, 824, 832). From his point
of view the *Aeneid* and flatus are essentially the same thing. Such
reductionism might imply a contempt for earthly things; but

Boethius's similarities to the Eagle's naturalistic perspective are merely superficial. Dante and Boethius rise above the sublunary world to evoke the celestial order, which is beyond the powers of human speech and writing to describe. The Eagle, on the other hand, gains his bird's-eye view by reducing language and meaning to their lowest naturalistic common denominator.

His naturalism is consistently maintained, and he shows a lecturer's love for his own pedantry. The argument on the operations of sound is, he implies, the serious part of his speech: " 'Now wil we speken al of game!' " (886) prefaces a series of tour-guide remarks, exactly when he is soaring high enough to remind Chaucer in his reverie of Boethius and St. Paul. The limits of the Eagle's interests argue against those critics who believe Book Two to show Chaucer's change of allegiance from authority to experience, from musty books to the fresh air of life. The Eagle is assuredly the voice of experience, but he proves to be no more credible than written authority. Although the narrator gives a qualified assent to the proof of how sound moves (872-74), the comically unfortunate avian terms of the Eagle's reply remind us that Chaucer is still as much a captive audience as he was in Book One, dreaming about the *Aeneid*:

> "A ha!" quod he, "lo, so I can
> Lewedly to a lewed man
> Speke, and shewe hym swyche skiles
> That he may shake hem be the biles,
> So palpable they shulden be."
>
> [865-69]

The Eagle's promise of "a preve by experience" (878), after all, simply forecasts a dream about the House of Fame.

In sum, Book Two adds experiential knowledge to the list of the sources for man's confusion in the world. Chaucer's comment on his flight recapitulates the inadequacies of the Eagle's teaching:

> But thus sone in a while he
> Was flowen fro the ground so hye
> That al the world, as to myn yë,

> No more semed than a prikke;
> Or elles was the air so thikke
> That y ne myghte not discerne.
>
> [904-09]

The Boethian resonances of reducing the world to a "prikke" are, as I have argued, undercut by the Eagle's naturalism, which shrinks the world by emptying it of intelligibility and human meaning. The alternative, inescapable below the moon, is fog and confusion. The Eagle's long catalogue of the love tidings Chaucer will hear (675ff.) recalls in its jumble and fragmentation the Libyan desert of Book One and the dream categories of the Proem. Experience proves to be uselessly clear in trivial matters, but as confusing as dreams and books in essentials. Significantly, the narrator sees "cloude" (978) very well; but he says that he is too old for astronomy lessons (995), and his vision is too poor for him to look at the stars.

Book Three

> "Però ti son mostrate in queste rote,
>   nel monte e ne la valle dolorosa
>   pur l'anime che son di fama note,
> che l'animo di quel ch'ode, non posa
>   né ferma fede per essempro ch'aia
>   la sua radice incognita e ascosa,
>   né per altro argomento che non paia."
>
> [*Paradiso* xvii.136-42]

[Therefore only the souls known of fame have been shown to you within these wheels, upon the mountain, and in the woeful valley; for the mind of him who hears rests not nor confirms its faith by an example that has its roots unknown or hidden, nor for other proof that is not manifest.]

Cacciaguida's explanation shows that the *Commedia* is also a poem about Fame, but Fame strictly subordinated to the workings of God's justice.[49] Chaucer, in contrast, allows the goddess a free hand in Book Three; and she distributes the parody of divine justice, arbitrarily determined renown. The promise in Book Two of a mock-theodicy is fulfilled. Fame—in her portrait itself (1367ff.) a caricature of Boethius's Lady Philosophy—sums up the blur of truth and falsehood in dreams, books, and experience; and she epitomizes the contingency and deceit of the sublunary world.

As the qualities of the goddess suggest, Book Three recapitulates Books One and Two. The House of Rumor and the palace of Fame are, as Sheila Delany has argued, "the loci, respectively, of experience and of literary tradition";[50] and they restate the problems already apparent in these sources of knowledge. The restatement is ample: this "lytel laste bok" (1093), in fact as long as the other two put together, proceeds as if in imitation of Fame's magnifying power (1290-92). This restatement is also so clear that there is no need to paraphrase its meaning in great detail. Fame reveals at length, by her responses to a series of petitioners, that her rewards are arbitrary and irrationally assigned. The House of Fame, where Vergil and Ovid appear once more, and the House of Rumor, which the Eagle takes a particular interest in from the start, fit what we have come to expect from them. The poets and other writers who preserve Fame's judgments for posterity are distributed on pillars, each a partisan—like Vergil and "Venus clerk, Ovide" (1487)—of the fame he bears up. The whirling wicker house of Rumor, the source of tidings, is full of tale-tellers who augment and distort what they have heard, and of tidings that become hopelessly blurred: "Thus saugh I fals and soth compouned / Togeder fle for oo tydynge" (2108-09).

There is, appropriately, a certain sense of anticlimax in Book Three, as amplification brings clarity to the teasing subtleties of the first two books. Even the narrator shows some impatience with his so-called reward. The pageantry of Fame's court has not given him much new information of any value; besides, he tells his "frend," he has been promised tidings,

> "But these be no suche tydynges
> As I mene of." "Noo?" quod he.

> And I answered, "Noo, parde!
> For wel y wiste ever yit,
> Sith that first y hadde wit,
> That somme folk han desired fame
> Diversly, and loos, and name.
> But certeynly, y nyste how
> Ne where that Fame duelled, er now,
> And eke of her descripcioun,
> Ne also her condicioun,
> Ne the ordre of her dom,
> Unto the tyme y hidder com."
>
> [1894-1906]

He already knows that Fame is capricious, and is not himself one of her followers (1873-82). In other words, his visit repeats the disappointments of his trip through the sky. Its novelties are interesting but trivial details, not deep truths; moreover, they are details that simply elaborate on the descriptions of Fame in Vergil and Ovid. As in the *Parliament of Fowls*, the wrong questions get answered; and the open-ended conclusion of that poem, where Chaucer awaits a dream of "som thyng for to fare / The bet" (*Parliament* 698-99), resembles the narrator's hope in Book Three to learn something, at least, in the House of Rumor:

> "For yit, paraunter, y may lere
> Som good thereon, or sumwhat here
> That leef me were, or that y wente."
>
> [1997-99]

It is unlikely, as the poem breaks off, that Chaucer will in fact learn anything very exciting. Book Three does, however, illuminate the meaning of the *House of Fame* precisely by its process of recapitulation and anticlimax, for it completes the pattern of expansion and collapse that has prevailed through the poem. Prayer displaces the catalogue of dream theories; the *Aeneid* gives way to a barren wasteland; the Eagle jokes—" 'Take yt in ernest or in game' " (822)—as he ends his lecture on sound; Chaucer's echoes of his visionary ancestors announce a trip to the palace of Fame, not the third heaven; the monumental pillars of Fame's authorities suddenly become a "ful confus matere," part of a hall as full "Of hem that writen olde gestes, / As ben on treës rokes nestes" (1515-16). The structural principle at work in these episodes forecasts the bloated debate on dream theory in the *Nun's Priest's Tale*, no sooner finished than ignored. In each instance, the comic effect is the literary equivalent of a pratfall: the speaker abruptly dismisses what he has just said at length, and usually with a great deal of pomposity or apparent confusion. But also implicit in such dismissals, and of more general importance, is the change of perspective they force upon the narrator: like the narrator of *Troilus*, he moves from detachment to bias, and then from commitment to disillusionment.

In Books One and Two Chaucer begins in a position of awe or discomfort, and progresses to a greater sense of security in his surroundings. He becomes increasingly involved in his experience, and more and more inclined to comment on it. But in each case, he is told that his perceptions are deluded (493, 992). There is a movement from detachment to interest in Book Three as well: in fact, the narrator is very much as he was in the first book. Once again he mixes the passivity of "Ther saugh I" with the more active responses of proverbs, moral platitudes, and comments of wonder and surprise. His growing involvement is most noticeable when the setting shifts from Fame's palace to the House of Rumor, where "I alther-fastest wente / About" (2131-32). This final scene of the poem is unfinished. But the successive collapse of every previous elaborated framework makes the probability of finding truth less and less likely; and one must predict yet another disillusionment.

The limitations of the narrator's knowledge illustrate a congenital human deficiency, as the constant interplay of bias and attempted objectivity shows that they have the same hopeless result. In Book Three, more explicitly than before, the mechanism of amplification and collapse gets at the artistic consequences of human limitation. It explains why Chaucer sees Colle tregetour, who can "carien a wynd-melle / Under a walsh-note shale" (1280-81), among the lesser servants of Fame:

> . . . alle maner of mynstralles,
> And gestiours, that tellen tales
> Both of wepinge and of game,
> Of al that longeth unto Fame.
>
> [1197-1200]

Magicians belong in this world of flux and illusion, where the beryl walls of Fame's palace have magnifying powers (1288-92). Fame's hall itself expands a thousandfold as more and more writers add their works to literary tradition (1493-96), each one demanding attention for his point of view, repeating and amplifying what others have written before, and squabbling with their interpretations of history. This international book depository begins as a noble stasis, in the calm of the eternally opposite viewpoints of Homer, Vergil, Ovid, Lucan, and the rest. But as it expands it gives way to rancor and contradiction, and at last to the narrator's exasperation:

> But hit a ful confus matere
> Were alle the gestes for to here,
> That they of write, or how they highte.
>
> [1517-19]

The pillars, after all, do not even provide a very detailed subject catalogue—let alone Library of Congress call numbers or a system of cross-referencing. Truth, as the story of Aeneas showed, is impossible to ascertain; in Book Three it proves difficult enough even to keep up with the proliferating interpretations of the past.

There is a nearly contemporaneous outburst against such confusion in the preface to the *Pupilla Oculi* (ca. 1385), an abridgment of the *Oculus Sacerdotis*, a manual for parish priests. Its author John de Burgo, chancellor of the University of Cambridge, laments: "As the world grows old, human nature deteriorates, life is shorter, opportunity for acquiring knowledge is lessened." The *Oculus* is too repetitive, and not carefully enough arranged; hence the need for his abridgment: "Other books are neglected by modern parish priests, because they are too prolix and modern men like brevity [*gaudent brevitate moderni*], or because they are too costly."[51] In the *House of Fame* Chaucer makes a comic response to such sentiments against the proliferation of books. After two thousand lines of preliminaries, he refuses to pass on the new tiding that he finally does hear (2136). Why add to the confusion?

> Folk kan synge hit bet than I;
> For al mot out, other late or rathe,
> Alle the sheves in the lathe.
>
> [2138-40]

There are also, however, some serious reasons for such hesitation, since the poet's choice has moral consequences, and tidings are of uncertain truth value. Exactly this problem provoked Dido's complaint against "wikke Fame" in Book One (349); and it will provoke Criseyde as well (*Troilus* V.1058-62). Vergil broadcasts Dido's deeds and sets her reputation forever. Even by writing down his dream Chaucer too is implicated in Fame's workings, as Book Three shows. For he is constricted by the goddess's amoral choices, which can devour a whole tradition. The name of the trumpeter Messenus survives because Vergil mentions him (1244); the others, "that in her tyme famous were" (1249), are now apparently forgotten. The inequity of renown preserves the names of immoral or presumptuous artists—Pseustis and Marsyas (1228-29)—but not of the humble "lytel herde-gromes, / That kepen bestis in the bromes" (1225-26). Yet the narrator's part in the process of spreading fame is not merely a passive one. He can dispense or withhold fame as he chooses: it would take too long, he says, to give the names of "alle these clerkes / That writen of Romes myghty werkes" (1503-04). And his purposes may be as whimsical as those of the goddess herself, as one comic *occupatio* suggests:

> There saugh I sitte in other seës,
> Pleyinge upon sondry gleës,
> Whiche that I kan not nevene,
> Moo than sterres ben in hevene,
> Of whiche I nyl as now not ryme,
> For ese of yow, and los of tyme.

> For tyme ylost, this knowen ye,
> Be no way may recovered be.
>
> [1251-58]

He does, nonetheless, find time to preserve—in jocular imitation of Dante's practice—the name of his contemporary, Colle the magician.

The concerns of the poet in such situations may be nugatory; and it does his status no good to be catalogued with minstrels and magicians among the servants of Fame. Nor is it pleasant to be associated with Eolus the rumormonger. Yet if poetry is imperfect, because of its inevitable connection to Fame, the *House of Fame* has shown that to be human is to be flawed. Chaucer is careful in Book Three to indicate the nobility, however fragile, of the poet's calling. The book is filled with throngs of people: the minstrels, musicians, and magicians outside the palace; the petitioners for Fame's grace; and the mob inside the House of Rumor. But inside Fame's hall there is a sudden quiet space, when the poets and historians are about to make their presence known: "Ful moche prees of folk ther nas, / Ne crowdyng for to mochil prees" (1358-59). These preservers of the past have their base counterparts in the heralds who puff the present, who ask for money (1315) and only "crien ryche folkes laudes" (1322). The poets and historians ask for no reward when they bear up the fame of the people and events of the past. In contrast to the gold of the heralds and of the palace floor, their pillars are

> Of metal that shoon not ful cler;
> But though they nere of no rychesse,
> Yet they were mad for gret noblesse,
> And in hem hy and gret sentence;
> And folk of digne reverence.
>
> [1422-26]

Petrarch's Laureate Oration, the noblest fourteenth-century statement of the poet's high vocation, argues that among his major rewards is the "immortality of one's name. This immortality is itself twofold, for it includes both the immortality of the poet's own

name and the immortality of the names of those whom he celebrates."[52] The poets in the *House of Fame* do not seek fame for
themselves: their pillars name the subjects of their poetry. When
renown comes to them unasked for, it is a fitting reward for their
humility.

Chaucer too, as a poet, responds to the allurements of Fame with
the dignity of his predecessors:

> "Sufficeth me, as I were ded,
> That no wight have my name in honde.
> I wot myself best how y stonde;
> For what I drye, or what I thynke,
> I wil myselven al hyt drynke,
> Certeyn, for the more part,
> As fer forth as I kan myn art."

[1876-82]

The absorption of the self in its vocation is, paradoxically, also its
highest fulfillment and expression. Yet if the poet's art allows him to
make the best of his human condition, his immediate rewards are
limited, and they blend pathos and comedy. Chaucer is promised
relief from his distress as one who is "disesperat of alle blys"
(2011-18). But the Eagle makes clear, as Africanus does in the
Parliament, the enforced detachment Cupid has imposed on his
poet: the reward of happy love tidings is not necessarily a satis-
factory substitute for a happy love affair. Apparently, those who
cannot do anything write; or, more precisely, those who write
cannot act.

This necessary disjunction of experience and perception leads the
poet more to a comic, resigned acceptance than to despair; and it
completes the thematic pattern of the poem. Chaucer has rephrased
Ovid's central awareness of human limitations; and he has done so
by using the Ovidian trick of building structures that immediately
fall apart. The *House of Fame* has examined in turn the impermanence and illusory quality of every subject it has touched:
books, experience, love, fame, and art. Chaucer's message in all this

is almost a Boethian one, but we are not offered Boethius's recourse. In fact, the moral of the poem is Ovidian, and it is not simply to retreat from the complicated, deceitful, fascinating world. The *House of Fame* portrays the inevitable effort and equally inevitable failure of man to describe and understand his experience and surroundings from the only perspective available to him. In this world where mutability touches everything, we are left with an awareness of the impermanence—but also the vitality, comic exuberance, and poignant beauty—of things that "wexe and wane sone, / As doth the faire white mone" (2115-16).

3

LOVE AND THE LAW OF NATURE

This chapter discusses two versions, one early and one late, of Chaucer's abiding interest in the uneasy relationship of man with his earthly surroundings. The *Book of the Duchess* and the *Parliament of Fowls*, despite the obvious differences between them, explore the same basic Ovidian issue: the contrast between Nature's blissful oblivion and human consciousness, with its potential for unhappy frustration; or the analogous contrast between a lost state of innocence under Nature's law and the world of decadent experience. The two works, moreover, share the interests of the *House of Fame*, but present them in purer, unmixed forms. The narrator of the *House of Fame* finds himself caught between bias and detachment. In the *Book of the Duchess*, an unhappy lover is tripped up by his subjective responses; in the *Parliament*, Chaucer is told that he will remain detached, willy-nilly. Like the *House of Fame*, these two poems are dream visions about love. But Chaucer augments their effect with a powerful statement of love's pervading, unitive force: "love is he that alle thing may bynde; / For may no man fordo the lawe of kynde" (*Troilus* I.237-38).

Irony and the Age of Gold in the *Book of the Duchess*

> Siecle vraiment heureux, siecle d'or estimé,
> Où toujours l'amoureux se voyoit contre-aimé.[1]

[Age truly happy, esteemed age of gold, when the lover always found himself loved in return.]

Ronsard's couplet recalls a theme common enough in classical
and medieval poetry: that the Golden Age, man's brief happy spring
on earth, was a time when Love ruled human relations, and love's
fulfillment was to be had for the asking. To the mind of the moralist
our Fall, from Arcadia or from Eden, has one cause and symptom:
"love is falle into discord";[2] wars displace peaceful friendliness. The
amorist's private passion is as much affected by the world's decline:
eros joins *amicitia* and *caritas* in a general decay, when innocence
becomes duplicity and contentment lapses into unsatisfiable longing.
This chapter argues that Chaucer—drawing on his French contemporaries and on Ovid—uses primitivistic myth to console John of
Gaunt for the death of his first wife. The consolation, such as it is,
proves to be secular, not Christian. Nature teaches the poet her law,
and she forces the modern lover to come to terms with the golden
past.

The narrator's characterization of himself is at the heart of the
poem. His interpretation of his experience shapes ours, though not
always in the way he intends; his part in the action of his dream
makes possible its resolution. He is an unhappy lover whose portrait
Chaucer takes, almost word for word, from the opening of
Froissart's *Paradys d'Amours*:

> Je sui de moi en grant merveille
> Comment je vifs quant tant je veille,
> Et on ne poroit en veillant
> Trouver de moi plus traveillant,
> Car bien saciés que par veillier
> Me viennent souvent travillier
> Pensées et merancolies
> Qui me sont ens au coer liies
> Et pas ne les puis deslyer,
> Car ne voeil la belle oublyer
> Pour quele amour en ce traveil
> Je sui entrés et tant je veil.[3]

[I greatly wonder how I stay alive when I stay awake so much.
And one could not find anyone awake more exhausted than I

am, for well you must know that while I stay awake thoughts
and melancholy ideas, which are bound inside in my heart,
often come to torment me. And I can't unbind them, because
I don't wish to forget the lady for whose love I am entered
into this torment and stay awake so much.]

Chaucer's one departure from his source shifts the subjective mode
of the French *complainte d'amour* toward something approaching
solipsism. Froissart presents the Ovidian paradox of the lover who
knows he is ill yet refuses to cure himself.[4] Chaucer intensifies the
paradox and makes it sinister by postponing for twenty lines
Froissart's quick admission that love is the cause of his sickness. In
the meantime, we hear the prolonged lament of a "mased thyng"
who cannot discriminate between joy and sorrow because he has lost
all feeling (10-12). Numbness of spirit has apparently also blunted
his ability to explain what is wrong with him. When the narrator
does belatedly admit to being a victim of unrequited love, his dif-
fidence and his vacillation between statement and denial suggest that
he is as much unable as unwilling to heal himself:

> But men myght axe me why soo
> I may not sleepe, and what me is.
> But natheles, who aske this
> Leseth his asking trewely.
> Myselven can not telle why
> The sothe; but trewly, as I gesse,
> I holde hit be a sicknesse
> That I have suffred this eight yeer,
> And yet my boote is never the ner;
> For there is phisicien but oon
> That may me hele; but that is don.
> Passe we over untill eft;
> That wil not be mot nede be left;
> Our first mater is good to kepe.
>
> [30-43]

The peculiarly sprightly tone of this confession prepares us for
Chaucer's characteristic opposition of game and earnest, made ex-

plicit when he jokingly promises Morpheus a featherbed, though
"me lyst ryght evel to pleye" (239). This tension defines the
narrator's state of mind, an unstable mixture of good-natured
obtuseness and pathetic compulsion. When he says the poem is to be
about sleeplessness instead of love, we may wonder how he hopes to
relieve the symptom of his illness if he ignores the cause. But the
potential comedy in this failure to see the forest for the trees is
qualified by the hopelessness of Chaucer's position. He has been ill
for so long that he has almost no expectation of relief. In story,
sleep, and dream he looks merely for diversions from his waking
obsession. If game happens to turn to earnest, if the diversions prove
to be the cure, the narrator may well echo Froissart's wonder at the
way results defy our intentions:

> On cerche bien ce qu'on ne poet trouver,
> Si troeve l'en souvent sans demander
> Ce qu'on ne cuide veoir ne encontrer.[5]

[One really looks for what one cannot find, and yet often
finds without asking what one does not think to see or come
upon.]

What Chaucer's narrator seeks and cannot find is a poem about
insomnia, the "first mater" to which he notoriously returns after
reading the story of Ceyx and Alcyone (218ff.). Nonetheless, if his
effort to control the movement of the poem is in the wrong
direction, the error is in part excusable. He proceeds, even in his
solipsistic use of Ovid's tale, according to expectations that are
perfectly appropriate to the genre of the lover's complaint. In several
of Chaucer's French contemporaries, Ceyx and Alcyone simply provide a pretext for the poet to consider his own concerns. Indeed,
their precedent suggests not that Chaucer's focus is wrong, but that
he is foolish to restrict his requested boon to a few hours of sleep
(263). In the *Paradys d'Amours*, for example, Froissart prays to
Juno and Morpheus for a dream in which he can make his complaint
to the god of love.[6] One of Deschamps's ballades wittily uses
Alcyone's dream as good counsel for the poet's own romantic needs:

> Saincte Juno, vueillez moy conforter,
> Car je n'ose n'escripre ne parler
> A ma Dame: quelque part qu'elle soit,
> Fay lui mes maulx en dormant figurer
> Par Morpheus; de conseil vueil ouvrer:
> Foulz est li homs qui bon conseil ne croit.[7]

[Holy Juno, would you solace me, for I dare neither to write nor to speak to my lady. Wherever she may be, make my sufferings—while she is asleep—take shape for her in the person of Morpheus. I want to act according to counsel; foolish is the man who does not believe good counsel.]

And the shy lover whom Machaut overhears in the *Fonteinne Amoureuse* hopes that Morpheus, in light of the Ovidian precedent, will carry a message of love to his lady.[8]

Such uses of Ovid's story depend on a refusal to dwell on its controlling, pathetic theme: the fulfilled, reciprocal love of Ceyx and Alcyone, who are surely one of the few happily married couples in classical mythology. Ovid stresses that they were equally ardent and that Alcyone filled Ceyx's dying thoughts and last words.[9] Their faithful, conjugal love continues after their metamorphosis, when the pity of the gods allows them relief from insupportable suffering and they become the birds that breed, nest, and calm the sea at the time of the winter solstice.[10] Chaucer refuses them this release: as is his practice, he deletes Ovid's simple miracle of metamorphosis. Yet the miraculous working of Nature, whose agency turns the narrator's game to earnest, depends on a transformation more subtle but as Ovidian in its effect. When Ovid's Io is turned into a cow, her failure to catch up quickly enough with her new form generates the Ovidian blend of pathos and comedy.[11] She has no arms to hold out in supplication, and her attempts to articulate her terror come out as moos. With an analogous result, the narrator of the *Book of the Duchess* suddenly finds himself in the wrong genre. What began as a poem about insomnia, with overtones of a lover's complaint, abruptly turns into an elegy; and, like Io, the narrator is slow to catch up with such a radical and unexpected shift.

So must be the reader. We have no reason to expect beforehand that Chaucer will replace what he deletes from Ovid's story: that the opening peace of the dream will supplant the tranquillity of the halcyon days; that Ceyx and Alcyone, denied their Ovidian metamorphosis, will reappear transformed by the dream as the man in black and "goode faire White" (948). On the other hand, we do have certain advantages of consciousness over the dazed dreamer, and we may well suspect that his responses will be increasingly inadequate to the demands of his situation. From the start the poem lets slip its key thematic words: Nature, sorrow, and love. But although the meaning of the narrator's dream experience will depend on the unfolding of their complex interrelationship, he is unable to juggle more than two of these terms at one time. Sorrowing insomnia is unnatural, he says; and his sympathy with Alcyone arises from the sorrow, not the love, they both feel:

> Such sorowe this lady to her tok
> That trewly I, which made this book,
> Had such pittee and such rowthe
> To rede hir sorwe, that, by my trowthe,
> I ferde the worse al the morwe
> Aftir, to thenken on hir sorwe.
>
> [95-100]

The peculiar self-pointing of these lines confirms earlier hints. Chaucer portrays himself as a man too obsessed by his own concerns to see anything else very clearly or dispassionately. He shows no interest in a union directly in contrast to his own unrequited love. A kindred sorrow and its possible remedy are his concern.

If the narrator's emphasis on Alcyone's sorrow results from an impaired vision of the world, his surprise at finding sorrow's remedy "a wonder thing" (61) shows how little he expects from his reading. There are two reasons for his initial detachment. The book he asks for is a "romaunce," full of "fables" about "thinges smale" (48-59), which can serve as a diversion from insomnia and sorrow. But the distance of fiction and romance from fact, the distance that makes the story available as "play" (50), also denies it a serious application to Chaucer's own plight. Moreover, the fable is set in the distant past:

> And in this bok were written fables
> That clerkes had in olde tyme,
> And other poets, put in rime
> To rede, and for to be in minde,
> While men loved the lawe of kinde.
>
> [52-56]

The remoteness of this "olde tyme" from the present is as much moral as temporal. As Chaucer's dream will confirm, the "lawe of kinde" is not simply "the characteristic religion of pre-Christian times," but specifically the natural law that governed the earth in its first, Golden Age.[12] As the world declined, Nature's rule was lost and men became progressively more brutal in their dealings with one another.[13] The "romaunce" is therefore irrelevant to the narrator precisely because men no longer love the law of kind. What was once "for to be in minde" is for him—and, by extension, for us—nothing more than a fairy tale. And if its central premise is the possibility of a perfectly fulfilled love relationship, then it is no wonder the romance pertains to modern experience only in its digression on sleep and in its indication of the universality of human sorrow. The perfect union of Ceyx and Alcyone is no longer possible; the narrator's hopeless love marks the modern norm.[14]

In so linking the ages of the world with particular gradations of love, Chaucer follows Jean de Meun's *Roman de la Rose,* in which Ami contrasts the degenerate present with the Golden Age.[15] The *Roman* cites the Ovidian tag "non bene conveniunt nec in una sede morantur / maiestas et amor"[16] [majesty and love do not suit each other well, nor do they linger in one dwelling-place]. Like other medieval love poets, Jean ignores the context of this joke on Jupiter and uses it to lament the loss of equality between men and women, which alone permits love to thrive. The jealous husband who treats his wife as property is a modern counterexample:

> onques amor et seigneurie
> ne s'entrefirent compaignie
> ne ne demorerent ensemble:
> cil qui mestroie les dessemble.
>
> [8421-24] [17]

[Love and lordship never joined company nor remained together. He who dominates pulls them apart.]

Deschamps's ballade "La loy souvent contraire à la nature" [law is often contrary to nature] establishes the same point with a good deal of wit, as it explores the relation of the declining world to love, "qui onques jour n'ama bien seignourie" [who never loved lordship much]. The "franchise commune" [universal generosity] of the Golden Age, when "chascuns avoit plaisir / De soy monstrer vray ami et amie" [all were pleased to show themselves as true lovers, male and female alike], has given way to the modern drabness of "espoux et espousée" [husband and wife]. Love has become "pale et brune" [pale and morbid], and has lost its "clarté." "Franchise" is now dead; the force of law, "qui veult nature anientir" [which wishes to destroy nature], has replaced man's once strong, but now lost, disposition to love.

The mordant refrain of Deschamps's ballade, "Ainsi fist on, mais on ne le fait mie" [People once acted this way, but now don't at all],[18] will be proved false in Chaucer's dream by the example of Blanche and John of Gaunt. Their union—though the conventional language of courtship dictates that the lady have "governaunce" (1286)—is in fact characterized by equality and perfect unanimity.[19] They are the modern equivalents of Ceyx and Alcyone:

> "Oure hertes wern so evene a payre,
> That never nas that oon contrayre
> To that other, for no woo.
> For sothe, ylyche they suffred thoo
> Oo blysse, and eke oo sorwe bothe;
> Ylyche they were bothe glad and wrothe;
> Al was us oon, withoute were."
>
> [1289-95]

Moreover, "White" and her knight remind us of a better past as much by the process of their courtship as by its perfect resolution. For the terms the knight uses to recount his life imply a parallel with the history of the world. Love and the rule of Nature's law define his own first age: his youthful mind was a *tabula rasa* on which love imprinted itself "kyndely" (778-84). He has served love alone

> ". . . sith first I kouthe
> Have any maner wyt fro youthe,
> Or kyndely understondyng."
>
> [759-61]

And though he now knows full well the corrosive effects of experience, love survives in his heart as a vestige of lost innocence:

> "I ches love to my firste craft;
> Therefore hit ys with me laft,
> For-why I tok hyt of so yong age
> That malyce hadde my corage
> Nat that tyme turned to nothyng
> Thorgh to mochel knowlechyng."
>
> [791-96]

The "malyce" and "to mochel knowlechyng" that have since corrupted his spirit and the world's do not triumph without contest. We are given many indications that Nature's beneficence does survive in the fallen world, if only as a blind sympathy for the sorrow of earthly creatures. The forces of Nature offer possibilities of relief and regeneration: the spring can forget the "povertee" and "sorwes" of winter (410-13); the knight's blood rushes to his fainting heart "by kynde" (494); and Pan, the "god of kynde," is "wroth" because of the knight's sorrow (512-13). [20] The most wonderful of these tokens of Nature's good will is the gift the narrator receives to assuage his insomnia and melancholy, which are also "agaynes kynde" (16). For his dream of a world presided over by "th 'emperour Octovyen" (368) promises a vision of the Golden Age, which he had read about without understanding. The attempts to identify Octovyen as Edward III [21] or, by a numerological pun, as Christ [22] have obscured what is surely the most likely possibility. Octovyen is

Augustus Caesar, and he is so named in the *Legend of Good Women*
(624) and in Machaut's *Jugement dou Roy de Behaingne*. [23] Indeed,
the medieval association of Augustan Rome with the Golden Age is a
persistent one, [24] and it appears in the fourteenth century not only
in such writers as Benvenuto da Imola and Petrarch, [25] but also in the
poetry of Deschamps: "Quant verray je le temps Octovien, / Que
toute paix fut au monde affermée?" [26] [When shall I see the
Octavian time, when utter peace was established in the world?].

The narrator's dream-world, then, is governed by the emperor of
the Golden Age and by the "kyndely" sympathy of Nature, and the
most prominent inhabitant of this world is a knight whose love fits
the traditional account of the prelapsarian ideal. But these dreamed
hints of golden stability and harmony do not remain unsullied.
Chaucer takes from Jean de Meun his description of the *locus
amoenus* where Flora and Zephirus live and where the earth strives
to outdo the heaven, "To have moo floures, swiche seven, / As in the
welken sterres bee" (408-09). In the *Roman de la Rose*, this setting
belongs to the "printens pardurable" [everlasting spring] of the
Golden Age.[27] In the *Book of the Duchess*, however, it is placed in a
wider, chastening perspective. The earth

> . . . had forgete the povertee
> That wynter, thorgh hys colde morwes,
> Had mad hyt suffre, and his sorwes,
> All was forgeten, and that was sene.
> For al the woode was waxen grene;
> Swetnesse of dew had mad hyt waxe.

[410-15]

The blithe unconsciousness of spring stands in poignant contrast to
our human inability to forget that winter will come again. As
Chaucer's phrasing intimates, the pure release of the opening of the
dream is only temporary: the narrator cannot escape sorrow for
long.

The disturbance of his May-morning joy is at first nearly im-
perceptible. A call to a hunt might normally awaken purely con-

ventional expectations: in the *Paradys d'Amours*, for example, an allegorical hunt of love follows Froissart's prayer to Juno and Morpheus for a dream.[28] But Chaucer's choice of words creates an undertone of uneasiness that prepares us for the lament to follow:

> And al men speken of huntyng,
> How they wolde slee the hert with strengthe,
> And how the hert had, upon lengthe,
> So moche embosed, y not now what.
>
> [350-53]

If the hart has *embosed* ("exhausted") himself, it must imply that he will easily be killed; given this certainty, the hesitance of the phrase "y not now what" darkens the lighthearted bustle of the hunters' preparations. The vague menace in these lines presages a more extensive uneasiness between man and Nature. Indeed, the hunt soon impinges on the *locus amoenus,* at first in an almost comic fashion as Chaucer's approach frightens away a paradisal assembly of animals (427-34, 443-44). The threat of sorrow becomes stronger with the appearance of the knight, whose wintry heart—like that of the amorous narrator in a typical medieval lyric—jars with the vernal bliss around him. He too is a hunter's prey: like the "hert," his "herte" is in mortal danger.[29] Nature helps each to escape death, though just barely (1312-13). The hart survives because of his natural cunning (381), the heart because of a sympathetic natural process (490-94) and the unwitting assistance of the narrator.

His assistance is unwitting because, repeating an earlier error, he misunderstands the reason for the knight's sorrow. Chaucer shifted the emphasis of Ovid's story to fit his own emotional needs: Alcyone's sorrow and sleeplessness were relevant to his situation, her fulfilled love was not. A similar distortion dominates his dream, as he finds an alter ego in the knight. As before, there is some excuse for his confusion. In a dream designed by convention to provide solace for himself,[30] its dreamer might well expect some commiseration from another unrequited lover. Moreover, much of the knight's description of his plight is phrased rather ambiguously, and

helps perpetuate the initial error.[31] The trope of the chess game
played with Fortune (618-86) could as easily describe a loss by
betrayal as by death. And the "poun errant" (661) with which
Fortune checkmates the knight could quite possibly be, as the narrator seems to believe, a successful rival who has stolen the knight's
beloved.

Whatever the justification for his confusion, the result is an
almost unbearable tension between our knowledge that "White" is
dead and his failure to comprehend the knight's lyric, which tells us
so (475-86).[32] The extent of his misunderstanding becomes clear
when he tries to console the knight with a rather glib reference to
Socrates and a series of authoritative exempla (717-39). These
exempla have a well-rehearsed air: the vitriol of the narrator's comments on Dido and the others (734, 737) suggests that he has often,
and without success, used them to rebuke himself. In fact, the important point about the exempla is their utter irrelevance to the
knight; they apply only to the narrator, or to someone exactly like
him. Medea murdered her children, and Phyllis, Dido, and Echo
committed suicide because of unrequited passion, not because their
lovers had died.[33] And surely the narrator's astounding claim that
Samson died for love of Delilah (738) simply underlines once again
his ability to adapt all remotely similar experience to his own distorted perceptual framework. Indeed, the most striking evidence of
his self-absorption is his failure to mention the one example obviously analogous to the knight's predicament: Ceyx and Alcyone.

Nonetheless, the ancient couple impose the pattern of their fulfilled love on Chaucer's dream; for in it he, as disgruntled modern,
directly confronts the golden past. His dream makes his reading
come alive. The stained-glass windows of his glittering bedchamber
portray two no longer possible kinds of fulfillment: the heroism of
the Troy story, and the lover's success in the *Roman de la Rose*
(326-34). The cold fact of their loss in a shrunken world becomes
more and more apparent as the dialogue of knight and narrator
allows us to compare the two men. No doubt the careful distinction
in Chaucer's use of "thou" and "ye" does reflect the tact of a civil

servant presuming to console a prince.[34] But it establishes a difference in stature that is moral as well as social: to use the metaphor
of Bernard of Chartres, a modern dwarf here meets an ancient
giant.[35] There may be a hint of this confrontation in the narrator's
painfully inappropriate art-of-love questions (745-48, 1130-43), inappropriate because the knight's account repeatedly evokes the artless
innocence of his courtship (e.g., 1160-74). After all, as Ovid pointed
out, artfulness in love became necessary only as the world declined,
when decadence and sophistication superseded natural simplicity in
human relations.[36] Elsewhere, it becomes unambiguously clear that
the knight is another Ceyx, misplaced in the age of iron. " 'But ther is
no man alyve her / Wolde for a fers make this woo!' " (740-41), the
narrator exclaims. He surely does not mean that modern men are like
Socrates immune to fortune; instead, as his own experience has shown,
no modern woman is worth getting very upset about. The virtues and
fidelity of an Alcyone are no longer to be found. In the fallen world
relativism replaces an absolute standard of value; one may grant
another his perception of worth and beauty, but only in terms that
imply a solipsistic delusion:

> "I leve yow wel, that trewely
> Yow thoghte that she was the beste,
> And to beholde the alderfayreste,
> Whoso had loked hir with your eyen."
>   [1048-51]

Thus, the narrator blunders through an attempt at consolation by
attacking the fickleness of love and women. Yet at every turn, the
platitudes his own unhappy love affair provides are exactly the ones
least appropriate to the knight's experience. This tension between
modern realities and ancient values explains his most confusing
response to the knight's account:

> "And yet she syt so in myn herte,
> That, by my trouthe, y nolde noght,
> For al thys world, out of my thoght
> Leve my lady; noo, trewely!"

> "Now, by my trouthe, sir!" quod I,
> "Me thynketh ye have such a chaunce
> As shryfte wythoute repentaunce."
>   "Repentaunce! nay, fy!" quod he,
> "Shulde y now repente me
> To love?"

[1108-17]

The vehemence of the knight's self-defense underlines the magnitude
of the other's error. To the narrator's mind, the ill luck of "such a
chaunce"[37] has absolved the knight from love's service without
erasing his remembered desire. He is shriven by his mistress's betrayal, but does not yet repent his misdirected love for her. The
dreamer is unable to escape the sorrows of love; from his point of
view, the knight seems oddly unwilling to do so.

The unwillingness is of course justified. It becomes apparent that
Blanche is, despite the narrator's doubts, well worth the woe. She is
Trouthe's "maner principal" and "restyng place" (1004-05), and
Nature's "chef patron of beaute / And chef ensample of al hir werk"
(910-11). Her artless, straightforward manner appears in her refusal
to use the "knakkes smale" of decadent coquetry (1024-33). She
takes on the stature of the ancient heroines; in fact, rhetoric makes
her one of them:

> "She was as good, so have I reste,
> As ever was Penelopee of Grece,
> Or as the noble wif Lucrece,
> That was the beste—he telleth thus,
> The Romayn, Tytus Lyvyus—
> She was as good, and nothyng lyk,
> Thogh hir stories be autentyk;
> Algate she was as trewe as she."

[1080-87]

These lines directly answer the jealous husband's charge against
modern women:

> "Si n'est il mes nule Lucrece,

> ne Penelope nule en Grece,
> ne preude fame nule an terre,
> se l'en les savoit bien requerre."
>
> [8621-24] [38]

["However, there is no Lucrece any more, nor any Penelope in Greece, nor any honest woman in the world, even supposing that one indeed knew how to look for them."]

In the *Book of the Duchess*, a modern exemplar of chaste fidelity defies the declining world and refutes the cynicism of Chaucer's narrator.

If Blanche can equal the noblest women of antiquity, the knight compares himself rather unfavorably to a number of ancient heroes (1056-72), though the point of his comparison is that he would still—even with their larger-than-life qualities—have " 'loved best my lady free' " (1055). The lover's courtesy that makes Blanche even more akin to the ancients than he is extends to the delineation of the innocence they both possess. The knight describes his "firste youthe" as a time when " 'ful lytel good y couthe' " (799-800), using a phrase that recalls the unconscious natural innocence of the "whelp, that fauned me as I stood, / That hadde yfolowed, and koude no good" (389-90).[39] Blanche, on the other hand, possesses a kind of innocence even more valuable than the knight's natural inclination to love and virtue:

> "She had a wyt so general,
> So hool enclyned to alle goode,
> That al hir wyt was set, by the rode,
> Withoute malyce, upon gladnesse;
> And therto I saugh never yet a lesse
> Harmful than she was in doynge.
> I sey nat that she ne had knowynge
> What harm was; or elles she
> Had koud no good, so thinketh me."
>
> [990-98]

Her virtue is both natural and something strived for; and she transcends the fallen world by recognizing and then dismissing its treacherous complexities.

Blanche thus keeps the Golden Age alive in the iron world. The paradox encompassed by her worldly innocence resolves itself as a moderation that defines her character:

> "She nas to sobre ne to glad;
> In alle thynges more mesure
> Had never, I trowe, creature."
>
> [880–82]

This "mesure" counters the extremes of change embodied in Fortune, who presides over the fallen world, just as Blanche's straightforwardness contrasts with Fortune's dissimulation (620–49). Though her death gives Fortune the chess game, Blanche in a sense has the final victory. For her "mesure" and wise innocence suggest the means by which the knight may escape his paralyzing sorrow and the series of antitheses—exactly mimicking the movement of Fortune's wheel—that now characterize his life (598–618). "To mochel knowlechyng" (796) is at the root of the narrator's sardonic view of the declining world; and it is precisely what threatens the knight, as he experiences mortality and the inevitable loss of earthly happiness. He cannot lose this knowledge. Man does not have the recourse of Nature, whose unconscious innocence allows it to accept the cycles of the seasons, of life and death, of joy and pain in a world tarnished by the loss of the Golden Age. Yet Blanche's innocence, achieved as it is by the full exercise of consciousness, does offer a human equivalent to Nature's resilience, indeed, a distinctively human refusal to give in to contingency and decay. In addition, Chaucer offers his narrator and the mourning knight the one recourse consciousness can give, the uniquely human ability to retain the past in memory and in a sense make it come alive once again. In this respect, the human actors of the *Book of the Duchess* copy Nature's annual return to bliss. The narrator finds, at the beginning of his dream, the unalloyed happiness of a spring morning. The knight, in his recounting of the progress of his love affair, evokes the freshness of his own first age (790-845, 1090-1107, 1171-80) and gains the serenity of remembered perfection (1287-97).

There is little indication in the poem that their relief from sorrow is any more permanent than the spring. The narrator is apparently not much happier after his dream than before (e.g., 99-100). And the knight's nearly successful attempt to bring remembered happiness back to life is brusquely cut off by the narrator's exclamation when he finally realizes how Blanche was lost (1298-1310). But a limited consolation does take shape in the narrator's belated recognition of what has been lost. Blanche's example shows his pessimistic view of the modern world to be not simply self-destructive but also only partially correct. He was able to find the story of Ceyx and Alcyone irrelevant to his own situation because of its distance in a better past. It proves impossible so to escape the lesson of Blanche and her knight because they are emphatically modern embodiments of "trouthe" and virtue. However much the world has declined from its first, golden age, Blanche shows that perfection can still exist and that the rewards of love can outweigh its terrors. Though we have little to stave off our sorrow at the mortality of such perfection, we at least can use the memory of its human exemplars as a defense against time and fortune. It is this possibility that gives meaning to Chaucer's comparison of himself as author (96) with the "clerkes . . . and other poets" of "olde tyme" (53-54), and to his vow, when he awakes book in hand, to make a poem of his dream (1324-33). The story of Ceyx and Alcyone was written "for to be in minde" (55) for the men of the Golden Age. The story of Blanche and John of Gaunt, the *Book of the Duchess* elegantly implies, can serve the narrator and us as a partial consolation for the sorrow of a fallen world.

The Discordant Concord of the *Parliament of Fowls*

The *Parliament of Fowls* is Chaucer's most sophisticated comment on the world ruled by Nature; indeed, it is in many respects the thematic epitome of his poetry. This dream vision re-explores the Ovidian themes of the earlier poems, but with a new clarity and economy. It sets out to unravel the paradox of love, which is the favorite subject of Chaucer's major poems, early and late. Chaucer's narrator tries to disentangle the paradox in a series of juxtapositions; but he succeeds in creating only a spurious clarity, and the conflicts he exposes are left unresolved. The narrator's failures of understanding are given depth by his enforced separation from the natural world around him. As fallen, conscious man faces instinctive Nature, the systems that the mind discovers in the world, or imposes on it, verge on collapse.

The first few stanzas of the poem recall the *Book of the Duchess* and the *House of Fame,* and open up a similar range of thematic issues. Once again the narrator is a dreamer, and once again his dream is provoked by his reading. Moreover, this dream too, like the one in the *House of Fame,* begins in a rather literary manner: Cicero's *Somnium Scipionis* gives Chaucer his dream-guide, and Dante is the source for the gate to Love's garden.[40] Just as the lover dreams of love and the knight of battle (99-105), so by implication the reader dreams of books. To dream of books is not a matter for reproach. It does, however, imply a certain distance from the complexities of experience, a distance even greater than the normal gap between reality and a dreamed wish-fulfillment: "The lovere met he hath his lady wonne" (105). Chaucer's narrator may read in order to understand; but his reading leads to more dreams about life, not to life itself:

> I wok, and othere bokes tok me to,
> To reede upon, and yit I rede alwey.
> I hope, ywis, to rede so som day
> That I shal mete som thyng for to fare
> The bet, and thus to rede I nyl nat spare.
>
> [695-99]

Yet the narrator's distance from experience—to *mete* ("dream") something is, unfortunately, not the same as to live it—is not entirely self-imposed. His dream, like the one in the *House of Fame*, is a payment for his poetic service to Love; and the payment, as before, is not a love affair, but additional material for his love poetry.

The *Parliament* is in this respect, like the *Book of the Duchess*, reminiscent of a good many medieval lyrics, in which a loveless narrator yearningly sees the amatory excitement and promised fruition of Nature quickening in spring. But the device, conventional as it is, also has deeper resonances. In most of his major works Chaucer explores the paradox of the non-lover writing about love. The *Parliament* explicitly raises the question of what it means to be a reader instead of a lover. When the promises of heaven and hell on the gate to Love's garden have left Chaucer paralyzed, Africanus pushes him through:

> "For this writyng nys nothyng ment bi the,
> Ne by non, but he Loves servaunt be:
> For thow of love hast lost thy tast, I gesse,
> As sek man hath of swete and bytternesse.
>
> "But natheles, although that thow be dul,
> Yit that thow canst not do, yit mayst thow se.
> For many a man that may nat stonde a pul,
> It liketh hym at the wrastlyng for to be,
> And demeth yit wher he do bet or he."
>
> [158-66]

The image is apt, for it raises the issue that is central in most of Chaucer's works: how do we know things, and how do we know if what we know is the truth? Books can lie, or at least disagree, as Vergil and Ovid differed about Dido, and the Troy-poets about Troy. Or, as proves to be true of Macrobius in the *Parliament,* they may simply answer the wrong question: "For bothe I hadde thyng which that I nolde, / And ek I nadde that thyng that I wolde" (90-91). Experience, as the wrestling image suggests, raises its own problems; it is by no means a fulfilling substitute for written authority. The wrestler knows a lot about wrestling, but loses detachment and objectivity by his involvement in process. The spectator can judge who is the better wrestler, but how can he tell the full meaning of the experience he observes? Chaucer's dreams are themselves in the realm of experience; yet, as the Proem of the *House of Fame* stresses, dreams are notoriously difficult to define or interpret. In the *Parliament,* the result of the dream is much the same as the result of the narrator's reading—not surprisingly, since the dream springs from the reading and in some sense mirrors it. Although we are not called upon to decide that either is a lie, they are both inconclusive, and do not satisfy the narrator's unstated needs (695-99).

The unsatisfying, loose-ended quality of the dream depends on, though it is not fully explained by, the inconclusiveness of the debate at Nature's parliament. Chaucer's use here of juxtaposition and unresolved dramatic contrast directly forecasts the debates in the *Canterbury Tales.* Specifically, the dispute about love among the birds, who are divided pretty much along class lines, has a great deal in common with Miller versus Knight. In each instance no resolution of the conflict seems possible, at least on the issue of truth. There are other issues at stake, to be sure; but Chaucer's comments as a spokesman for genteel behavior and social rank are too self-consciously witty to be considered entirely serious. In the *Canterbury Tales,* his disingenuous apology for the Miller's "harlotrie" (I.3167-86) is so intrusive that it breaks the illusion of verisimilitude: we remember that Chaucer himself of course wrote this "cherles tale." What the apology primarily accomplishes is to show him as a character rushing to join the "gentils" who so much liked the *Knight's Tale* (I.3113). His remarks in the *Parliament* on the "large golee" (556) of the "lewednesse behynde" (520) run awry for a different reason. For the birds' comments about the folly of *fin amour* are in fact cogent: however human their characters seem to be, they are after all simply birds, who are driven to mate by natural impulse, not by love as humans define it. As in the *Nun's Priest's Tale,* where a rooster's notion of beauty sometimes jars rather sharply with our own (VII.3161), there is a comic wavering between human attitudes and avian realities. Indeed, the debate becomes increasingly hilarious once we realize that the birds are feeling an avian version of estrus and can barely restrain the pressing urgency of their drive to copulate and reproduce, an urge that Nature, as the vice-gerent of God, has given them. Nature herself is well aware of the need for haste: " 'And for youre ese, in fotheryng of youre nede, / As faste as I may speke, I wol me speede' " (384-85); even one of the three tercel eagles promises, on such grounds, to be brief (464-68). The impatience of the lower birds is predictable, indeed welcome, once it becomes disconcertingly apparent that the three courtly lovers have debated all day long (489-90). They resent, quite rightly, being trapped in the wrong genre; and their just resentment prevents any confident arbitration of the debate on the nature of love.

There is also, of course, unresolved dramatic conflict in the courtly debate of the three eagle suitors, each with a different claim to the formel. Their unfinished courtship, set against the union of the other birds and the joy of the concluding roundel to spring, contributes crucially to the tentative mood of the poem's ending. Although the formel will, in a year's time, have to choose one eagle or another as her mate, she is at least given that much delay for her present inclination not to love at all. Except that she has freely chosen her detached position, the formel mirrors the narrator's state of mind: half in paralysis before the alternatives of a choice, half tentative about even choosing whether or not to choose.[41]

Nature responds to the formel's quandary with a rational solution:

> "But as for conseyl for to chese a make,
> If I were Resoun, certes, thanne wolde I
> Conseyle yow the royal tercel take."
>
> [631-33]

Nonetheless, it is important that we leave up in the air, as the formel does, what her choice will eventually be.[42] Love is not rational; and Nature after all is not Reason,[43] even if, as sometimes happens in the *Roman de la Rose,* their advice occasionally coincides. The response of the other birds is absolutely correct, and sums up a problem that can be resolved only by the formel's decision: " 'How sholde a juge eyther parti leve / For ye or nay, withouten any preve?' " (496-97). There is no compelling argument, in the love logic of this *demande d'amour,* for favoring one suitor over the others: the first has the highest social rank; the second is of a lower degree but has loved the formel longer; the third has loved not long but deeply. Judicial combat—the solution of the *Knight's Tale*—is averted, though the three eagles voice their willingness to fight it out (540). And Nature's futile appeal to Reason complements the indecisive love debate between the higher and lower birds. If this were a poem in which Reason, Love, and Nature always coincided, the narrator presumably would be content simply to expound Scipio's dream. Instead, he explores a "lower" form of love; and in Love's earthly garden, the appeals of social hierarchy give a genteel answer, not one that can be considered an absolute truth.

These inconclusive debates present in miniature the structure of the whole poem. The *Parliament* opens with an awed recital of the confusing, paradoxical qualities of love: *ars longa, vita brevis*; and "the dredful joye, alwey that slit so yerne" (1-3). At first sight the task of the poem will be to unravel the confusion and resolve the paradox of love's nature. Appropriately, its structure is built by repeated division and subdivision: Macrobius versus the garden; the two inscriptions on the garden gate; Venus versus Nature; the three competing eagles; courtly views of love versus more down-to-earth ones. But what happens at the end of the poem happens each time before, as Chaucer works out an Ovidian paradigm. The clarity gained by division produces no resolution; we are left with opposing but unreconciled viewpoints, thesis and antithesis with no synthesis. Moreover, at the very moments when division lends clarity to an issue, we discover that the clarity is artificial, an unstable separating out of elements that are all too ready to blur together again into the paradoxes that begin the poem and continue to be love's reality.

The first such division, between Macrobius and the garden, creates not so much a false clarity as a distinction so encompassing as to be not very useful for the narrator's concerns. Scipio's dream is about love as the cosmic bond of the universe, next to whose immensity and sweeping order "the lytel erthe that here is" (57) merits the wise man's contempt, since "oure present worldes lyves space / Nis but a maner deth, what wey we trace" (53-54). Love, in this rarefied scheme of things, is defined as "commune profyt" (47); its adherents will be rewarded, Scipio is told, by eternal life in "a blysful place" (48). As this summary suggests, there are some striking analogies between Cicero's picture of universal order and the Christian one: the promise of an afterlife, with reward or punishment; the comparable positions of "comune profyt" and of charity as man's way to find truth by love. Yet even though Chaucer does delete some of Cicero's specifically pagan ideas,[44] he is careful to preserve the pagan atmosphere of the dream, chiefly by reporting the heterodox notion that even "brekers of the lawe" and "likerous folk" will eventually be "foryeven al hir wikked dede" and be allowed to "come into this blysful place" (78-83). The reason for doing so is clearly its distancing effect: if Chaucer had chosen St. Paul for his bedtime reading, the *Parliament of Fowls* would be a very different poem. As it stands, Chaucer is able to express some dissatisfaction (90-91) when he has completed his reading of Macrobius. He is also able subtly to bring into question the truth value of what he has read, when he says: "And therupon, a certeyn thing to lerne, / The longe day ful faste I redde and yerne" (20-21). For "a certeyn thing" has two possible meanings: both "a particular thing" and "something that is certain."[45] Cicero is not gospel truth, "something certain," nor does he answer the "certeyn thing" that Chaucer is interested in. As the narrator's own dream shows, that certain thing is how love works in a less rarefied sense, how it operates in the world. Cicero presented a picture of universal order, ruled by Love, in which the mire and complexity of earthly concerns are dissipated and resolved. The rest of the *Parliament* returns us to the quandaries of its opening paradoxes, to the "myrakles" and "crewel yre" of love as it manifests itself on earth.

The inscriptions on the garden gate sum up the antithetical

possibilities of earthly love and appropriately—given their source in
Dante—describe them with hellish and heavenly connotations. The
clarity of opposition between the two inscriptions has misled a good
many readers of the *Parliament*, in precisely the way that the "two
Venuses" have distorted interpretations of the *House of Fame*. The
temptation has been to make the poem into an analogue of Boccaccio's *Amorosa Visione* or of a ballade by Oton de Grandson,
where there are two gates to the garden of love.[46] According to this
reading, one has only to choose the correct side of the gate in order
to achieve love's heaven and avoid its hell.[47] But Chaucer's point,
quite unmistakably, is that the same gate leads to both extremes,
just as a single Venus, in the *House of Fame*, both aids Aeneas and
brings about Dido's tragedy. There is no way of knowing beforehand
whether one will find heaven or hell, or both, in love's garden;[48]
hence, the narrator's paralysis in front of the gate:

> These vers of gold and blak iwriten were,
> Of whiche I gan astoned to beholde,
> For with that oon encresede ay my fere,
> And with that other gan myn herte bolde;
> That oon me hette, that other dide me colde:
> No wit hadde I, for errour, for to chese,
> To entre or flen, or me to save or lese.
>
> [141–47]

He is, as he says, like "a pece of yren set" "betwixen adamauntes
two / Of evene myght" (148–49); and his indecision here echoes his
dazed reflection on love at the beginning of the poem: "Nat wot I
wel wher that I flete or synke" (7).

Africanus's solution is to shove Chaucer through the gate, and
inform him that " 'this writyng nys nothyng ment bi the, / Ne by
non, but he Loves servaunt be' " (158–59). The narrator's leap into
experience can remain a rather tentative one, confined to a dream
and without extreme consequences of either sort. He gets past the
necessity of choice by being told that he does not have to choose.
Indeed, he will not be permitted to do so; and the limits on his

freedom of will create some degree of pathos. For the price of detachment is muted response, an inability to taste the sweet as well as feel the bitter: " 'For thow of love hast lost thy tast, I gesse, / As sek man hath of swete and bytternesse' " (160-61). The most one could hope is that the narrator's detachment, whatever the cost to himself, might allow him to tell the rest of us how to find love's joy and escape its torment.

Nothing of the sort happens, of course. The antithesis of the two inscriptions on the gate repeats itself in the garden; but we are shown no narrow path to heaven, no wide one to hell. Critics have often been tempted to find exact equivalences: "This gate seems to symbolize two distinct kinds òf love to be found in the garden; love according to Nature, which promises ever-green joy, and love of a more courtly kind which leads to barren sorrow and despair." [49] The trouble is that the pairs of opposing terms are in analogous but not exactly identical relationships. As many critics have said, Venus in her temple does manifest the disagreeable side of love. Indeed, Chaucer darkens the already maleficent tone of his source, a description in Boccaccio's *Teseida*, by adding to it a list of doomed lovers from the *Inferno*. Nonetheless, the more one looks at this antithesis of Venus and Nature, the less sharply defined it seems.

The reason for the blurring is implicit in the Chartrian myth of the goddess Nature, which Chaucer adopts directly from the *De Planctu Naturae* of Alanus de Insulis, and as it comes filtered through Jean de Meun's *Roman de la Rose*. Venus in this system stands for the human notions and trappings of love, which lead to unrequited longings as well as to courtly elegance; and she so stands in contrast to Nature's simple demand for fecundity and regeneration, uncluttered by the distortions and malaises of consciousness. [50] Yet, as distinct as their attributes are, the two goddesses merge: Venus is part of Nature's realm, and serves her larger purposes of regeneration and the fight of the plenum against the ravages of time. As Alanus's Nature explains, "Venerem in fabrili scientia peritam, meaeque operationis subvicariam, in mundiali suburbio collocavi, ut ipsa sub meae praeceptionis arbitrio . . . humani generis seriem in-

defessa continuatione contexeret" [in the outskirt world I stationed
Venus, who is skilled in the knowledge of making, as under-deputy
of my work, in order that she, under my judgment and
guidance . . . might weave together the line of the human race in
unwearied continuation].[51] Proprietary rights are, accordingly, left
rather vague in Chaucer's dream: there are not two gardens, any
more than there are two gates. As Clemen has pointed out, the fact
that Chaucer sees Cupid "under a tre" (211) "reminds us that the
poet has not passed into some new region; he is still in the same park
whose individual trees had been enumerated at the outset of the
description."[52] Venus's temple likewise is an enclosed, hothouse
space within the airy *locus amoenus* of Nature's domain—just as, in
the *Book of the Duchess*, the self-conscious, sorrowing Man in Black
punctures the natural innocence of his Golden Age setting. Chaucer
implies a link between what he sees of the garden before he enters
the temple and what he sees after he comes out. The catalogue of
trees (176-82) presages the catalogue of birds (330-64): each is a
conventional part of the usual description of the plenum of life,
filling every niche of Nature's domain, falling under her tutelage and
beneficent rule.

The catalogues also force on us an increasing awareness of
ambiguity and the blurring of what were at first clearly defined
oppositions. This blurring occurs even within Venus's temple: if the
emphasis there is on the evils of human sexuality, it must be admitted that some of its good, or at least morally neutral, qualities are
presented as well. One can hardly find fault with Curteysie and
Gentilesse; and Plesaunce, Lust, and Delyt are open to contradictory
interpretations.[53] Furthermore, if Venus's temple contains some
good attributes among the predominantly bad, Nature's realm has
bad among the good. To say this is to oversimplify matters con-
siderably, from a theological viewpoint.[54] But it is fair to say that
the catalogues of trees and birds, describing individual species by
their function in Nature's plan, contain a great deal that is disagreeable and—from a limited human perspective—morally questionable.
The fullness of Nature contains "the cofre unto carayne," "the

cipresse, deth to playne," and "the dronke vyne" as well as "the
byldere ok" and "saylynge fyr" (176-80); "the drake, stroyere of his
owene kynde" and "the cukkow ever unkynde" as well as "the
wedded turtil, with hire herte trewe" and "the raven wys" (355-63).
Indeed, in the catalogue of birds especially there is a preponderance
of unpleasant attributes. Nature's realm, even in its purified, eternal
setting as a *locus amoenus,* is not all roses and sunshine. Yet the
birds which seem most disagreeable—to the extent, unfortunately,
that they echo the immoral qualities of human beings—fulfill their
mysterious functions in Nature's scheme, and are included in her
constant injunction: be fruitful and multiply.

Nature's unfailing purpose does directly oppose the inscription
that describes love's hell as a wasteland of sterility and of unrequited, unfulfilled longing (134-40). Elsewhere in fourteenth-
century poetry such an antithesis is conventionally used to set off a
conscious, loveless narrator from the unconscious, fulfilled creatures
of the world in spring. In several instances man is contrasted
specifically with the birds. Gower so begins his *Confessio Amantis:*

> And that was in the Monthe of Maii,
> Whan every brid hath chose his make
> And thenkth his merthes forto make
> Of love that he hath achieved;
> Bot so was I nothing relieved,
> For I was further fro my love
> Than Erthe is fro the hevene above,
> As forto speke of eny sped.
>
> [I.100-07]

The comparison in fact frames the poem; Gower repeats it toward
the end of Book Eight:

> Ferst to Nature if that I me compleigne,
> Ther finde I hou that every creature
> Som time ayer hath love in his demeine,
> So that the litel wrenne in his mesure
> Hath yit of kinde a love under his cure;
> And I bot on desire, of which I misse:

> And thus, bot I, hath every kinde his blisse.
>
> [VIII.2224-30]

This *topos* has a special appropriateness for St. Valentine's Day
poems, because the separation of man from nature is at its sharpest
on the day when all the birds choose their mates for the coming
year. The contrast between mating birds and an unrequited human
lover appears in Chaucer's own "Complaynt D'Amours" (*Works*, p.
541). It also shows up in one of Gower's ballades, in terms that
recall quite pointedly the *Parliament of Fowls:*

> Chascun Tarcel gentil ad sa falcoun,
> Mais j'ai faili de ceo q'avoir voldroie:
> Ma dame, c'est le fin de mon chançoun,
> Qui soul remaint ne poet avoir grant joie.[55]

[Every gentle tercel has his falcon, but I have lacked what I
would wish to have; my lady, this is the end of my song; he
who remains alone cannot have great joy.]

Yet Chaucer's purposes in the *Parliament* are more complicated.
The closest analogue to his blurring of Venus and Nature, of the
human and the animal, is Oton de Grandson's *Songe Saint Valentin,*
which also gives human attributes to the birds assembled on St.
Valentine's Day.[56] The narrator takes "grant soulas" (78) from the
joy of the mating birds, paired off "deux et deux" (75). He himself,
it appears, is an unrequited lover; and he learns that a peregrine
falcon, alone among the birds, shares his plight. The falcon is far
away from his loved one, in status as well as distance: he is afraid to
ask for her as his "par" (242) ["companion" or "mate," but also
"equal"], because her social rank and inherent worth are so much
higher than his. When the dreamer awakes, he meditates at length on
the differences between birds and human beings, and is unable to
suppress a certain amount of envy at the easy, unreflective success of
birds in love (315ff.). Among people things are more difficult:

> Les oyseaulx a leur gré choisissent,
> Et lez gens pour aimer eslisent

> La ou leur plaisance s'acorde.
> Dont bien souvent y a discorde,
> Car a l'un plaist, a l'autre non.

[328-32]

[The birds choose at will, and people elect to love where their pleasure decides—from which there is very often discord, for it is pleasing to one, to another not.]

Yet, although "Amour est chouse naturelle" (340) [love is something natural] , Grandson asks for no easy retreat from consciousness into the blissful oblivion of

> . . . les oyseaulx et les bestez
> Qui n'ont point de sens en leurz testez,
> Et ne doubtent paour ne honte,
> Et de dongier ne tiennent compte,
> Mais vivent sans entendement.

[344-48]

[the birds and the beasts who don't have any sense at all in their heads, and do not care about fear or shame, and do not take reckoning of refusal, but live without conscious judgment.]

Though man's consciousness opens the possibility of misery, it also allows a happiness in love beyond the powers of animate nature to achieve (334-39, 349-56).

Grandson's rather complex response to the contrasts between man and other earthly creatures leads us to Chaucer's meaning in the *Parliament of Fowls*. As in *Le Songe Saint Valentin*, complications arise from the fact that there are unrequited lovers among the birds as well as among men. In fact, the blurring of human and animal is somewhat stronger in Chaucer. Grandson's solitary falcon is, after all, little more than a stand-in for the lovelorn narrator. The three tercel eagles of the *Parliament,* on the other hand, are like the narrator only in being unfulfilled. Through them Venus invades Nature's realm, and partially frustrates the "evene acord" (668) by

which all the other birds are happily paired off. Diana shares the
blame, it is important to remember: the formel is not yet willing to
choose a mate. By their intrusion upon the instinctive world of
Nature, the two goddesses exacerbate our human awareness of the
problems of consciousness.

Chaucer, as always, responds to this issue with an Ovidian
paradox, by treating man's distance from natural harmony with a
mixture of deeply felt regret and comic ruefulness. The *Parliament*
no doubt does show "the disruptive force of individual
personality":[57] the happiest creatures in the poem are the ones least
aware of learning, conscious motive, and genteel behavior. Yet whatever envy we may feel for the unreflective happiness of creatures
must be a temporary one. Ignorance is not really bliss. Chaucer's
point is certainly not that courtly love and consciousness are simply
bad, or that uninhibited sexual activity, on behalf of the instinctive
drive to reproduce, is the answer to the eagles' problems, let alone
the narrator's.

After all, man is stuck with his consciousness, for better as well as
for worse.[58] In the *Parliament of Fowls* human consciousness does
lead to a paralysis of choice about issues which have no apparent
solution. But it is well—as Theseus reminds us at the end of a similar
demande d'amour—"to maken vertu of necessitee" (I.3042). The
opening lines of the *General Prologue* offer a guide to recognizing
the positive side of our predicament. There, too, the tonal effect of
contrasting man and nature is double-edged; and, as in the *Parliament,* humanized birds mark the point of transition between
Nature's realm and our special province within it (I.9-11). The magnificent simplicity of Nature, renewing the world, following the
archetypal pattern of God's plan, gives way within the first eighteen
lines to the many-motived chaos of scurrying human beings. But if
the shift from Nature in its pure form necessitates a loss of
simplicity and uncluttered harmony, the entrance of man also makes
possible the bursting vitality and energy of the Canterbury pilgrims
and their tales. The *Parliament of Fowls,* with its uneasy balance of

stasis and energy, and its discordant range of perspectives on the meaning of love, thus foreshadows the exuberant variety of the Canterbury stories, with all their unresolved conflicts of viewpoint, social class, and moral scope.

THE LEGEND OF GOOD WOMEN:
PALINODE AND PROCRUSTEAN BED

This chapter discusses the last of Chaucer's dream visions and the collection of stories it introduces, the *Legend of Good Women*. At first glance, it will seem out of sequence in two ways: I talk about the *Legend* before *Troilus and Criseyde*, and the legends themselves before their *Prologue*. The legends come first in this chapter because it is easier to describe Chaucer's method than his purpose; it makes sense to show what he is doing in the poem before one decides why he is doing it. The *Legend* directly follows the *Parliament of Fowls* in this book partly because they both contain dream visions, and illuminate each other when looked at side by side. Moreover, although the *Legend* is explicitly a palinode for *Troilus*, it counters equally well the terms of the *Parliament*. Both of the earlier poems are willing, as they approach the problems of earthly love, to allow paradox and ambiguity. In the *Parliament* Chaucer lays before us a paralysis of choice, an unsettling balance of opposing viewpoints. In *Troilus* there is at least a resolution of sorts, imposed by the inescapable fact of history and the narrator's need to explain Criseyde's betrayal. One of his sputtered disclaimers reduces the human complexities of the poem to a black-and-white battle between the sexes; it makes an ironic preamble to the *Legend of Good Women:*

> Bysechyng every lady bright of hewe,
> And every gentil womman, what she be,
> That, al be that Criseyde was untrewe,
> That for that gilt ye be nat wroth with me.

> Ye may hire gilt in other bokes se;
> And gladlier I wol write, if yow leste,
> Penelopes trouthe and good Alceste.
>
> Ny sey nat this al oonly for thise men,
> But moost for wommen that bitraised be
> Thorugh fals folk; god yeve hem sorwe, amen!
> That with hire grete wit and subtilite
> Bytraise yow! And this commeveth me
> To speke, and in effect yow alle I preye,
> Beth war of men, and herkneth what I seye.
>
> [V.1772-85]

The god of love is quick to take this cue for another kind of imposed solution. The fitting punishment for a male poet who has revived the story of Criseyde is to spend the rest of his life composing saints' lives about "goode wymmen, maydenes and wyves, / That weren trewe in lovyng al hire lyves" and the "false men that hem bytraien" (F 481-89).

Cupid shows himself to be a rather literal-minded reader. In fact, Chaucer responds convincingly to the charges against him: to recount one woman's infidelity is not to attack all women (F 456ff.). There is no way for us to tell whether Cupid's naiveté as a critic summarizes an adverse reaction to *Troilus* among the women of the court; or whether Chaucer in fact presented the *Legend* to Queen Anne "at Eltham or at Sheene" (F 497). I find it hard to believe, however, that Chaucer's penance has even the seriousness of Queen Elizabeth's notorious command to Sir John Harington, not to return until he had translated the rest of *Orlando Furioso*. For the *Legend of Good Women* is no more straightforward than most other literary palinodes. In particular, Chaucer has learned the comic lessons of the *Remedia Amoris* and of the *Ars Amatoria*, Book Three, which also pretends to take the woman's side of things.[1] As Ovid prepares to arm women for erotic combat, he must first respond to the outraged cry of a nervous male in the audience:

> dixerit e multis aliquis "quid uirus in anguis
> adicis et rabidae tradis ouile lupae?"

parcite paucarum diffundere crimen in omnes;
spectetur meritis quaeque puella suis.

[III.7–10]

[Some one of the many will have said: "Why do you add
venom to snakes, and hand over the sheepfold to the raging
she-wolf?" Refrain from extending the guilt of a few women
to them all; let each woman be judged on her merits.]

After all, if Helen and her sister were rather nasty to the sons of
Atreus, if the earth did swallow Amphiaraus alive because of his
wife's betrayal (11–14), one must not forget the great counter-
examples of virtuous women: Penelope, Laodamia, Alceste, and
Evadne (15–22). Chaucer's palinode, which praises two of these
women, goes even further than Ovid's. Cupid orders Chaucer to
impose a prefabricated system, the literary form of the saint's life,
on the flux and ambiguity of human experience. But the poet's
simple-minded efforts belie the complexity of the women he attempts to enshrine. The narrator's failures of understanding in the
Legend go beyond those of the earlier dream visions; and this time
they are even more emphatically not his responsibility. Under
orders, the *Legend of Good Women* claims to resolve debate by
erasing what came before. In fact, like most palinodes, it simply adds
another voice to an unresolved dispute.

I

The imposed partiality of the *Legend* is the source of its narrator's difficulty. Chaucer elsewhere entitles the work the "Seintes
Legende of Cupide" (*Canterbury Tales* II.61); and it becomes apparent that in Cupid's religion this "Seintes Legende" replaces the
famous late thirteenth-century collection of Christian saints' lives,
the *Legenda Aurea*. Chaucer canonizes ten of love's martyrs: Cleopatra, Thisbe, Dido, Hypsipyle, Medea, Lucrece, Ariadne, Philomela,
Phyllis, and Hypermnestra. On a quick reading the names are unexceptionable: we feel no particular sense of distortion or in-

congruity in the linking together of so heterogeneous a company, so long as all they are called on to do is be martyrs for love. Certainly such lists are straightforward enough elsewhere, in the *House of Fame* (388-426) as much as in Christine de Pisan's avowedly feminist *Epistre au Dieu d'Amours*. The flatness of a catalogue ensures the suppression of unwelcome detail, even when it is mentioned. For example, the allusions in the *Prologue* to suicide and incest do not seem to have any special moral weight: "Phillis, hangyng for thy Demophoun, / And Canace, espied by thy chere" (F 264-65).[2] Their particulars are lost in a list of names; and the two heroines do not seem out of place among their companions in the ballade—Hero, Dido, Laodamia, and the rest.

The problems arise when Chaucer tries to flesh out this catalogue with the hyperbole of saints' lives, and when rhetoric forces Cupid's saints to compete with Christ's. For the details the narrator has to work with too often resist his efforts to prod them into a hagiographical mold. Cupid's command to tell simply the gist of each life (F570-77) leads to a wonderfully comic exercise in censorship and distorted emphasis. When his sources have anything scurrilous to say about his heroines, the narrator resorts to silence or, more often, to an *occupatio* that comes just a little bit too late. Since Chaucer's method has been accurately described only by one unpublished study of the poem,[3] it is worth reviewing in some detail. One must admit that some of his distortions are explicable only as private jokes: for their recognition they require us to read Chaucer with his sources also in hand. Others are accessible to anyone who has an elementary acquaintance with classical mythology. But the cumulative effect of Chaucer's deletions is compelling: we cannot avoid recognizing a consistent pattern of censorship.

One should look first at the *Legend of Cleopatra*, since Chaucer himself is forced by the god of love to begin there (F 566). This first martyr's life is harder to discuss than the later ones, because Chaucer's source is uncertain. Nonetheless, the extant medieval accounts of "Cleopatràs lussurïosa" (*Inferno* v. 63) are unanimous in their outrage at her immorality. Boccaccio's *De Mulieribus Claris* is particularly vehement; it outlines with care her lustfulness, avarice, incest, probable murder of her brother-husband, and seduction of Julius Caesar.[4] Chaucer does not mention these unsavory episodes, but he is perfectly well aware of them: at several points they lie barely beneath the surface of his relatively bland narrative. After Antony's death, the narrator tells us, "His wif, that coude of Cesar have no grace, / To Egipt is fled for drede and for destresse" (663-64). Vincent of Beauvais[5] and Boccaccio describe the specifics of Octavian's refusal: "Capta vero Alexandria, cum Cleopatra ingenio veteri in vanum tentasset, uti iam dudum Cesarem et Antonium illexerat in concupiscentiam suam, sic et iuvenem Octavianum illicere"[6] [when Alexandria had in truth been seized, Cleopatra tried in vain with her old craft, just as long before she had enticed Caesar and Antony to her concupiscent desire, so to entice young Octavian]. An even more astounding deletion occurs earlier, when Chaucer describes his heroine's beauty with one trite simile and moves on to a sweeping *occupatio*:

> And she was fayr as is the rose in May.
> And, for to make shortly is the beste,
> She wax his wif, and hadde hym as hire leste.
>   The weddynge and the feste to devyse,
> To me, that have ytake swich empryse
> Of so many a story for to make,
> It were to longe, lest that I shulde slake
> Of thyng that bereth more effect and charge;
> For men may overlade a ship or barge.
> And forthy to th'effect thanne wol I skyppe,
> And al the remenaunt, I wol lete it slippe.
>
> [613-23]

Ships are common enough metaphors for poems; but an overloaded barge inevitably brings to mind some of the more luxurious events in Cleopatra's life.[7] The narrator's metaphor is doubly unfortunate, since the *Legend* in fact becomes overloaded with ships; in place of the wedding, Chaucer recounts the battle of Actium. The sea-battle takes up a quarter of Cleopatra's allotted time; and its prominence is not even justified by a spotlight on Antony, who is hardly mentioned.[8] The joke may be that Chaucer the male poet warms to the wrong task; as in the *Knight's Tale* (I.2605ff.), alliteration seems to mark the narrator's excitement at describing combat. Yet this diversion of our attention is also opportune in another respect. Chaucer's haste in moving beyond Cleopatra's wedding is understandable, given the sinister undertones of "hadde hym as hire leste": Vincent of Beauvais speaks of "lascivus Antonius correptus amore Cleopatre" [wanton Antony overcome by love of Cleopatra].[9] Boccaccio too refrains from dwelling on the marriage of the "wicked woman" and the "effeminate," Orientalized Antony, but his *occupatio* does not completely suppress the decadence of their wedding feast: "Et ut arabicas unctiones et odoratos Sabee fumos et crapulas sinem" [I shall not discuss the Arabian ointments, the perfumes of Saba, and the drunken revels].[10]

The narrator's delay in escaping his sources becomes habitual, and it continues to make problems for his task as a hagiographer. He avoids the difficulty of explaining away Pasiphaë by not mentioning her at all in the *Legend of Ariadne.* But he does let Scylla, the daughter of Nisus, appear as a seduced and abandoned heroine: a timely *occupatio* (1914, 1921) passes over her parricide and Minos's righteous horror when she claims his love as her proper reward.[11] Good women suffer as much as the bad ones benefit from his procedure. In the *Legend* about Hypsipyle, "that whylom Thoas doughter was, the kyng" (1468), the "whylom" recalls the heroine's most famous virtuous action. For Thoas ruled Lemnos "eo evo . . . quo rabies illa subivit mulierum insule mentes, subtrahendi omnino indomita colla virorum iugo" [at the time when women were seized by madness and withdrew their untamed necks from the yoke of men].[12] The male messenger who meets Chaucer's Jason at the shore (1479-86) underlines a silent emendation: there were in fact no men left on the island when he arrived. In Chaucer's acknowledged source, *Heroides* VI, Hypsipyle regrets that the Lemnian women did not give Jason's band a more murderous welcome: "Lemniadesque viros, nimium quoque, vincere norunt. / milite tam forti causa tuenda fuit!" (53-54; also 139) [the Lemnian women know all too well how to subdue men. My cause should have been guarded by so courageous a soldiery]. Yet when the Lemnian women killed all the men on the island, Hypsipyle helped her father to escape; and the narrator, by not distinguishing this woman from the others, pares away her heroic *pietas* to a languid, indifferent virtue. The pressures to make a saint of every woman who appears have the same result in the *Legend of Hypermnestra*; and there the narrator ignores the hint his own verse sets out: "That of the shef she sholde be the corn" (2579). Chaucer lets slip enough to make a hash of the story as he tells it: the cruel father wonders which one of his nephews will kill him (2660), but orders only Hypermnestra to become a murderess. The deletion of her forty-nine sisters, who all dutifully butchered their newlywed husbands (*Heroides* XIV), tries to save the reputation of women en masse, but in fact deprives Chaucer's heroine of a setting that emphasizes the singularity of her virtuous act.

Not all of Amor's devotees have such high claims to sanctity, nor do they respond to the narrator's call for female solidarity. There are even several examples of conniving at the martyrdom of other women. Chaucer leaves to his audience the task of drawing inferences: Cleopatra did, after all, have something to do with Antony's desertion of Octavia (593); and Hypsipyle herself knows the main reason why Jason has not returned to her (1572). Even sisters are not to be trusted. At the beginning of the *Legend of Ariadne*, the narrator scolds Theseus:

> Me thynketh this, that thow were depe yholde
> To whom that savede thee from cares colde!
> And if now any woman helpe the,
> Wel oughtestow hire servaunt for to be,
> And ben hire trewe lovere yer be yere!

[1954-58]

The trouble with defining things on this *quid pro quo* basis is that Chaucer has emended his source: in his version Phaedra, not

Ariadne, is the one who comes up with the plan to save the hero.[13] Chaucer's Ariadne in fact turns out to be both an ingénue and a fortune-hunter. She already has plans to marry off Phaedra to Hippolytus (2099), even though Theseus, as we have just been told, is only twenty-three (2075). And she daydreams about their future together as duchesses, " 'And sekered to the regals of Athenes, / And bothe hereafter likly to ben quenes' " (2128-29).

Chaucer's sources are most intractable, and hilariously so, in the *Legend of Medea* and the *Legend of Philomela.* The *Historia Destructionis Troiae* of Guido delle Colonne supplies most of Medea's story, including an apparently innocuous detail. Oetes orders his daughter to sit beside Jason at dinner (1601-02). But Guido tacks on an antifeminist moral; Oetes was a fool to allow his daughter such freedom:

Scimus enim mulieris animum semper virum appetere, sicut appetit materia semper formam. O utinam materia transiens semel in formam posset dici suo contenta formato! Set sicut de forma ad formam procedere materie notum est, sic mulieris concupiscentia dissoluta procedere de viro ad virum, uti esse creditur sine fine, cum sit quedam profunditas sine fundo, nisi forte pudoris labes aliqua abstinencia laudanda concluserit sub terminis honestatis. Qua ergo, O rex Oetes, ductus audacia tenere puelle latus extranei viri lateri consuisti?[14]

[For we know that the will of a woman always desires a man, just as matter always desires form. O would that matter, once passing over into form, could be called contented with its having been given form! But just as it is customary for matter to proceed from form to form, so it is for the dissolute concupiscence of woman to proceed from man to man, so as to be—it is believed—endless, with as it were a kind of bottomless depth, unless perchance some praiseworthy self-denial has confined the stains of disgrace under the limits of respectability. How then, O king Oetes, misled by temerity, did you join together the side of a delicate girl with the side of a strange man?]

In the *Legend of Medea* the Aristotelian metaphor changes sex, in order to condemn Jason,

> That is of love devourer and dragoun.
> As mater apetiteth forme alwey,
> And from forme into forme it passen may.
>
> [1581-83]

Jason lives up to his reputation, "doth his oth, and goth with hire to bedde" (1644); but Chaucer's version omits Guido's report of Medea's unquenchable lust.[15] These are the hidden jokes of a translator; there are also more obvious distortions. At the end of *Hypsipyle* Chaucer follows Ovid's heroine slightly too far. Though he suppresses her name-calling against Medea the "barbara venefica" (*Heroides* VI.19) [foreign witch], he does translate her malevolent prayer: "that she moste bothe hire chyldren spylle, / And alle tho that sufferede hym his wille" (1574-75).[16] The narrator's slip causes him problems, even though he manages not to repeat the same mistake in the *Legend of Medea.* For he does direct us (1678-79) to *Heroides* XII, in the course of translating a few innocuous lines from Ovid (XII.11-12, 19-20). And Ovid's Medea outlines how she betrayed her father, dismembered her brother Absyrtus (109-15), and tricked Pelias's daughters into killing their father unwittingly (129-32). She fulfills Hypsipyle's curse, falling at last into a frenzy as she prepares to murder her own children (209-12).

In the *Legend of Philomela,* Tereus offers the nastiest possible example of male villainy. Yet it is difficult to assign Philomela the role of an entirely passive martyr. The narrator, gripped by his own story, censors it slightly too late to keep us from remembering what happened:

> O sely Philomene, wo is thyn herte!
> God wreke thee, and sende the thy bone!
> Now is it tyme I make an ende sone.
>
> [2339-41]

Once alluded to, the grisly stew the two sisters make of Procne's son

Itys is impossible to forget, in part because of the narrator's awkwardness in suppressing the end of his story:

> Allas! the wo, the compleynt, and the mone
> That Progne upon hire doumbe syster maketh!
> In armes everych of hem other taketh,
> And thus I late hem in here sorwe dwelle.
>   The remenaunt is no charge for to telle,
> For this is al and som: thus was she served,
> That nevere harm agilte ne deserved
> Unto this crewel man, that she of wiste.
> Ye may be war of men, if that yow liste.
>
> [2379-87]

His retreat into bland piousness barely covers over the horror of Ovid's account (*Metamorphoses* VI.424-674).

Hyperbole works in the other direction as well: if all the women in the *Legend* are saints, all the men must be made—so far as it is possible—to seem the opposite. The narrator has a difficult time at first, before his rhetoric gets warmed up. The opening legends describe two couples, the first of rather dubious character, the second a pair of innocents. But one can hardly make moral distinctions within the couples: both Antony and Cleopatra, both Pyramus and Thisbe die for love. Though Chaucer does his best to make Pyramus a villain (798-801), the shape of Ovid's story forces its own pathetic response to the mutual fate of the two lovers. The hagiographer of women has to give in:

> Of trewe men I fynde but fewe mo
> In alle my bokes, save this Piramus,
> And therfore have I spoken of hym thus.
> For it is deynte to us men to fynde
> A man that can in love been trewe and kynde.
> Here may ye se, what lovere so he be,
> A woman dar and can as wel as he.
>
> [917-23]

The task of finding male villainy becomes easier as the legends

progress. Some heroes open themselves to invective: Jason is the
"rote of false lovers," because "there othere falsen oon, thow falsest
two!" (1368, 1377).[17] Details can also be altered when the source is
not vehement enough. Aeneas sneaks off while Dido is sleeping, and
accidentally on purpose leaves his sword next to her bed (1332). His
perfidy is especially unforgivable because Dido gave him so many
nice presents (1113-25); in Vergil Aeneas is the gift-giver.[18] Hercules,
in the *Argonautica,* warns Jason against falling for Hypsipyle,
because love leads to loss of manhood and degeneracy.[19] Chaucer's
Hercules acts as Jason's procurer; he pledges his honesty to
Hypsipyle with a grisly vow that Deianira will help him to fulfill:
" 'As wolde almighty God that I hadde yive / My blod and
flesh . . .' " (1538-39). In Guido's *Historia,* Jason's expressed willingness to die makes Medea offer him her aid (p. 20). Chaucer's Jason
does things in the reverse order, in a belated attempt to appear
heroic:

> "Youre man I am, and lowely yow beseche
> To ben my helpe, withoute more speche;
> But, certes, for my deth shal I nat spare."
>
> [1626-28]

By the time we get to the final *Legend,* the most innocent preliminaries to the story provoke an indignant aside: Hypermnestra
had a father, "That was of love as fals as evere hym liste" (2571);
her father's brother had many sons, "As swiche false lovers ofte
conne" (2565).

To characterize all men as villains obviously erases some rather
useful distinctions between people. The narrator's judgment is
comically indiscriminate, as the rapists Tarquin (1883-85) and
Tereus cast their pall over the rest of the sex:

> Ye may be war of men, if that yow liste.
> For al be it that he wol nat, for shame,
> Don as Tereus, to lese his name,
> Ne serve yow as a morderour or a knave,
> Ful lytel while shal ye trewe hym have—

> That wol I seyn, al were he now my brother—
> But it so be that he may have non other.
>
> [2387-93]

The effort to make all women seem to be saints has the same caricaturing effect. The heroines lose their diversity and individuality in order to suffer martyrdom passively. Sometimes departure from the sources is nearly inevitable: it would not do to have Hypsipyle and the Lemnian women dress up in armor, and be the pursuers instead of the pursued. But usually the preconceived pattern of sanctity defeats its own intent by enervating female heroism.[20] I have mentioned that the deletion of Hypermnestra's sisters takes away the proper setting for her heroic defiance of her father. So does the narrator's whole treatment of the story: forced into the "abandoned heroine" mold, she comes to seem as much a comic figure as a pathetic one. The horoscope of her nativity, we are told, predisposed her to nonviolence: "That Ypermystra dar nat handle a knyf / In malyce, thogh she shulde lese hire lyf" (2594-95). In these lines astrology brings into sharp focus what the narrator imposes in a more subtle fashion on all his heroines: it takes away Hypermnestra's noble exercise of will, when she decides that the duties of a wife outweigh those of a daughter. It also wholly changes the tone of a later passage, which Chaucer translates from Ovid:

> "Allas! and shal myne hondes blody be?
> I am a mayde, and, as by my nature,
> And bi my semblaunt and by my vesture,
> Myne handes ben nat shapen for a knyf,
> As for to reve no man fro his lyf.
> What devel have I with the knyf to do?
> And shal I have my throte korve a-two?
> Thanne shal I blede, allas! and me beshende!"
>
> [2689-96]

Ovid's heroine (*Heroides* XIV.53-66) reflects on her father's cruel command and her sisters' bloody example; she thinks about killing herself, but decides at last to save her husband and face her father's wrath. Chaucer's heroine simply demonstrates her predestined passivity, as she worries about getting her hands dirty.

The narrator's insistence on creating a clear, black-and-white opposition between the sexes, at the expense of truth to his sources and to the complexities of human character, is reminiscent of the Eagle's comic reductiveness in the *House of Fame*. It is even closer to the procedure of one of the *Canterbury Tales*, which also makes a Procrustean bed of literary form. The *Monk's Tale* and the *Legend* have the same hagiographical flattening and formalization of detail: the requirements of structure force experience to fit preconceived patterns. Sometimes the fit is perfect, or nearly so: the legends of *Lucrece, Thisbe,* and *Phyllis* do not seem jarringly out of place. Most of the time, though, we are made aware that a strong exercise of narrative control, in the selection and arrangement of detail, is necessary to make a story become a *Legend*.

Selectivity is of course necessary in any narrative, and appeals to relevance are utterly conventional in medieval poetry. There is no surprise in Chaucer's deletion of Aeneas's "aventures in the se," because "it acordeth nat to my matere" (953, 955). Nor is there, at first glance, any reason to become suspicious of a similar caveat at the end of *Troilus:*

> And if I hadde ytaken for to write
> The armes of this ilke worthi man,
> Than wolde ich of his batailles endite.
> But for that I to writen first bigan
> Of his love, I have seyd as I kan,—
> His worthi dedes, whoso list hem heere,
> Rede Dares, he kan telle hem alle ifeere.
> [V.1765-71]

Yet these lines are strongly reminiscent of Ovid's witty introduction to the *Amores*; and Chaucer too reveals a comic hint of regret at having chosen the wrong subject matter.[21] Moreover, this stanza shows the narrator backed into a corner, and it immediately precedes his apology to the gentlewomen in the audience: he prepares for the *Legend* by his promise that "gladlier I wol write, if yow leste, / Penelopes trouthe and good Alceste" (1777-78). Ironically, in the *Legend* itself Cupid's insistence on a stringent selection of detail enforces a much greater, constantly imposed narrative control; the poem silently counters the *Troilus* narrator's repeated avowals of his detachment, and his passive acquiescence to the inexorable movement of his source and of past events. The *Legend* also counters, in this respect, the practice of the source it most frequently turns to, Ovid's *Heroides.* Ovid's heroines too are all of a type; but, however interchangeable their rhetoric may be, they at least achieve some individuality and dramatic force by being allowed to tell their own stories. Like the Wife of Bath, they are stereotypes; but also like her, they gain humanity in their performances, as they explore the agonies of betrayal and despair. The narrator of the *Legend*, in contrast, forces passivity on his heroines: he tells, and he controls their narratives.

His control is, paradoxically, most obvious at the points when he quotes from the *Heroides* and lets his heroines speak for themselves. Chaucer in effect plays an Ovidian trick on Ovid's heroines, much as Ovid himself does in the *Ars Amatoria*, where he puts their towering passions to trivial use. I have already argued that Chaucer's selection of detail from the letters of Hypsipyle, Medea, and Ariadne reveals a disingenuous manipulation of his sources. The most outrageous comedy of this sort appears in the *Legend of Phyllis*, where the narrator admits that he is tired of describing male villains (2454-57). Like father like son (2395); Demophoon tricked Phyllis in exactly "the same wey, the same path" (2463) that Theseus used to seduce Ariadne: "As wel coude I, if that me leste so, / Tellen al his doynge to and fro" (2470-71). Why bother preparing the detailed background for a moral that has already been made time after time? The constrictions of literary form, more than of Demophoon's heredity, deprive him of any interest as an individual:

> Me lyste nat vouche-sauf on hym to swynke,
> Ne spende on hym a penne ful of ynke,
> For fals in love was he, ryght as his syre.
> The devil sette here soules bothe afyre!

> But of the letter of Phillis wol I wryte
> A word or two, althogh it be but lyte.
>
> [2490-95]

In fact, the second half of the legend becomes a florilegium of
Heroides II. The effect is curious, since the first half also depends on
Phyllis's letter for its narrative of events. As Eleanor Winsor Leach
has pointed out, Chaucer "in effect tells the story twice."[22] The
second time through, Phyllis is allowed to speak in her own voice;
but Chaucer cuts her off, after the first eight lines of her letter:

> But al hire letter wryten I ne may
> By order, for it were to me a charge;
> Hire letter was ryght long and therto large.
> But here and ther in rym I have it layd,
> There as me thoughte that she wel hath sayd.
>
> [2513-17]

There may be a hint, in this search for purple passages, that Phyllis is
not normally very articulate; the narrator, in any case, finds it easier
to copy some else's work than to invent his own. He abandons, in
boredom or fatigue, the difficult task of sorting through historical
evidence; simple aesthetic appreciation makes lesser demands.

Yet the *Legend of Phyllis* and especially the *Legend of Dido*
suggest that more is at stake than a comic, willful falsification or
avoidance of history. Chaucer is again concerned with one of the
central issues in the *House of Fame* and in *Troilus*: the poet's
responsibility to keep the past in memory and revivify the fame of
the dead; and his difficulty in finding the truth, and representing it
accurately. The narrator's failures of understanding are predictable,
given the Ovidian pattern; but they also voice a concern that is
conventional in later medieval literature.[23] Boccaccio gives it a
particularly eloquent expression in the preface to his *De Genealogia
Deorum*, a late, humanistic version of the medieval impulse to make
a *summa* by compiling and harmonizing the divergent written
records of the past:

Everywhere, to your heart's desire, I will find and gather, like
fragments of a mighty wreck strewn on some vast shore, the
relics of the Gentile gods. These relics, scattered through
almost infinite volumes, shrunk with age, half consumed, well-
nigh a blank, I will bring into such single genealogical order as
I can, to gratify your wish.

And yet I shudder to embark on so huge a task. . . . Who in
our day can penetrate the hearts of the Ancients? Who can
bring to light and life again minds long since removed in
death? Who can elicit their meaning? A divine task that—not
human! The Ancients departed in the way of all flesh, leaving
behind them their literature and their famous names for
posterity to interpret according to their own judgment. But as
many minds, so many opinions.[24]

The responsibility of the poet to disentangle and arbitrate between
his sources is awesome. Though Thomas Gascoigne's account of
Chaucer's deathbed repentance—delayed, Gascoigne says, as long as
Judas's—is apocryphal, it does express a version of the problem with
special vividness: "sicut Chawserus ante mortem suam sepe clamavit,
'Ve michi! Ve michi! quia revocare nec destruere jam potero illa que
mala scripsi de malo et turpissimo amore hominum ad mulieres, et
jam de homine in hominem continuabuntur' "[25] [just as Chaucer
before his death often cried aloud: "Woe is me! Woe is me! because I
will now be able neither to call back nor to destroy those evil things
that I have written about the evil and most shameful love of men for
women, and henceforth they will be passed on from man to man"].
The poet bears a moral responsibility for what he writes, even for
what he copies. If he lies, knowingly or not, he is to blame for
passing on to later generations a false version of the past.

The story of Dido and Aeneas, as I argued in chapter 2, is the
locus classicus for medieval treatments of this problem; and the
contradictory accounts in Vergil and Ovid set up the alternative
possibilities of truth and meaning. In Book One of the *House of
Fame*, Chaucer's narrator is paralyzed as he attempts to decide
where his sympathies belong. The *Legend of Dido* takes a simpler

course, by adopting Ovid's—that is to say, Dido's—side whole-heartedly. Even though most of the *Legend* is a summary of the first four books of the *Aeneid*, there is nonetheless an implicit tension between Chaucer's sources. A promise to follow the "lanterne" of "Virgil Mantoan" (924-26) quickly becomes complicated: "In Naso and Eneydos wol I take / The tenor, and the grete effects make" (928-29). After following Vergil for over four hundred lines, Chaucer makes a sudden shift, confusing because unannounced: "But, as myn auctour seith, yit thus she seyde; / Or she was hurt, byforen or she deyde" (1352-53). Ovid now openly becomes the "auctour"; in fact, he has influenced the tone of the *Legend* throughout. "This Eneas" (1226, 1264-65, 1285)[26] is treated un-fairly from the start: his appearance as someone "lyk to been a verray gentil man" (1068; also 1074) belies his unsavory reality. Chaucer copies the Ovidian embroidery on the story; his Dido too is pregnant (1323) (see *Heroides* VII.133; vs. *Aeneid* IV.327-30). He in fact goes further than Ovid in fabricating damning bits of evidence.[27] Chaucer's Dido does not mention the vow she had made to be faith-ful to Sychaeus's memory. His Aeneas accepts Dido's gifts, leaves his sword by her bed—in the *Aeneid* he gives it to her much earlier, as one of a number of presents (IV.646-47)—and makes the wild promises of a seducer when they are alone together in the cave.

Moreover, as Robinson notes, Chaucer "ignores, or minimizes the importance of the intervention of the gods."[28] The narrator wonders whether Venus could in fact have made her son temporarily invisible (1020-22); and whether Cupid actually took the likeness of Ascanius, "This noble queen enamored to make / On Eneas" (1143-44). In the *Aeneid* Juno and Venus summon up a storm, in order to interrupt the hunt and force Dido and Aeneas together (IV.105-28); Chaucer's most disingenuous emendation describes the aftermath:

> And shortly, from the tempest hire to save,
> She fledde hireself into a litel cave,
> And with hire wente this Eneas also.

> I not, with hem if there wente any mo;
> The autour maketh of it no mencioun.

> [1224-28]

Actually, Vergil's Juno loudly announces (IV.124-27) that she too will be present, in order to bind Aeneas to Dido in marriage. With the gods thus deprived of their fearful, compelling power, Aeneas is doubly at fault. Though the narrator concedes that Aeneas later sailed "Toward Ytayle, as wolde his destinee" (952), his "destiny" here becomes merely his own invention, a grandiose excuse for deserting a woman he has become tired of. In the *Aeneid* and in the *House of Fame* (429-32) Mercury appears to Aeneas to remind him of his calling. In the *Legend of Dido*, Aeneas simply reports the supposed visit and bursts into "false teres."[29]

Like the people in the whirling House of Rumor, the narrator of the *Legend of Good Women* thus passes on distorted versions of the stories he learns from others. One way to avoid such distortion would be to copy out one's source verbatim: the *Troilus* narrator, in fact, repeatedly claims to be doing nothing more (e.g., II.8-18). Even so, difficulties arise, because language, customs, and meaning change in the course of time (II.22ff.): nor can one count on careful work from the Adam Scriveyns of the world.[30] Moreover, some selection and reorganization are almost unavoidable, as past records are brought to life again to fill different, present needs. Chaucer cannot simply quote the whole of Phyllis's letter; nor can he be content to transcribe the *Aeneid*: "I coude folwe, word for word, Virgile, / But it wolde lasten al to longe while" (1002-03). The pressures of time, as much as the demands of structure, force the poet to interpose himself between his source and his audience. The result is not nearly so complex and zany as Borges's Pierre Menard, whose twentieth-century novel *Don Quixote* has exactly the same words as its predecessor by Cervantes, though necessarily a quite different meaning;[31] but for Chaucer too, the poet's filtering and abridgment of the past inevitably alters the old books he draws on.

As Harry Bailly frequently reminds the Canterbury pilgrims (e.g.,

II.16ff.; VII.931), the poet needs to be concise if he is to keep the attention and interest of his audience. Bad art loses the effectiveness of its moral message, as the *Monk's Tale* shows; to instruct, the tale-teller must also delight. Yet the problems of using the past are as much in the poet's audience as in himself. The poet's limitations remind us of our own blindnesses, when he uses the mistakes of the dead to instruct the living:

> O sely wemen, ful of innocence,
> Ful of pite, of trouthe, and conscience,
> What maketh yow to men to truste so?
> Have ye swych routhe upon hyre feyned wo,
> And han swich olde ensaumples yow beforn?
> Se ye nat alle how they ben forsworn?
> Where sen ye oon, that he ne hath laft his leef,
> Or ben unkynde, or don hire som myscheef,
> Or piled here, or bosted of his dede?
> Ye may as wel it sen, as ye may rede.
>
> [1254-63]

The comic overtones of this apostrophe partly obscure its depiction of a serious issue. As Troilus says in response to Pandarus's preaching: " 'What knowe I of the queene Nyobe? / Lat be thyne olde ensaumples, I the preye' " (I.759-60). One reason for the failure of Troilus and the "sely wemen" to heed the past is the congenital defect of man's "blynde entencioun" (I.211); another is that there is no way for a human being to escape certain kinds of sorrow. Furthermore, the *Legend*, as in this comic apostrophe, demonstrates that the clearest didactic lessons depend on presenting the past in a potted form: as proverbial wisdom, or as oversimplified exempla. Even then its message is not always taken to heart: the garrulous Manciple learned at his talkative mother's knee the fable of the crow who spoke rashly; the story passes from generation to generation with no discernible effect. The moral proposed in the *Legend of Good Women* is too extreme to be very useful, but also owes its clarity of statement to its outrageous exaggeration. For in *Troilus*, the lifelike complexity of characters and motives makes it exceedingly difficult for us to take away any easy didactic message. The complexities of history, when combined with the limitations of the poet and his audience, conspire against a simple congruence of art and moral *sentence*. Inevitably, with both comic and tragic results, "Ther nys nat oon kan war by other be" (*Troilus* I.203).

For this reason, one must remember the context of the *Legend of Good Women*, that it is a palinode for *Troilus*. Chaucer does not ask us simply to invert the terms of these saints' lives, turning them into antifeminist satire. For they do not answer a male bias with a female one, but replace a pose of benevolent detachment with a predetermined moral message. One would be in part correct, though anachronistic, to say that the *Legend* shows what happens when art becomes propaganda. More important, and truer to Chaucer's cast of thought, the *Legend* and *Troilus* together reveal that the difference between an ironic narrowing of the poet's vision and the poet with his powers fully extended is insignificant compared to the gulf between either and the heavenly perspective we accept by faith but cannot attain on earth. As its *Prologue* brilliantly shows, the *Legend of Good Women* has a function in Chaucer's work analogous to that of Peter Quince's play in *A Midsummer Night's Dream* (V.i.). Oversimplification and distortion serve not only to poke fun at literary and moral simple-mindedness, but also to show the truth of Theseus's judgment, that "the best in this kind are but shadows."

II

This reading of the *Legend* may at times have appeared too subtle, since I have argued that what Chaucer deletes from his source is often as much a part of the poem's meaning as what he includes. But there are examples in later literature of this kind of subtlety, demanding of the reader an equally intimate knowledge of the classics:[32] Gulliver quotes the notorious liar Sinon, without naming him, for a supposedly authoritative statement of his own truthfulness. There are also such examples elsewhere in Chaucer. Pandarus quotes a few innocuous lines from Oenone's letter to Paris, which

Troilus claims not to have read (I.654ff.); the rest of *Heroides* V forecasts the fall of Troy. Chaucer's procedure in the *Legend*, as in *Troilus*, may argue for a fourteenth-century court audience with an astonishingly sophisticated awareness of classical mythology. Yet its *Prologue* reveals beyond question that the *Legend of Good Women* is not simply a boring task imposed on an unwilling poet by outraged female listeners, or simply a preparatory exercise for the *Canterbury Tales*. In the *Prologue* Chaucer invents a myth, that Alceste, the wife of Admetus, was metamorphosed into a daisy (F 512); and his myth elucidates the meaning of the rest of the poem.

Chaucer's myth develops from a miniature genre of fourteenth-century courtly literature, the marguerite poem.[33] The primary reason for paying homage to one's mistress in the guise of a flower, particularly this flower, is obviously the potential pun in its name. Wordplay in such contexts is habitual: Froissart admits, in the *Joli Buisson de Jonece*, that when he awakes he prays to St. Margherite as a matter of course;[34] in *L'Espinette Amoureuse*, he devises an anagram with the names Jehan Froissart and Margherite.[35] Once the marguerite-daisy is chosen to stand in for its human namesake, natural history provides these poems with their conventional imagery. For the daisy has two distinctive characteristics, summed up in Bernardus Silvestris's *De Mundi Universitate*: "Quaeque die clauso sibi clauditur et reserato / Se reserat solem sponsa secuta suum" [and she who is closed upon herself at close of day and, at the day's reappearance, reappears herself, responding to the sun like a bride].[36] The fourteenth-century marguerite poems all dwell on these two features. In Machaut's *Lis et Marguerite*, the daisy opens at dawn, and follows the movement of the sun in its course (250-54), drawn almost as if by a conscious awareness of its beneficent, life-giving power (255-58).[37] The reason for the flower's faithful mimicry appears in Froissart's *Dittié de la Flour de la Margherite*:

> Car le soleil, qui en beauté l'afine,

> Naturelment li est chambre et courtine,
> Et le deffent contre toute bruïne.
>
> [58-60] [38]

[For the sun, which ripens it in beauty, is by nature its bed-chamber and canopy, and defends it against all mist.]

When the sun sets, the daisy closes up, in order to protect itself from the terrors of the night. Machaut describes the reasons for its protective withdrawal:

> Mais c'est mervilleuse chose,
> Quar quant la marguerite est close,
> En ses fueilles enseveli,
> Ha son tresor aveques li—
> C'est sa greinne qui samble or fin.
> Et croy qu'elle le fait a fin
> Que sa greinne ne soit gastée,
> Ravie, tollue, ou emblée.
>
> [235-42]

[But this is a marvelous thing, for when the marguerite is closed up, buried in its petals, it has its treasure with it—that is its grain, which resembles fine gold. And I believe that it does this so that its grain may not be spoiled, ravished, taken away, or stolen.]

Deschamps summarizes the whole process in his ballade "Eloge d'une dame du nom de Marguerite":

> Vous vous ouvrez quand li soleil s'esveille,
> A la clarté monstrez vostre chief sor;
> Quant il couche, vous cloez vostre oreille
> Et ne doubtez leu, panthere ne tor.
>
> [19-22] [39]

[You open yourself when the sun arises; to the light you show your golden head. When he beds down, you close your ear and are not afraid of wolf, panther, or bull.]

The daisy's mimicry of solar movement is suitable for a flower that looks like the sun; even its name, as Chaucer reminds us, alludes to the greater "ye of day" (F 184). The *Prologue* to the *Legend* recounts the flower's other conventional attributes, and like the French marguerite poems emphasizes the fragility of its equipoise:

> And whan that hit ys eve, I renne blyve,
> As sone as evere the sonne gynneth weste,
> To seen this flour, how it wol go to reste,
> For fere of nyght, so hateth she derknesse.
> Hire chere is pleynly sprad in the brightnesse
> Of the sonne, for ther yt wol unclose.
>
> [F 60-65]

Chaucer combines these conventional images with a convention of much longer standing: the description of earthly love as a religion.[40] In this respect too, the *Legend* looks back to *Troilus,* where Chaucer defined his role as a love poet by the papal formula *servus servorum Dei* ("I, that god of loves servauntes serve")(I.15), and where Pandarus stumblingly invoked " 'Immortal god . . . that mayst nat dyen, / Cupide I mene' " (III.185-86). The *Prologue* thus places itself in a tradition that goes back to such twelfth-century jeux d'esprit as the *Love-Council of Remiremont,*[41] as it parodies the language of "oure legende," the religion to which—the narrator tells us—St. Augustine belongs (1689). Amor accuses Chaucer of being a heretic " 'ayeins my lawe' " (330), who must recant and undergo penance; Chaucer is to become love's James of Voragine, his "Seintes Legende of Cupide" the equivalent of the *Legenda Aurea.* Amor also makes a promise: " 'Ne shal no trewe lover come in helle' " (553). The lover's reward is apparently to be eternal life in Cupid's *locus amoenus:* " 'I mot goon hom (the sonne draweth west) / To paradys, with al this companye' " (563-64). In this context Chaucer's invented myth, identifying Alceste with the marguerite, gives the flower a shocking significance. For when we hear that the narrator is present at the daisy's "resureccioun" (110), and are reminded of the basis of Alceste's fame, we suddenly realize that she takes the place, in Cupid's religion, of Christ the Redeemer:

> She that for hire housbonde chees to dye,
> And eke to goon to helle, rather than he,
> And Ercules rescowed hire, parde,
> And broght hir out of helle agayn to blys.
>
>   [513-16]

Alceste is indeed preeminent among love's saints, but the rhetoric that attempts to make her Christ reveals its own inadequacy. The narrator worships her flower as "the clernesse and the verray lyght / That in this derke world me wynt and ledeth" (84-85).[42] But the daisy steals its pale fire from another "day's eye," the sun; and it is impossible to forget in this context that the sun is a traditional symbol of Christ. Just as the flower mimics the appearance and movement of its far greater counterpart, so Alceste anachronistically performs a true *imitatio Christi*, but on a miniature scale. The difference in magnitude between God and love goddess also becomes evident in the imperfection of the daisy's mimicry. It can bear only daylight; Cupid must retire to his version of paradise at sunset, and his flower folds up for the night.

The one-sidedness of Cupid and the daisy is fitting, for they rule a world defined by contingency, half-statement, and partial vision. Chaucer presents a touching idyll of spring and birdsong:

> Forgeten hadde the erthe his pore estat
> Of wynter, that hym naked made and mat,
> And with his swerd of cold so sore greved;
> Now hath th'atempre sonne all that releved,
> That naked was, and clad him new agayn.
> The smale foules, of the sesoun fayn,
> That from the panter and the net ben scaped,
> Upon the foweler, that hem made awhaped
> In wynter, and distroyed hadde hire brood,
> In his dispit hem thoghte yt did hem good
> To synge of hym, and in hir song despise
> The foule cherl that, for his coveytise,
> Had hem betrayed with his sophistrye.
> This was hire song, "The foweler we deffye,
> And al his craft."
>
>   [125-39]

We are told in Grandson's *Songe Saint Valentin* and in the *Parliament of Fowls* that the birds choose new mates every year; here, ironically, they swear on the blossoms to be true to one another (157). Earth's forgetfulness and the birds' brave defiance are affecting, because we cannot participate in the blissful oblivion of nature in spring; we know that winter and the fowler will soon enough return.[43]

By its attempt to impose a willed forgetfulness, the *Prologue* to the *Legend* predicts the comically one-sided perspective Amor dictates for Chaucer's palinode. Its world is one in which contraries battle each other: heaven and hell, past and present, authority and experience, flower and leaf join night and day, winter and spring. In *Troilus and Criseyde* Chaucer emphasized his detachment and impartiality. In the *Legend* Cupid forces him to choose sides. The *Prologue* shows him being prodded from one stance to the other, despite his efforts to disengage himself from controversy:

> But natheles, ne wene nat that I make
> In preysing of the flour agayn the leef,
> No more than of the corn agayn the sheef;
> For, as to me, nys lever noon ne lother.
> I nam withholden yit with never nother;
> Ne I not who serveth leef, ne who the flour.
>
> [188-93]

The elegant, and unresolvable, courtly quarrel between the adherents of the flower and those of the leaf[44] is germane to the task Cupid will impose on the narrator. One of Deschamps's ballades favors the flower, another praises the leaf:[45] we infer that rhetoric can with ease set up a case for either side. It can also support falsehood as readily as truth. For, given the usual metaphorical associations of winnowed grain, Chaucer's profession of neutrality between not only flower and leaf but corn and sheaf (190; G 74) is comically suspect. Indeed, Cupid elsewhere complains, in the later version of the *Prologue*: " 'But yit, I seye, what eyleth the to wryte / The draf of storyes, and forgete the corn?' " (G 311-12; also G 529); and at the beginning of both versions Chaucer laments that the "corn" of poetic words has already been reaped by earlier poets (74; G 62). In fact, the narrator will dismiss every unamenable fact in his sources as chaff. In the service of Amor's religion, one must proclaim the correct *sentence*, even at the expense of truth.

Cupid, unsurprisingly, shows himself to be inconsistent. One of the primary charges he makes against Chaucer is that the poet showed unfair bias in his treatment of Criseyde, perhaps—Alceste says in his defense—because he was ordered to do so (366-67). Given what is to follow, this notion is richly comic. It is also totally incorrect, as any reader of *Troilus* knows. In fact, the narrator of *Troilus* establishes every possible ground for objectivity: he is, so he says, simply translating a Latin source; he is not a lover (at least not a successful one), and has no emotional stake in the subject of his poem; the story took place long ago, and has the distance of unalterable historical fact (II.13-21). Even so, as the poem unfolds he finds his objective stance impossible to maintain; but he abandons it pretty much in Criseyde's favor. He defends her against her accusers, delays his account of her betrayal, and is defeated in the end only by the historicity of the story: he cannot change what happened at Troy.

He also cannot be absolutely certain that he knows what actually happened. As in the *House of Fame*, we are made aware in *Troilus* that the narrator is kept at a distance from the historical past by the written sources he is forced to rely on: he is unable to say whether Criseyde had any children (I.132-33); he knows of Criseyde's betrayal only from the books written by "folk thorugh which it is in mynde" (IV.18). In the *Prologue* to the *Legend*, this issue arises in part because of a joke at the expense of modern women, as Chaucer alludes to the myth of the declining world. Cupid offers him examples of female " 'goodnesse / By pref, and ek by storyes herebyforn' " (G 527-28). But the *pref* of experience appears in an unreliable dream about ancient heroines; and the injunction to "honouren and beleve / These bokes, there we han noon other preve" (27-28) has a comically unfortunate application, given the apparent dearth of any good women more recent than Ovid's.

> "These olde wemen kepte so here name
> That in this world I trowe men shal nat fynde
> A man that coude be so trewe and kynde
> As was the leste woman in that tyde."
>
> [G 301-04]

The incipient contrast between women of the past and women of the present suddenly becomes one between "these olde wemen" and living men. Boccaccio's good women too were "hethene, al the pak" (G 299); but the force of their example in a declining world is to make modern, Christian women ashamed to be so much less virtuous.[46] In Chaucer's *Prologue* the declining world abruptly changes sex.

Yet the guardians of fame themselves are at least partly to blame for Chaucer's complete reliance on ancient exemplars. Cupid argues that there are, among women,

> ". . . evere an hundred goode ageyn oon badde.
> This knoweth God, and alle clerkes eke,
> That usen swiche materes for to seke."
>
> [G 277-79]

If there are in fact any clerks who take pains to find exempla favorable to women, they are certainly not the ones the god of love mentions. His list includes the most notorious antifeminist documents in the Middle Ages: the *Epistola Valerii ad Ruffinum* and "Jerome agayns Jovynyan" (G 281). Clerkish bias joins the other poetic problems of the declining world: almost every "goodly word" has already been used; all the "fresshe songes" have been sung (77-79). It is tempting to look to the ancient, purer past for a simple unifying perspective, something to set against the modern strife between leaf and flower: "For this thing is al of another tonne, / Of olde storye, er swich stryf was begonne" (195-96).

But the clear simplicity of the Golden Age, which the *Book of the Duchess* nostalgically celebrated, is out of reach in the *Legend of Good Women*: the battle between the sexes and the problems of human knowledge do not by any means disappear as one goes back in time. The narrator is forced to make a claim as charmingly simple, and as misleading, as the birds' accusation of the sophistical fowler. In his anguish Troilus tried to refute Cassandra by describing Criseyde as another Alceste (V.1527-33); rhetoric pushes the narrator of the *Legend* to repeat Troilus's mistake. Yet the *Legend* indirectly shows that neither sex has a monopoly on treachery and evil. Chaucer's unavailing defense of his earlier work is perfectly just:

> "But trewly I wende, as in this cas,
> Naught have agilt, ne doon to love trespas.
> For-why a trewe man, withouten drede,
> Hath nat to parten with a theves dede;
> Ne a trewe lover oght me not to blame,
> Thogh that I speke a fals lovere som shame.
> They oghte rather with me for to holde,
> For that I of Creseyde wroot or tolde,
> Or of the Rose; what so myn auctour mente,
> Algate, God woot, yt was myn entente
> To forthren trouthe in love and yt cheryce,
> And to ben war fro falsnesse and fro vice
> By swich ensample; this was my menynge."
>
> [462-74]

To attempt to find *trouthe* where there is none does not, as the *Legend of Good Women* neatly proves, accomplish very much. If the daisy opens with every dawn and the birds make spring seem eternal, darkness and winter will not on that account delay their return.

THE NARRATOR AND HIS DOUBLE

The emphasis of this book has been on Chaucer's dream visions. Ovid's influence on detail is apparent in each of the four works; but I have mainly tried to show how a broad Ovidian perspective serves to unify the meaning of Chaucer's earlier poetry, with its skeptical exploration of the sources of human knowledge and the extent of man's limitations. In the final two chapters, I would like to suggest, in a highly selective fashion, that an Ovidian perspective can also help us to understand Chaucer's greatest works. It is necessary to be selective, given the complexity of *Troilus* and the *Canterbury Tales*; and possible, because the criticism of these late works has been more comprehensive. In them the force of Ovid's influence is by no means diluted, though the clear indebtedness of the dream visions is replaced by a more subtle Ovidian suffusion. An Ovidian paradigm helps, in this chapter, to clarify the meaning of *Troilus* and the *Knight's Tale*; and in chapter 6, the *Nun's Priest's Tale* as an epitome of the *Canterbury Tales*. By the time of his mature works, Ovidian techniques and points of view are the bedrock of Chaucer's poetic vision.

I

At the beginning of Book Two of the *Ars Amatoria*, Ovid interrupts his catalogue of lover's stratagems in order to recount the story of Daedalus, Icarus, and their disastrous flight. By this point in the poem, we are prepared for long digressions, connected to the art of love only by comically implausible assertions of relevance: in Book One Ovid tells us, for instance, that the rape of the Sabine women

set a fine Roman precedent for dalliance at the theater (101-34).
Even so, Ovid's ingenious return to his topic, when it immediately
follows Daedalus's pathetic, vain cries for his drowned son, is as
jarring in substance as it is in tone: "non potuit Minos hominis
conpescere pinnas, / ipse deum uolucrem detinuisse paro" (II.97-98)
[Minos was unable to restrain the wings of a man; I am preparing to
have held back a winged god].

The banality of this statement disguises only briefly the fact that
the comparison of real interest here is not between the narrator and
Minos, or Daedalus and Cupid. Instead, the rest of the *Ars Amatoria*
suggests that the narrator, a self-styled *magister* of love, is in many
important respects like Daedalus; and that his students, fledgling
lovers, are comic versions of the unfortunate Icarus. The self-
appointed tasks of the two teachers are similar: " 'sunt mihi naturae
iura nouanda meae' " (II.42) [I must invent the laws for my natural
order]. Daedalus the supreme *artifex* has discovered how to master
the air; Ovid, who dubs his trained lovers *artifices* (III.47), claims to
have reduced the blind emotion of love to a rational science: "quod
nunc ratio est, inpetus ante fuit" (*Remedia* 10) [what is now a
system was violent impulse before]. There is in both of them a kind
of presumption, in the narrator's case impudence, that stands in
ironic contrast to their Polonian loquacity and caution. Daedalus's
fussy avowal to his son, " 'me duce tutus eris' " (II.58) [with me as
your guide you will be safe], has its comic equivalent in the narrator's disclaimer: "non ego per praeceps et acuta cacumina
uadam, / nec iuuenum quisquam me duce captus erit" (I.381-82) [I
would not rush over precipice and pointed summits; nor will any
youth with me as his guide be seized]. Their presumption is
punished, as the arts they have devised come up against intractable
reality. Youthful impatience frustrates the success of each system.
Icarus, "incautis nimium temerarius annis" (II.83) [too rash in his
careless age], suffers the harsher fate; Ovid's students simply fall in
love. As Ovid repeatedly laments, once emotion overwhelms rational
detachment, strategy flies out the window. Even the *magister* himself becomes at times a "medicus turpiter aeger" (*Remedia* 314) [a

disgracefully sick physician]. His remedies lack potency precisely when they are most needed:

> aut noua, si possis, sedare incendia temptes
> aut ubi per uires procubuere suas.
> dum furor in cursu est, currenti cede furori:
> difficiles aditus impetus omnis habet.
>
> [*Remedia* 117-20]

[You should try, if you can, to calm fires either when they are new, or when they have subsided by their own force. While the raving passion is coursing, submit to its racing madness; every violent impulse has difficult approaches.]

Impetus sums up those forces in the world and in human nature which work against the possibility of rational control, in the arts both of love and of aerial navigation. Icarus's wings fall off, and the lover's rudderless ship is tossed around the ocean.

The poem too, by ancient convention, is a ship; and Ovid's ship runs wildly out of control (II.429-30), with Palinurus the helmsman swept overboard (*Remedia* 577). Just as Ovid the teacher loses control of his lessons and his students, so Ovid the poet repeatedly shows himself losing control of his poem. His most notorious lapse is at the beginning of the *Amores,* where we see him all set to write another *Aeneid*, until Cupid comes along and dictates a less elevated subject-matter and meter. In the *Ars Amatoria* Ovid has his own poetic madness to blame; in the middle of giving amatory advice to women, the *magister* suddenly remembers his sex and self-interest: "quo feror insanus?" (III.667) [whither am I, like a madman, being impelled?]. These analogous failures of poet, *magister,* and master artificer are jokes with a serious point. Daedalus and the comic teacher of love appear in the *Ars Amatoria* as versions of the poet, and they explicate the meaning of his name. For the art of the poet as a *maker* is to perceive reality and reproduce its structure; the art of the *magister* and of Daedalus is that structuring itself. All three characters illustrate the limitations of human knowledge and action, when they reveal themselves to be imperfect artists. The result can be pathetic as well as comic; but when Icarus falls to his death, the experienced teacher falls in love, or the poet submits to a comic vatic madness, the effect is a keen portrayal of human fallibility, as it faces the unmalleable force of desire or of external, nonhuman reality.

Chaucer too, in several of the *Canterbury Tales,* experiments with the idea of a narrator putting a surrogate version of himself inside his poem. In one instance the correspondence seems of minor or at least uncertain importance, an artist's signature like Alfred Hitchcock's boarding a bus in one of his films: the carpenter's knave in the *Miller's Tale,* like his creator, is named Robin, is "a strong carl for the nones," and is skilled at breaking open doors (I.3469-70; I.545, 550). Elsewhere the surrogate relationship offers a dramatic revelation, as the pilgrim, consciously or not, tells a tale about himself, either as he is or as he wishes he could be. The Merchant would prefer to be identified as Justinus, but his loathing for January does not completely disguise the unpleasant similarities between them. The Pardoner divides himself among his characters: he combines the qualities of the young revelers looking for death and the mysterious old man who cannot find it. The Wife of Bath, in the guise of the old woman in her fairy *Tale,* brings off triumphantly—and with comic self-awareness—a rejuvenation of herself that is harder to effect in reality. In the *Reeve's Tale* a thinly disguised, fictional Miller receives the drubbing the Reeve is afraid to give the real one: " 'For whan we may nat doon, than wol we speke; / Yet in oure asshen olde is fyr yreke' " (I.3881-82). The two clerks, even more northern and rustic than their narrator, get a sexual reward that the Reeve, despite his "grene tayl," is now able to relish only with a prurient, vicarious delight: " 'for thogh oure myght be goon, / Oure wyl desireth folie evere in oon' " (I.3879-80).

In these *Tales,* however, Chaucer follows a different paradigm from Ovid's: that is, the surrogate relationship as it appears in Boccaccio's *Teseida* and *Filostrato.* The dedicatory epistle of the *Teseida* tells Fiammetta: "if you remember well, you will be able to recognize in what is related of one of the lovers and of the young lady who is loved, things said and done by me to you and by you to me, if you were not false. Which of the two it is, I will not reveal because I know that you will discern it."[1] Such lovers' secrets appear in the *Filostrato* as well: Troilo sees Criseida for the first time at the festival of the Palladion, interpreted to be a pagan substitute for Easter; Boccaccio's love for Fiammetta, we know, dates from Easter 1336.[2] Moreover, the Proem to the *Filostrato* makes clear that Boccaccio means the poem to be cathartic, a device for relieving part of his amorous pain: "And the means was this: in the person of some impassioned one, such as I was and am, to relate my sufferings in song. I began therefore to turn over in my mind with great care ancient stories, in order to find one that would serve in all color of likelihood as a mask for my secret and amorous grief. Nor did other more apt for such a need occur to me than the valiant young Troilus. . . ."[3] The example of the protagonist, caught up in the confused turmoil of love, can help the narrator distance himself from his own unhappy experience. Boccaccio's interest is the same as Chaucer's in the *Wife of Bath's Tale* or *Reeve's Tale*: the psychological resonances of having an actor in a fiction stand in for its teller.

Given the fact that Chaucer follows Boccaccio's paradigm in some of the *Canterbury Tales,* it is striking when he chooses not to do so in the very works he adapts from the *Teseida* and the *Filostrato*. Instead, he alters these two Italian romances in exactly the same way, by replacing Boccaccio's version of the surrogate relationship with the Ovidian one. The narrators of the *Knight's Tale* and *Troilus* find their surrogates in characters who are distanced from the action of the poem and who act as detached observers and shapers of order, just as Ovid the poet and *magister* compares himself to Daedalus the master artificer. The Knight identifies himself with Theseus, not with Palamon or Arcite; and the narrator of *Troilus* is an analogue to Pandarus, not to the hero of the poem.[4] As I will argue in detail, this shift to an Ovidian pattern serves to make a characteristically Ovidian statement as well, for the shapers of order fail in their efforts, or at best achieve a sharply qualified success. Their narrators too, at a much greater remove from the distant past they recreate in verse, show themselves to be perplexed and hindered by the problems of process, order, and detachment that so concern their doubles.

There is a third example in Chaucer's poetry of this Ovidian structural pattern: the pairing of Harry Bailly and the narrator of the *Canterbury Tales*. It works primarily in the *General Prologue*, since afterward Chaucer resigns his poetic shaping and structuring powers to the illusion of verisimilitude (I.725ff.), the reader's whimsy (I.3176-77), and the control of the Host. One could easily demonstrate that this third pair repeats the Ovidian qualities of the first two: both Chaucer and Harry Bailly skillfully manage to put the Knight first, but their attempts to discern and maintain decorum and order quickly run into hilarious difficulties thereafter. Yet the *Knight's Tale* and *Troilus* are best considered by themselves. Chaucer probably wrote them at roughly the same point in his career;[5] and they display similar poetic concerns. Moreover, each work illuminates obscurities in the other. The example of Theseus helps us understand what Pandarus is up to; and the much examined role of the narrator in *Troilus* clarifies some less familiar qualities of the Knight as a storyteller.

II

The idea that Pandarus and the *Troilus* narrator are much alike is not new.[6] Chaucer's alterations of the *Filostrato* make them become versions of each other. Pandaro is the cousin of Criseida; Chaucer's Pandarus is Criseyde's uncle, someone who, like the narrator, looks at young love from an older man's perspective. Boccaccio's ardent narrator invokes his lady as poetic inspiration: "tu mi sei Apollo, / Tu se' mia musa" [thou to me art Apollo, thou art my muse].[7] Chaucer's has no lady to call on; by default, and for reasons of poetic decorum, Tisiphone becomes his muse. He, as he laments,

> Ne dar to love, for myn unliklynesse,
> Preyen for speed, al sholde I therfor sterve,
> So fer am I from his help in derknesse.
>
> [I.16-18]

In some moods Chaucer's narrator thinks himself lucky to be so unscathed by "the fir of love, the wherfro god me blesse!" (I.436); elsewhere he reveals, as the narrator of the *Parliament* does, that he is caught between fact and longing. Pandarus too is in an impossible, paradoxical position: he is a servant of love whom the god arbitrarily chooses not to reward.[8] Consumed by a long-lasting, unrequited passion (I.810-12, IV.484-90), he asks Troilus to " 'bid for me, sith thow art now in blysse, / That god me sende deth or soone lisse' " (III.342-43); the narrator asks the happy lovers in his audience to say a similar prayer for those "That ben despeired out of loves grace" (I.42), half implying that he himself feels such despair.

Pandarus does generally manage to hide his unhappiness with a comic vitality; only when caught unawares "in a studye" (II.1180),[9] or in the privacy of his lonely bed (II.57-63), does he reveal his true state. The detachment that age and unsuccess impose expresses itself in the comedy he brings to almost every scene, starting with his first, when he shakes Criseyde's name out of the reluctant Troilus: " 'A ha!' quod Pandare, 'here bygynneth game' " (I.868) (see esp. III.113-22). The narrator too, with the added distance of someone recording the remote past, finds comedy in the process of Troilus's courtship, especially in the first letter the convert to love writes to Criseyde (II.1065-85). These two onlookers are detached enough from Troilus's whirling absorption in his affair for the narrator to express foreknowledge (V.28), and Pandarus foreboding (V.505-08), when Criseyde leaves for the Greek camp. Yet each of them observes the central action of the story with a benevolence that overrides, at least for a time, his detachment. The narrator's well-wishing necessarily operates from a distance, since the progress of events is so emphatically out of his control. But he can nonetheless express his compassion for lovers in general (I.50), and for Troilus's plight in particular. Pandarus's active benevolence of course unites the two lovers; and the narrator urges his surrogate on, praying that "Janus, god of entre" will bless his first meeting with Criseyde (II.77), and that God will help "to quenchen al this sorwe! / So hope I that he shal, for he best may" (III.1058-59).

Like Chaucer's narrator, Pandarus is a servant of love's servants
(I.15), like him "the sorwful instrument / That helpeth loveres, as I
kan, to pleyne" (I.10-11). The Ovidian paradox of the sick physician
who can nonetheless cure others (I.659ff.) appears in his defense of
himself as the "blynd man" who keeps his feet when another, "that
koude loken wide," falls (I.628-29). The narrator uses, surprisingly,
much the same image to characterize his own relation to the story:

> Ek though I speke of love unfelyngly,
> No wonder is, for it no thyng of newe is;
> A blynd man kan nat juggen wel in hewis.
>
> [II.19-21]

An even more startling correspondence between them appears.
Pandarus humbly concludes his offer to help Troilus with: " 'Yif me
this labour and this besynesse, / And of my spede be thyn al that
swetnesse' " (I.1042-43). His words echo Chaucer's at the beginning
of the poem:

> But natheles, if this may don gladnesse
> Unto any lovere, and his cause availle,
> Have he my thonk, and myn be this travaille.
>
> [I.19-21] [10]

The nearly identical phrasing of these generous self-denials implies
that the narrator is, like Pandarus, a go-between; and he in fact vows
to have compassion for lovers, "As though I were hire owne brother
dere" (I.51). Though he distinguishes himself from the active energy
of Pandarus's intervention, he must as Venus's clerk (III.41) nonetheless admit his responsibility as the reviver of Lollius's story; and
he recites it to help the cause of the lovers in his audience. Like
Pandarus, he responds to the story as it unfolds by following with
decorous emotions (I.13-14) the sweep of its events. To be sure,
Chaucer's narrator is more hesitant than his double: his praises of
love's beneficence, unlike Pandarus's (I.813-19), seem to some
degree forced from him (I.246-59; III.1359-79), because they never
entirely suppress his awareness of the tragedy to come. Yet he does,
when necessary, rise to the rhetorical occasion. He offers us a word-

for-word translation of Troilus's song, when Lollius has provided
only its "sentence" for his use: empathy must fill in the details
(I.393-99). And the beautiful hymn to Venus at the opening of
Book Three is, significantly, stolen from Boccaccio's Troilo, who
praises the goddess in these terms after his second night with
Criseyde. If only for a short time, the narrator thus succeeds in
making a vicarious emotional identification with the bliss of his
hero.

Pandarus, notoriously, pushes such vicarious emotion to a comic,
voyeuristic extreme by his refusals to admit that three is a crowd:
" 'myn avys anoon may helpen us' " (I.620; also I.994; III.952,
1095). He shows an artist's reluctance to let his creation alone, and
an exuberant delight in his artifices: he pulls the two lovers around
"by the lappe" (III.59, 742), pokes his niece when her response to
Troilus's sorrow is too restrained (III.116), and hurries her off to
bed as quickly as possible: " 'This were a weder for to slepen
inne; / And that I rede us soone to bygynne' " (III.657-58). Moreover, in the two central episodes of Book Three—the lovers' meetings
at the houses of Deiphebus and Pandarus—there are astonishing
reminders that all three characters are present, every time we are in
danger of forgetting that fact. Each of the two men eavesdrops on
Criseyde's conversations with the other: Troilus interrupts Pandarus
in order to plead his own cause (III.127, 953-59); Pandarus keeps
reappearing as the lovers prepare to go to bed together (III.1094,
1135, 1188). The narrator too, as he describes the preparations for
Criseyde's visit to her uncle's house, nearly makes vicarious delight
become participation:

> This tymber is al redy up to frame;
> Us lakketh nought but that we weten wolde
> A certeyn houre, in which she comen sholde.
>   [III.530-32]

"Us" embraces even the audience. The poet's function as a go-
between and our own voyeuristic impulses as readers come to the
foreground with a jolt when Pandarus makes his most outrageous
false departure from the bedroom scene:

> And with that word he drow hym to the feere,
> And took a light, and fond his contenaunce
> As for to looke upon an old romaunce.
>
> [III.978-80]

As Troilus aptly says, when he laments his sorrow, " 'Men myghte a book make of it, lik a storie' " (V.585). The freezing of life into literary form offers us an intimacy with its characters yet makes us aware of our detachment from the reality of their fate.

This mixture of interest and detachment appears in both Pandarus and the narrator: even in the raptures of Book Three, their comic interruptions qualify the wholeheartedness of their involvement and give it a self-conscious, reflective air. As the downward curve of the story takes over, they go through parallel motions of disengagement. The narrator retains enough of an identification with Troilus to sneer at Diomede's sugared hypocrisy (V.946-47) and to forestall the anger of his audience: "And shortly, lest that ye my tale breke," he tells us, Diomede "refte" Criseyde "of the grete of al hire peyne" (V.1032, 1036). But such responses are as ineffectual as Pandarus's attempts to console the hero. The only option the two go-betweens have, finally, is to abandon Troilus to the sinking ship of his love. Who could describe Troilus's sorrow? the narrator asks:

> Thow, redere, maist thi self ful wel devyne
> That swich a wo my wit kan nat defyne.
> On ydel for to write it sholde I swynke,
> Whan that my wit is wery it to thynke.
>
> [V.270-73]

The alternative to exhaustion is violent repudiation:

> "My brother deere, I may do the no more.
> What sholde I seyn? I hate, ywys, Criseyde!
> And, god woot, I wol hate hire evere more!"
>
> [V.1731-33]

Given the Ovidian metaphor Boccaccio and Chaucer use for both poem and love-affair (I.416; II.3; III.910, 1291; IV.282; V.638-44), we may in fact think of *Troilus* as a procession of rats leaving a

sinking ship. The order of departure is important. Pandarus and the
narrator abandon Troilus's love and the poem only at their endings.
Calkas is the first rat to leave (I.64-84); and our distaste answers a
betrayal that is as much aesthetic as political. For if his response to
foreknowledge is the correct one, there is no reason for Chaucer to
keep on writing or for us to keep on reading: we too, after all, know
that Troy will fall. Another wise old man, Egeus in the *Knight's
Tale*, responds to the vicissitudes of earthly life with philosophic
resignation; Calkas scurries to get on the winning side. But they both
stand in contrast to the artificers who refuse to abandon hope, even
in an obviously losing effort.

In *Troilus* the resonances of a single image imply the correspondence of the two kinds of artifice. Chaucer describes
Pandarus's deliberations on how best to approach Criseyde by the
analogy of an architect planning a house before he begins to build it
(I.1065-71). The traditional associations of this image—like the *ars
longa, vita brevis* at the beginning of the *Parliament of Fowls*—are in
fact with the poetic, not the amatory art: Geoffrey of Vinsauf uses
the figure to outline the proper procedure for the poet-rhetorician to
follow.[11] Moreover, its source is Boethius's portrayal of *Deus artifex*
(*Boece* IV.pr. 6, 82-89).[12] The disparities between God and his
human imitators become obvious in the flawed artifices of poet and
go-between. For their precarious constructions choose to ignore the
Trojan War, in order to focus on Troilus's love affair (I.141-47).
Pandarus, with less foreknowledge than the narrator, has more of an
excuse for the blinders on his vision. He quotes the least important
part of Oenone's letter to Paris (I.652-65); he tells Criseyde that his
news for her is not that the Greeks have sailed away, but something
five times better (II.126); he uses the arrival in Troy of a Greek spy
as a pretext for a second visit (II.1112-13). Most astonishingly, he
uses the conjunction of Saturn and Jupiter in Cancer, almost
certainly to be understood as an omen of the fall of Troy,[13] as a way
of predicting a convenient heavy rainstorm. But the events of the
war, in the persons of Calkas and Antenor, frustrate his efforts to
create his own, ordered world of love.[14] The larger course of history
takes events beyond the power of his control.

They are out of the narrator's control as well: he is simply translating Lollius, and his poem is about the unalterable past. The scope
for his skills as an artificer is restricted—at one point, with ironic
humor, simply to finding rhyme words for a story that unrolls itself
(II.10–11). As an artificer the passive narrator directly opposes
Pandarus, whose bustling activity prods the two lovers together: " 'O
verray god, so have I ronne! / Lo, nece myn, se ye nat how I
swete?' " (II.1464-65). Once he has made his choice of subject
matter, decorum dictates in a good Horatian fashion his poetic
response (I.13-14). Troilus's ship of love is tossed around the ocean
(I.416-17); so is the narrator's poem (II.1-7). He cannot escape the
bell curve of Troilus's experience once he has undertaken to tell the
story, as the proems to the five books of *Troilus* brilliantly show.[15]
The muses, decorously appropriate to their points on the curve, are
invoked to fill the poet's empty vessel; he calls on Calliope to infuse
him with *sentement*:

> For now is nede; sestow nat my destresse,
> How I mot telle anon right the gladnesse
> Of Troilus, to Venus heryinge?
>
> [III.46–48]

Later in the same book we are asked: "What myghte or may the sely
larke seye, / Whan that the sperhauk hath it in his foot?" (1191-92).
The "sely larke" is, first of all, Criseyde, who "felte hire thus itake"
(1198). But as the rest of the stanza shows, it is also the narrator,
forced by his material to rhapsodize:

> Though that I tarie a yer, som tyme I moot,
> After myn auctour, telle of hire gladnesse,
> As well as I have told hire hevynesse.
>
> [1195-97]

He is not forced to do so for very long; and his passivity comes
out in the farewell he offers to Venus, Cupid, and the muses at the
end of Book Three: "syn that ye wol wende, / Ye heried ben for ay
withouten ende" (1812-13). The following proem, which asks that
he be helped to finish the poem in its fourth book (IV.26-28), has
been taken to be a remnant of Chaucer's first version of *Troilus,* an

out-of-place detail in an untidy revision. But the terseness of the
proem to Book Five fits another explanation of the narrator's inability to finish *Troilus* in four books. Given the Ovidian precedents,
Chaucer may well be offering one more indication that the poem is
out of his control.[16] His hurry at the beginning of Book Four
prefaces a general sense of impatience in the last two books to get
done with an increasingly disagreeable task. In Book Five even the
objective heavenly markers of time are in a hurry to get things over
with, to move past the date appointed for Criseyde's return: "And
Cynthea hire charhors overraughte / To whirle out of the Leoun, if
she myghte" (1018-19).

The conclusion to Book Five, which promises the *Legend of
Good Women* (1777-78), shows the narrator's awareness that he
cannot, despite his passivity, wholly escape responsibility for the
story he has told. Indeed, at first sight his responsibility must be in
some respects greater than Pandarus's. He does, after all, know
before he begins that Troilus's love will fail (I.378). Yet Pandarus in
some important senses knows as much. He expresses a perfect awareness of the arbitrary workings of Fortune:[17] since Troilus has felt
the goddess's bad effects, it may now be his turn to have better luck
(I.850-54). Even at the high point of the affair, in the bliss of Book
Three, Pandarus warns his friend to be as careful in keeping Criseyde
as he was in winning her: " 'For worldly joie halt nat but by a wir' "
(1636); and the worst kind of fortune is " 'to han ben in pros-
peritee, / And it remembren whan it passed is' " (1627-28). When
things begin to fall apart Pandarus is surprised, not at the fact of
mutability, but merely at the speed with which Fortune has turned
against Troilus: " 'Who wolde have wend that, in so litel a
throwe / Fortune oure joie wolde han overthrowe?' " (IV.384-85).

The poetic effect of Pandarus's foreboding is somewhat akin to
the irony of Criseyde's giving Stoic speeches on the inevitable
transience of earthly happiness (III.813-16; IV.834-36). As in the
Knight's Tale (I.993, 2911, 2941), Chaucer is careful to remind us of
the fact that his characters are pagan—with an awareness of
mutability as sharp as any Christian's, but without the Christian's

recourse.[18] The difference is stressed at several points by a half-comic, jarring use of religious language: " 'O god of love in soth we serven bothe,' " says Diomede to Criseyde (V.143). Pandarus's response to young love is the most striking such instance, as delay underlines the irony: " 'Immortal god,' quod he, 'that mayst nat dyen, / Cupide I mene, of this mayst glorifie' " (III.185-86). Pandarus quickly deflates his own rhapsody: " 'But ho, no more as now of this matere' " (190); he seems to have as much awareness as we do of the insufficiencies and arbitrary judgments of his god. Like Theseus in the *Knight's Tale,* he responds to an apparently arbitrary and malign universe with *pitee* and *gentilesse*; and his efforts to bring ordered happiness out of emotional torment, while sometimes comic, are by no means ignoble.

The narrator faces the problems of love and order from a standpoint that is in some essential ways different from Pandarus's. He is, after all, a Christian, and has available from the start a definition of true love that is beyond the reach of his characters, except as an unsatisfiable yearning. Even so, the people in Troy have to deal with dilemmas that are human, not simply pagan: the vocabulary of love is ambiguous; language uses the same words to describe earthly rapture and heavenly bliss. Indeed, the narrator is forced by the development of his story to clarify and focus the meaning of his vocabulary. He begins with the ambiguities of reference, and hint of blasphemy, inherent in the description of love as a religion (I.15). In Book Three, the terms of his rhapsody to love's power are indistinguishable from Troilus's: their referents are impossible to pin down. The same words encompass both pagan and Christian, both earthly and heavenly meanings. As Troilus exclaims:

> . . . "O Love, O Charite,
> Thi moder ek, Citherea the swete,
> After thi self next heried be she,
> Venus mene I, the wel-willy planete."
> [III.1254-57]

The need for distinctions is brought home abruptly when the

narrator makes his astonishing response to the night of love: "Why ne hadde I swich oon with my soule ybought, / Ye, or the leeste joie that was there?" (III.1319-20). As Troilus's love affair falls apart, and the "fetheres brighte of Troie" are pulled away by Fortune (V.1546), the narrator discovers the recourse available to him and to us, but not to his characters. Our pity is enhanced by their distance in the darkness of the past: in their "blynde entencioun" these pagans knew enough to place love above all other values, but did not have the revelation of Love that can bring certainty.

Yet the "blynde entencioun" is ours as well, and the similarities between Christian narrator and pagan go-between are finally more significant than their differences. If the ending of *Troilus* shows that faith is available to us in our earthly state, the poem as a whole has proved that knowledge and certainty are not. We are left, as in all of Chaucer's poems, with a simultaneous awareness of human nobility and of human limitations. The effort of Pandarus and the narrator to serve love by giving order to blind impulse is Ovidian. So too is their failure, brought about by the insufficiencies of love itself. The tensions between order and the forces that frustrate its realization are given even clearer statement in the *Knight's Tale,* to which this chapter will now turn. But *Troilus and Criseyde* offers a poignant examination of the pretensions of human artifice, in literature and in life, and the pathetic nobility of the artist's presumption.

III

In the past twenty-five years many critics have noted that order is the central concern of the *Knight's Tale.*[19] Chaucer heightens his emphasis on order by the changes he makes from his source, Boccaccio's *Teseida.* They are pervasive, and range in prominence from the introduction of Theseus's Boethian discourse on the First Mover to the minute details of the ordered society and its opera-tions: Arcite's progress up the social ladder of Theseus's court (1429ff.) has no counterpart in Boccaccio. The most important of these changes have to do with character. From the time that

Palamon and Arcite first appear, half-dead, clad "bothe in oon armes" (1012), they are much harder to tell apart than the heroes of the *Teseida.* Whatever individuality they gain from their extended speeches is countered by the Olympian perspective of the narrator, who at several points reduces them to chessmen in an abstract problem of order. Such flattening of character is even more pronounced in Emelye. In Boccaccio, she has a strongly defined personality: she flirts with Palemone and Arcita when they first see her, pretending to be unaware of their gaze (III.19); she recognizes Arcita in his disguise (IV.61); she reacts to Arcita's impending death with bitter, eloquent sorrow (X.68ff.). In Chaucer's tale she is reduced to a passive responder to events beyond her control. Chaucer shifts the center of interest entirely by a compensatory fleshing out of two other characters. He invents important speeches for Theseus, who presides over the story: most notably, the ironic comments after the fight in the grove, and the First Mover speech. And, as happens in *Troilus,* Chaucer makes us aware of the narrator as a character. The Knight is not an inobtrusive medium for his story; his perceptions, as they shape ours, are self-revelatory.

We become increasingly aware, moreover, of similarities between Theseus and the Knight-narrator.[20] When one thinks back on the *Tale* from some distance, it is often difficult to remember which one of them made a particular comment: their attitudes toward life and love are exactly the same. They both have strong military interests, and an intense delight in the details of pageantry and tournaments. Theseus's care in setting up the tournament and building the arena is matched by the Knight's zest in describing his preparations. The Knight's loving detail in arming the two companies (2491ff.) is largely Chaucer's invention, as are the enthusiastic comments on the excellence of the company (2101ff.) and the joy that would come, "in Engelond or elleswhere" (2113), if such an occasion were to arise again: "To fighte for a lady, *benedicitee!* / It were a lusty sighte for to see" (2115-16). His most obvious expression of enthusiasm is the famous slip into alliterative verse, in the excitement of reciting the battle (2600ff.). Yet both Theseus and the Knight counter such enthusiasm with an austere and rather coldly indifferent reaction to life and death. We cannot expect them to be bright-eyed innocents; nonetheless, appropriate as their detachment is to seasoned veterans, it still comes as a surprise. The Knight's comment at the approach of Arcite's death is shocking: "And certeinly, ther Nature wol nat wirche, / Fare wel phisik! go ber the man to chirche!" (2759-60). At the very beginning of the *Tale* Theseus's kindred callousness appears in action: he punishes Thebes with total destruction (990). The Knight's description of the *pilours'* work in the battle's aftermath is notably harsher than Boccaccio's; using a word that occurs nowhere else in Chaucer's poetry, he mentions three times the heap (*taas*) of dead bodies in which Palamon and Arcite are found (1005, 1009, 1020).

Theseus and the Knight also share an older man's detached view of the folly of youthful love. And if Egeus shows that bodily decrepitude is not necessarily wisdom, the young lovers are indeed ignorant. Chaucer makes their love debate when they first see Emelye at least half-comic, by adding a large measure of contentiousness to Boccaccio's account; an echo of their split-second shift from blood brotherhood to mortal enmity comes up later, when each helps the other to arm before they begin hacking and hewing in blood up to their ankles (1660).[21] The Knight jokes about Palamon's "youlyng" (1278), using a word that appears nowhere else in Chaucer. Like the narrator of *Troilus,* he is a non-lover who distinguishes himself from his audience (1347) and from the characters in his story:

> Into a studie he fil sodeynly,
> As doon thise loveres in hir queynte geres,
> Now in the crope, now doun in the breres,
> Now up, now doun, as boket in a welle.
>
> [1530-33]

Theseus's response is exactly the same, as he comments on the "heigh folye" (1798) of love, and the absurdity of the two knights trying to kill each other for the love of a woman who does not know that they exist (1809-10). He softens into sympathy for their plight, as a reformed rake himself (1813-14). Yet Theseus is certainly a rather austere ex-lover: whether or not there are any symbolic overtones to his subjugation of "the regne of Femenye" (877)—there are in the *Teseida*—his expressed concerns are far from amorous, and his marriage to Ypolita is hardly a love-match. In more than one sense the Knight's summary of his May hunt is accurate: "For after Mars he serveth now Dyane" (1682).

Theseus's austerity is the Knight's as well, as the contrasting portrait in the *General Prologue* of his son the Squire suggests (I.87-98). It combines with a rather condescending view of women, and a peculiarly naive assessment of their actions. The Knight's *occupatio* about the rites of Diana's temple retreats before female mysteries with a gesture half of modesty, half of comic prurience (2284-88).[22] Emelye's passivity, to his mind, befits her sex: "(For wommen, as to speken in comune, / Thei folwen alle the favour of Fortune)" (2681-82).[23] Widows, we are told, for the most part mourn loudly, and must do so, "Or ellis fallen in swich maladye, / That at the laste certeinly they dye" (2825-26). They are not the only women to weep. In a scene Chaucer invents, Ypolita and Emelye burst into tears "for verray wommanhede" (1748) at Theseus's summary judgment of Palamon and Arcite; such "gentil men . . . of greet estaat" should not face execution, especially since "no thyng but for love was this debaat" (1753-54). The Queen and her sister repeat almost word for word the Theban widows' prayer (950-51): " 'Have mercy, Lord, upon us wommen alle!' " (1757). The Knight betrays at least a slight impatience with their sentimentality when he describes Theseus's response: "his herte hadde compassioun / Of wommen, for they wepen evere in oon" (1770-71). Yet women's tears twice act to temper Theseus's severity and detachment, by awakening the *pitee* appropriate to his *gentillesse* (920). Like the *Troilus* narrator and Pandarus, the Knight and Theseus both assume—in spite of their ironic, detached perspectives—a benevolence that asserts itself in action, in their efforts to shape and maintain ordered structures of various kinds. Their

fruitful activity is suitable to their chivalric vocation. The benevolence that triggers action both creates order and gives it a humane
dimension, by fulfilling the demands of sentiment before those of a
tidy pattern. The artificer tries to assert some measure of control
over human experience; ironically, he is provoked to action by
events that prophesy the inevitable failure of all his efforts.

The case of Theseus is the more familiar. There is no question of
his interest in order and hierarchy: the society he governs clearly
works according to degree and with a concern for the niceties of law
and decorum (1209, 1710-13, 2573, 2735). Yet a good deal of
recent criticism of the *Knight's Tale* has been at pains to show that
Theseus's efforts to create order are singularly ineffective, that they
in fact serve only to bring about further suffering.[24] There is much
in the *Tale* to support such readings; even the "heigh labour" that
goes into building Arcite's funeral pyre has the unexpected result of
disaster for the wood gods and dryads, "Disherited of hire
habitacioun, / In which they woneden in reste and pees" (2926-27).
The repeated subversion of order contributes centrally to the
Knight's bleak view of life and human possibility. Nonetheless,
Theseus is hardly to blame if his impulses toward equity lead to
impermanent solutions. In one instance, at least, the frustration of
his efforts is even half-comic. As an expression of mercy and of his
friendship with Pirithous, he releases Arcite from prison. No ransom
is paid (1205); the release is almost an instance of unmerited grace,
from Arcite's point of view, but an exceptionally inopportune one,
since it takes him away from Emelye: " 'Allas, that evere knew I
Perotheus!' " (1227). Neither Palamon nor Arcite is happy; each
envies the other his prison or "freedom." In such a curious situation,
Theseus's efforts cannot win.

More important, this episode marks an important shift in our
understanding of Theseus; the two lovers will catch up with our new
sense of him only after their battle in the grove. At the beginning of
the *Knight's Tale* Theseus is emphatically at the top of Fortune's
wheel, and Palamon and Arcite are at the bottom—apparently "for
everemoore" (1028-32). He has decided the fate of the two men for

purposes of his own, inscrutable either to them or to us. In Boccaccio's version the knights are "dannati . . . ad etterna prigione" (II.98) [condemned to eternal imprisonment].[25] Boccaccio explains the Duke's motives: it would be a sin, he thinks, to execute them, and he commutes their sentence to life imprisonment (II.98). The Knight, on the other hand, tells us three times only that Theseus will accept no ransom (1024, 1032, 1176), emphasizing by repetition an extraordinary, and mysterious, situation.[26] His arbitrary, unfathomable, and harsh action seems to justify Arcite's belief " 'That he . . . is my mortal enemy' " (1553). Theseus appears at the beginning of the poem to govern by "tirannye" (1111); in the *Teseïda,* by contrast, he shows some compassion toward Palemone and Arcita from the start, by going out of his way to see that their wounds are taken care of (II.89). Even after his release, Chaucer's Arcite can speak of " 'wrecched Palamoun, / That Theseus martireth in prisoun' " (1561-62). But the relationship of the three men changes during the scene in the grove, when the mercy Theseus showed to the Theban women extends itself to the two lovers. The distant, elevated ruler at last comes down to earth, within the range of our comprehension, in a series of benevolent temperings of an originally harsh and rigid sense of order. He releases Arcite for friendship's sake; he sets up a tournament in order to give some form to the chaos of conflicting impulse; and, as the tournament begins, he moves to prevent bloodshed: "Wherfore, to shapen that they shal nat dye, / He wol his firste purpos modifye" (2541-42).[27] Our rapidly growing sympathy with his good intentions is greatly abetted by the appearance elsewhere of a real cruelty and indifference to human values. Both Theseus and the gods come up with solutions to the puzzle of the two lovers' conflicting claims. Theseus's is humane; the legalistic gods manage to find a particularly cold-blooded one.[28] In this connection, it is fitting for Arcite to quote the Boethian (and Ovidian) commonplace that love is of greater force than positive law (1165-68). For if the dispute between Palamon and Arcite shows the disruptive power of love, Theseus shows its unitive force. As he says to Emelye, when he urges her to accept Palamon, " 'gentil mercy

oghte to passen right' " (3089). His own summation of the diverse
strands in his character—seeming distance and compassion, detachment and benevolence—appears at the end of the *Tale*. The famous
First Mover speech combines the faith that Love orders the universe
with the deep awareness that mutability is its earthly manifestation.
His final ordering act repeats this lesson of paradox. The moral he
gleans from Arcite's death, essentially "Don't cry over spilt milk,"
allows his demand for the marriage of Palamon and Emelye in " 'O
parfit joye, lastynge everemo' " (3072).

The events of the *Knight's Tale* and Theseus's own expressed
attitudes should keep us from attaching any easy sentimentality or
wide-eyed belief in good fortune to this final action. Instead, the
oddness of its finality—nothing, after all, has lasted "everemo" in the
world of this poem—underlines Theseus's essential trait: with great
resilience, unhampered by events or by his clear awareness of the
cruelty of Fortune and the world, he keeps on fighting to assert and
establish order. This trait distinguishes him from Boccaccio's Teseo:
the hero of the *Teseida* says the words (XII.6) that Chaucer gives to
Egeus (2843-46), a resigned, Stoic reaction to mutability. This trait
is also his most noteworthy link with the Knight, both as a character
in the *Canterbury Tales* and as the teller of his own tale.

For in the course of the *Tale* we become as conscious of the
Knight's structuring of his narrative as we are of Theseus's attempts
to order the events within it. At the very beginning the Knight
intrudes, breaking the illusion of his story (875-92); and such self-
conscious intrusions come to be a frequent occurrence. An intrusive
narrator and an indifference about maintaining illusion are characteristic of a great deal of medieval narrative, and certainly of medieval
romance narrative. Yet in the *Knight's Tale* these conventional
markers serve unconventional purposes. The Knight's comments remind us that the tale belongs to him, not simply to an anonymous
narrative voice; and they perform the dramatic function of adding
depth to his portrait in the *General Prologue*. Their effect is
heightened by the Knight's distance from his characters: like the
Troilus narrator, he is reviving events of the remote past. Another

kind of distance, in part created by such historical awareness, is even more important. The Knight reduces history to a symmetrical pattern. The astrologically significant physiognomies of Lycurgus and Emetreus[29] elegantly define the opposition between them; in the *Teseida* there are no such extended descriptions of the men who fight on behalf of the two lovers. The Knight's interest in narrative control and pattern comes out most clearly in his frequent use of *occupatio,* and in his application of a kind of equal-time rule to the contending lovers:

> Now wol I stynte of Palamon a lite,
> And lete hym in his prisoun stille dwelle,
> And of Arcita forth I wol yow telle.
> [1334-36; also 1449-50, 1488-90]

The *demande d'amour* at the end of Part One, "Who hath the worse, Arcite or Palamoun?" (1348), works in much the same way: it stops the action, makes us analyze the abstract possibilities of order in the situation as it stands, and then forces us to submit to process once more as the story starts up again.

The effect of such devices is cumulative, but the *Knight's Tale* beyond question insists on our noticing the artifice of its narrator—the *Miller's Tale,* for example, is as carefully but not so obviously structured. Perhaps the most important indication of such artifice is the one we at first find least unusual, the hyperbole and over-statement one expects to find in a romance. Romance hyperbole allows a cavalier attitude toward time; the pressures of urgency dissipate with unreal situations and characters. Thus Arcite endures the torments of love-sickness in Thebes for "a yeer or two" (1381), and he spends the same vague period of time as a "page of the chambre of Emelye" (1426-27). Another three years as one of Theseus's squires (1446) bring the total to seven, the number of years Palamon has spent alone in prison after Arcite's release (1452). The resolution of the conflict between the two lovers is a painfully slow process.

Yet the most significant instances of such overstatement are elsewhere. Just as Theseus repeatedly sets up structures of order that are quickly undermined, so the narrator's hyperbole bestows an illusory permanence upon situations. Theseus, we are told,

> . . . lyveth in joye and in honour
> Terme of his lyf; what nedeth wordes mo?
> And in a tour, in angwissh and in wo,
> This Palamon and his felawe Arcite
> For everemoore; ther may no gold hem quite.
>
> [1028-32]

When Arcite is released from prison and returns home to Thebes, "Ful ofte a day he swelte and seyde 'Allas!' / For seen his lady shal he nevere mo" (1356-57). The almost immediate reversal of these supposedly final arrangements undercuts any naive belief in the concluding resolution of the *Tale,* where Theseus's hyperbolic invocation of marriage as a " 'parfit joye, lastynge everemo' " (3072) directly precedes the Knight's own hyperbole, as he shifts to the historical present tense of a fairy-tale ending (3097-3108). In effect, Theseus and the Knight conspire to impose a happy ending on the poem.

The ending of the *Knight's Tale* has the tidy, self-conscious artificiality of Shakespeare's comedies, with their neatly paired couples going off, not always willingly, to the social resolution symbolized by marriage. It is artificial precisely because it does not follow logically from the nature of the world, order, and justice, as they have manifested themselves in the course of the narrative. Artificial, but not inappropriate or foolish. Neither the Knight nor Theseus is simply a sentimentalist; the *Tale* has exposed countering examples of the detachment, even brutality, that they both can muster. Instead, the Knight's interruption of the *Monk's Tale* suggests his intent at the end of his own:

> "Hoo!" quod the Knyght, "good sire, namoore of this!
> That ye han seyd is right ynough, ywis,
> And muchel moore; for litel hevynesse
> Is right ynough to muche folk, I gesse.

> I seye for me, it is a greet disese,
> Whereas men han been in greet welthe and ese,
> To heeren of hire sodeyn fal, allas![30]
> And the contrarie is joye and greet solas,
> As whan a man hath been in povre estaat,
> And clymbeth up and wexeth fortunat,
> And there abideth in prosperitee.
> Swich thyng is gladsom, as it thynketh me,
> And of swich thyng were goodly for to telle."
>
> [VII.2767-79]

The Knight, by saying that happy endings are nicer, is not revealing himself to be a pollyanna. He transcends the Monk's viewpoint in the way that Theseus goes beyond the Stoic wisdom of Egeus. Theseus's First Mover speech emphasizes the decay and death of all earthly things, but it begins with the vision of a "faire cheyne of love" (2988), whose effects may be inscrutable but which at least sets a pattern of love and order for us to believe in and imitate. Theseus's experience of the world must force him to agree "realistically" with his father's pessimistic point of view. Yet he unceasingly fights against the forces of disorder, whether they come from below in the form of man's blind impulse to love, or from above as the arbitrary judgments of the indifferent gods. Likewise, the Knight's vision of the world is scarcely less bleak than that of the *Monk's Tale*. But in the Knight's tale as in his own life, the chivalric ideal asserts its enduring force. Following the august example of his ancient exemplar, Chaucer's "verray, parfit gentil knyght" refuses to acquiesce in a passive acceptance of things as they are.

ORDER AND ENERGY IN THE CANTERBURY TALES: THE NUN'S PRIEST'S TALE

This book has had a great deal to say about narrators. I have argued that the speaking voices of Chaucer and Ovid, despite their obvious differences (one lacks experience, the other is sated by it), show their inadequacies in much the same fashion. Several of them admit to bias: the conscripted hagiographer of the *Legend of Good Women*; the lovers in turmoil of the *Amores, Heroides,* and *Book of the Duchess.* The others may, willingly or not, claim objectivity: the disinterested historian of *Troilus*; the detached observers of the *Parliament* and the *House of Fame*; the Ovidian *magister* of love and its remedies. But Chaucer and Ovid both point to an inescapable human predicament by revealing the insufficiencies of their narrators, whether biased or disinterested, bookish or reluctantly committed to love's service.

In the *Canterbury Tales* Chaucer makes use of both guises. "Chaucer the pilgrim," as the representative of his traveling companions, claims simple reportorial accuracy (I.3167-75); he is disinterested, though the *General Prologue* reveals that his impartiality is in fact a too ready willingness to accept other people's valuation of themselves. The tellers of the *Tales*—including "Chaucer" when he recites *Sir Thopas* and *Melibee*—have more of a stake in their performance: there is, after all, a free dinner to be won. Interest also takes the form of revealed bias, since the *Tales* often serve the dramatic function of illuminating the characters of their tellers. The result, at the heart of the work, is a series of contradicting viewpoints placed in conflict with one another. In some instances—the *Reeve's Tale,* or Friar versus Summoner—the

quarrel springs from personal animosity and vengefulness. In others—
Miller versus Knight, or the so-called Marriage Group—one finds a
usually genial confrontation of opposing philosophies of life, and of
large-scale views of the world. Chaucer's concern in both sorts of
conflict generally becomes the portrayal of dramatic interaction.
Moreover, following the pattern of his earlier works, he leaves the
opposing viewpoints of his pilgrim-narrators in a state of unresolved
tension. Truth is as elusive in the *Canterbury Tales* as it is in the rest
of Chaucer's poetry.

Yet if the *Tales* and their tellers remain in unresolved opposition,
the indeterminacy heightened by the unfinished state of the work,
Chaucer has provided a clearly marked, polished beginning and end,
which in a formal sense set forth an introduction to the conflict of
limited viewpoints, and a way of escaping from it.[1] This final
chapter will look at the boundaries of the *Canterbury Tales* from an
Ovidian perspective, with special attention to the most Ovidian tale
of all. Its argument will, in a certain sense, continue where chapter 5
left off, with the Ovidian conflict of *ratio* and *impetus,* which under
various guises—as order and energy, or as stasis and flux—is the
central structuring principle in Chaucer's poetry, as much as it is in
Ovid's. The conflict appears in the *House of Fame,* which reproduces
the tension between the precarious order Ovid gains by freezing his
characters into tableaux, and the violence of impending metamorphosis. Chaucer uses a similar device in *Troilus,* when the
narrator stops the action in Book Five in order to give character
sketches of Diomede, Criseyde, and Troilus (799-840); here, as
throughout in more muted terms, he pulls back against the inexorable forward movement of his story. And in the *Knight's Tale*
too, as I have just argued, formal structures cope ineffectually with
the forces of love and disorder.

The theme of the *Knight's Tale* in fact suits its position in the
Canterbury Tales; for Fragment One, as it moves from the *General
Prologue* to the *Cook's Tale*, makes a shift—both in its details and in
its large contours—from order to energy, from tidy form to the risk
of sprawling chaos. As in the *Metamorphoses,* the shift has moral

implications: the Knight's noble vision gives way to the Cook's dirty joke.[2] Indeed, given the traditional contexts for describing man's sinful state, it is hard entirely to avoid looking for signs of the Fall even in the opening lines of the *General Prologue,* where the innocent splendor of Nature fulfilling God's plan is set against the diversity of will in human beings. But the obvious inadequacy of such a reading leads to a recognition that simple order gives way to explosive vitality, as much as to moral chaos. Father Sky and Mother Earth, in the guise of the personified months, join the "smale foweles," sleeping "al the nyght with open ye" for excitement (I.9-10), to make Nature seem human; but the claims of the pathetic fallacy pale before the flamboyant complexity of true human motives. At first, the wonderful simplicity of Nature's uncluttered, unconscious purposiveness may evoke a comic version of Caligula's response to the messiness human beings bring to the world: "Would that the Roman people had but one neck!" On reflection, we realize that what we take for moral degeneration and the disintegration of order may simply be a momentarily vexing loss of clarity—that, as Theseus learns in the *Knight's Tale,* one cannot always achieve a tidy pattern. There is an analogous paradox in the *Metamorphoses,* especially at such moments as Caesar's hilarious apotheosis (XV.843-70) or Arachne's ill-fated spinning contest (VI.1-145): change brings decay, but life as well; and process, even with all its uncertainties and terrors, is preferable to the coldly formal stasis of the Augustan gods and political order.

As he does at the end of *Troilus,* Chaucer stops the action in order to describe the actors, though this time his tableaux come at a less surprising point, the beginning of the poem:

> But nathelees, whil I have tyme and space,
> Er that I ferther in this tale pace,
> Me thynketh it acordaunt to resoun
> To telle yow al the condicioun
> . Of ech of hem, so as it semed me,
> And whiche they weren, and of what degree,
> And eek in what array that they were inne.
>
> [I.35-41]

Once the pilgrimage begins, the demands of verisimilitude take matters out of his control: the Host is to be in charge, and even his strong will does not always succeed in mastering the diverse impulses of the other pilgrims. Yet the narrator's catalogue of characters itself shows that confusion is close at hand even when order is being asserted most carefully. The list proceeds overall from the top of society to the bottom, though as we move from one particular pilgrim to the next the logic of progression is not always clear. It also begins with an extremely old-fashioned division of the estates of men. But before warriors and clergy, neatly grouped in threes, can be followed by plowmen, the urban classes intervene; and, after the packed detail of their portraits, the Plowman seems a shadowy figure, as different from his companions in his vague, atavistic lineaments as his brother the Parson is in the ʻhomely straightforwardness of his ideal of serving others.

The first six pilgrims, in groups of three, are also linked together with a clarity of logic that afterward vanishes. The Squire, who "carf biforn his fader at the table" (100), properly takes a position subordinate to the Knight, and is himself higher in degree than the Yeoman. The three religious pilgrims mark progressively wider deviations from the ideal. Their differences appear in the extent to which they consciously misapply the language of God's love to cupidinous desires: the Prioress adopts the name of a romance heroine with features to match, follows "curteisie," and wears jewelry that proclaims *Amor vincit omnia* (121, 152-53, 132, 162); the Monk loves "venerie," that is, "prikyng and . . . huntyng for the hare," and wears a love-knot (166, 191, 197); the Friar brings the tendencies of the first two into the open, glorying in his wantonness and promiscuity, as "a noble post" of his order (211-14, 258). Such subtle reverberations of language soon become about the most emphatic indicators of relation; in the morass that follows the first six portraits, we are forced to search out the narrator's principles of order by retracing his subjective associations of significant detail.[3] The portraits of the Man of Law and the Franklin are adjacent because the two men are traveling together; the same accident connects the portraits of the guildsmen and the Cook. The Merchant,

"sownynge alwey th'encrees of his wynnyng" (275), precedes the
Clerk, who is laconic and careless of money. The country Franklin is
juxtaposed with the city guildsmen. The Physician and the Wife of
Bath are both experts in remedies of various kinds; the "remedies of
love" (475) the Wife knows contrast in turn with the Parson's
remedies of Love, as the extravagance of her clothing does with the
complete absence of detail about his. Some characters, especially
those in traditional social categories with clear-cut moral duties, may
be defined by the extent to which they fulfill the ideal set for their
behavior. Others are versions of the "verray, parfit praktisour" (422)
in an essentially amoral way: they are allowed to define themselves
by their technical skill alone.[4] The portraits vary in length, with no
correspondence to the social ranks of the people described. The
order of details within the portraits varies as widely; and physical
features mix with moral ones in an unsystematic fashion.

Chaucer appends an apology to his catalogue of the pilgrims:

> Also I prey yow to foryeve it me,
> Al have I nat set folk in hir degree
> Heere in this tale, as that they sholde stonde.
> My wit is short, ye may wel understonde.
>
> [743-46]

His regret is fitting, if disingenuous, since he has used several
competing methods of defining the social hierarchy.[5] The *General
Prologue* portrays a society in a state of flux: institutions decay;
people change their social class, as the anonymous, interchangeable
guildsmen hope to do. The divisions of such a society in the abstract
must stand in the way of the narrator's efforts to present it in an
orderly fashion. Its restlessness in the concrete likewise resists the
structuring of Chaucer's double, the Host. Like the narrator, he
shows himself to be well aware of social hierarchy: indeed, the first
two pilgrims he calls on to draw lots are the Knight and the Prioress,
who headed Chaucer's two opening triads. With absolute propriety,
not entirely hidden by Chaucer's disclaimer "Were it by aventure, or
sort, or cas" (844), the Knight is chosen to tell the first tale. But
after the *Knight's Tale,* itself specifically concerned with the

problems of order in the world, Harry Bailly is no more successful
than the narrator was in keeping things tidy. He calls on the Monk
for " 'Somwhat to quite with the Knyghtes tale' " (I.3119), and
answers the drunken Miller's insistence that his " 'noble tale for the
nones' " be allowed to do just that (3126-27):

> . . . "Abyd, Robyn, my leeve brother;
> Som bettre man shal telle us first another.
> Abyd, and lat us werken thriftily."
>
> [3129-31]

When the Miller threatens to break the game contract and " 'go my
wey' " (3133), the Host gives in. His resignation is echoed by the
parallel apology of the narrator, who warns us against this "cherles
tale" (3169), offers us the opportunity to read another, and asks us
to "put me out of blame; / And eek men shal nat maken ernest of
game" (3185-86).

Everyone would agree that the Miller justifies his rudeness by the
brilliant vitality of his *fabliau,* a benign, large-spirited response to the
Knight's courtly view of love and life. Like its counterpart in the
Parliament of Fowls, this debate remains unresolved: the *Miller's
Tale* answers the Knight's point by point, in its large structure—both
tales describe two lovers contesting each other for the same woman—
and in its verbal detail (e.g., 2779, 3204).[6] The Reeve, however,
lowers the level of discourse and turns debate into vindictive
squabble by his deciding

> "For leveful is with force force of-showve.
> This dronke Millere hath ytoold us heer
> How that bigyled was a carpenteer,
> Peraventure in scorn, for I am oon.
> And, by youre leve, I shal hym quite anoon;
> Right in his cherles termes wol I speke."
>
> [I.3912-17]

His literal-minded answer to what seems a largely imaginary injury
reduces the poetic artifice of narrative to a mean-spirited polemic.
The *Cook's Prologue* and unfinished *Tale,* which end Fragment One,

complete the process of disintegration that has been going on since the opening lines of the *General Prologue.* This final degeneration of order at least takes place with plenty of good humor. Roger's reaction to the *Reeve's Tale*—"For joye him thoughte he clawed him on the bak" (I.4326)—attempts to turn the *Canterbury Tales* into a succession of dirty jokes; his own tale appropriately ends, as it now stands, with the wife who "swyved for hir sustenance" (4422). And Harry Bailly is willing enough, at least for the moment, to let locker-room humor take over. The Cook answers his good-natured invitation to a ribald flyting with equal good humor (4356-62); in this regard, at least, he contrasts with the querulous Reeve.

The Cook appears once more, in the *Manciple's Prologue,* in a different mood but a symmetrical position. Just as he ushers in the debates that occupy the center of the *Canterbury Tales,* so he prefaces the transcendence of debate, and of all other earthly concerns, at the end of the work. The mood of the last three Prologues becomes progressively more eerie: the Canon's Yeoman's sweat and discolored complexion; the Cook's drunken stupor, dazed eyes, and gaping mouth; the gathering darkness of the *Parson's Prologue,* where twenty-nine degrees of daylight remain for the twenty-nine pilgrims, and Chaucer's shadow is divided in two equal parts as the moon rises in Libra, the scales that suggest the coming of God's Judgment.[7] The last four tales together announce the theme of Chaucer's own Retraction. The Manciple and the Parson both emphasize that they are not "textueel" (IX.235, 316; X.57). By this they mean, to some extent, that they are plain speakers, after the pattern of St. Cecilia in the *Second Nun's Tale* (VIII.428ff.); but they also show themselves to be indifferent to any of the frills attached to book learning or the poetic art. The Parson refuses to "geeste 'rum, ram, ruf,' by lettre, / Ne, God woot, rym holde I but litel bettre" (X.43-44); his tale will be in prose. The Manciple "wol noght telle of textes never a deel" (IX.236), and denies to language its powers of ornament and possible hypocrisy: one woman is called a "lady," another a "wenche," though "Men leyn that oon as lowe as lith that oother" (222). His reductionist impulses answer the specialist's argot of the *Canon's Yeoman's Tale,* which showed the potential of language for non-communication: the Canon's Yeoman's pell-mell catalogues (VIII.790ff.) intimate an essential disjunction between word and meaning, sign and thing, and they lead him only to the unnamable stone the alchemist searches for in vain (1452-71). But as a plainspoken sermonizer the Manciple is not so effective as the Parson: his frankness, as the Host points out, opens himself up for retaliatory exposures of his own sharp practices (IX.69-75). When the preacher's *ethos* collapses, Bacchus must be called on to bring about a wordless reconciliation; the Manciple and the Cook act out a debased restoration of concord.

As a sermon, the *Manciple's Tale* ironically prefaces the *Parson's.* The Manciple's garrulous mother—using Ovid's fable of the crow, and proverbs galore from the Bible and the *Disticha Catonis*—passes on to her garrulous son the conventional wisdom about the virtues of silence.[8] Even when dressed up in fictions to sweeten its message, wisdom apparently cannot be transmitted—at least not with the ease possible in the miraculous days of the early church, when Cecilia could provoke mass conversions by verbal argument and saintly example. The Parson's modern saintliness makes possible his candor and utter indifference to the worldly distinctions of class and polite language (I.504, 517, 522-25), and his efficacy as a spiritual guide. Yet though he opposes the Manciple in these respects, his no-nonsense attitude toward language is the same, and it prepares us for Chaucer's Retraction. The Manciple in fact nearly recreates the concluding scene of the *House of Fame* when his mother implicitly attacks the whole enterprise of Chaucer's poetry: " 'My sone, be war, and be noon auctour newe / Of tidynges, wheither they been false or trewe' " (IX.359-60). The rest is silence.[9] The end of the *Canterbury Tales* thus transcends words and a delight in poetic artifice by moving beyond them—first by an ironic disintegration, then with utter seriousness—to the absolute simplicity of supernatural truth, where no words are necessary and human language cannot follow.

Chaucer also, however, provides another, less austere resolution, in which the comic human resources of language and rhetoric try on their own to reintegrate the disordered, unresolved conflicts of the *Canterbury Tales.*[10] The Nun's Priest concludes Fragment Seven and, even at first sight, convincingly one-ups his predecessors in the fragment by alluding to their tales and incorporating their language in his own. Pertelote repeats almost verbatim the worldly wisdom of the wife in the *Shipman's Tale* (VII.175-77): " 'We alle desiren, if it myghte bee, / To han housbondes hardy, wise, and free' " (2913-14). Chauntecleer echoes rather stridently (3052-57) the Prioress's complacent trust in God's justice: "Mordre wol out" (576). The Nun's Priest's momentary, abortive pretense of being a minstrel recalls the "Now holde youre mouth, *par charitee*" (891) of *Sir Thopas:*

> Now every wys man, lat him herkne me;
> This storie is also trewe, I undertake,
> As is the book of Launcelot de Lake,
> That wommen holde in ful greet reverence.
>
> [3210-13]

His comically exaggerated misogyny extends to woman's counsel, "ful ofte colde," which made poor Adam lose his Paradise, "Ther as he was ful myrie and wel at ese" (3259). In the *Tale of Melibee,* by contrast, Prudence reminds us: "Thus sholde ye understonde the philosophre that seith, 'In wikked conseil wommen venquisshen hir housbondes.' / And ther as ye blamen alle wommen and hir resouns, I shal shewe yow by manye ensamples that many a womman hath ben ful good, and yet been, and hir conseils ful hoolsome and profitable" (1093-94). The Nun's Priest even echoes Harry Bailly, who put the Monk on his dignity by saying that he would have been a fine "tredefowel" (1945). The story of the treadfowl nonpareil converts the Host from "rude speche and boold" (2808), when he first calls on the Nun's Priest, to his wonderful, hilarious confusion of literary and sexual prowess:

> "This was a murie tale of Chauntecleer.

> But by my trouthe, if thou were seculer,
> Thou woldest ben a trede-foul aright."
>
> [3449-51]

The most outrageous allusions are to the *Monk's Tale.*
Chauntecleer offers an unintentionally ludicrous account of St.
Kenelm's martyrdom (3110-21); and the Nun's Priest attempts to
cast the rooster himself as the hero of a *de casibus* tragedy:

> But sodeynly hym fil a sorweful cas,
> For evere the latter ende of joye is wo.
> God woot that worldly joye is soone ago;
> And if a rethor koude faire endite,
> He in a cronycle saufly myghte it write
> As for a sovereyn notabilitee.
>
> [3204-09)

The *Monk's Tale* in fact points most clearly to the reason for all
these allusions: the *Nun's Priest's Tale* does not simply echo its
predecessors; it subsumes them in its own complicated vision. The
shift within the tale from the simple world of the "povre wydwe" to
the exuberance of Chauntecleer's realm repeats the larger pattern of
Fragment Seven. The preceding tales are all severely limited, either
by narrowness of perspective or by narrative incompetence. Yet even
in the company of the Shipman's cold commercialism, the horrifying
childish piety of the Prioress, and the wonderfully disastrous effort
by "Chaucer the pilgrim" himself, the *Monk's Tale* is the most
limited in structure and comprehensiveness of vision. Before the
Knight interrupts, it promises to be an endless series of tragedies, in
which a wildly incongruous group of people, who have little else in
common, all fall from the top of Fortune's wheel to the bottom. As
in the *Legend of Good Women,* literary form becomes a Procrustean
bed; details are lopped off or added, as necessary, to make the
subject of the narrative fit its preconceived structure. But morality
needs the aid of poetic delight in order to achieve its effect: the
Host, rushing to agree with the Knight's exasperated interruption,

clearly has been put to sleep by the Monk's monotonous litany (2782-83). An overly simple form not only falsifies reality but loses the attention of its audience.

What the *Nun's Priest's Tale* brilliantly does, in contrast, is to give us such a bewildering variety of perspectives that we end up with no notion of the vantage point we should adopt in order to understand its meaning. The frame of the story, the widow's simple, self-sufficient poverty, shifts quickly to the courtly pretensions hidden in her barnyard, just as her plain fare contrasts with Chauntecleer's overly rich diet (2923). The widow's own "bour" and "halle" are "ful sooty" (2832); but her "yeerd . . . , enclosed al aboute / With stikkes, and a drye dych withoute" (2847-48) becomes, by rhetorical magnification, the castle and moat of the courtly rooster. This move inside the barnyard also marks a shift, comically an-alogous to the narrator's own situation, from an entirely female environment—even the widow's farm animals are female[11]—to a world of male peacock splendor. The noble hero asserts his courtli-ness and his maleness with equal vigor: Chauntecleer the "gentil" rooster (2865) has on his comb the specifically heraldic colors "coral" red, "asure," "lylye" white, and "burned gold" (2859-64);[12] and he proudly treads his hens, at once "his sustres and his paramours" (2867). As this last phrase indicates, comic indecision never allows us any single perspective on the barnyard and its in-habitants. The narrator breaks the illusion of the beast fable at the moment he rationalizes it: Chauntecleer and Pertelote warble

> In sweete accord, "My lief is faren in londe!"
> For thilke tyme, as I have understonde,
> Beestes and briddes koude speke and synge.
>
> [2879-81]

Time and again, we are brought back abruptly to a broader view-point, by such details as the tender age of the rooster's mistresses (2873), Pertelote's demand " 'Have ye no mannes herte, and han a berd?' " (2920), and the "beautee" of her " 'face, / Ye been so scarlet reed aboute youre yen' " (3160-61).

The tale winds down with a brilliant return from wildly flamboyant heroic rhetoric to the quotidian perspective of the dairywoman. The hens, grief-stricken at Chauntecleer's calamity, evoke Hasdrubal's wife, who burned herself, and—by even more unlikely association—burning Rome and the keening senator's wives (3363-74). When "this sely wydwe and eek hir doghtres two" (3375) join the chase with "Colle oure dogge" (3383), they join the host of female lamenters, but with a sturdily practical action. Epic tragedy turns into the pursuit of a farmer's pest; "Jakke Straw and his meynee" (3394) replace the heroic figures of the past as a suitable analogue for the commotion.

Such uncertainty of perspective also occurs within Chauntecleer's domain. In the long discussion of dream theory, the voices of authority and experience oppose each other; but almost nothing results from the controversy, which takes up nearly half the *Tale*. The satanic apparition in the rooster's dream is so obviously a fox (2899-2905) that the quarrel seems superfluous, and Pertelote's effort to explain the colors of the creature wonderfully funny (2928-36).[13] The outcome might imply that her voice of experience is less trustworthy than Chauntecleer's appeal to the authority of famous prophetic dreams. But the rooster in fact dismisses his own argument—and does so with as much conviction as he shows in mistranslating Latin (3164-66). Likewise, the narrator's later digression on free will and predestination (3234-50) proves to serve no function at all: "I wol nat han to do of swich mateere; / My tale is of a cok, as ye may heere" (3251-52). An immense superstructure of rhetoric can be flicked away by whim or by a sudden shift in perspective.

The most remarkable instance of such a shift comes immediately after the long debate on dreams, when the details of syntax make Chaucer's meaning evident:

> And with that word he fley doun fro the beem,
> For it was day, and eke his hennes alle,
> And with a chuk he gan hem for to calle,
> For he hadde founde a corn, lay in the yerd.

> Real he was, he was namoore aferd.
> He fethered Pertelote twenty tyme,
> And trad hire eke as ofte, er it was pryme.
> He looketh as it were a grym leoun,
> And on his toos he rometh up and doun;
> Hym deigned nat to sette his foot to grounde.
> He chukketh whan he hath a corn yfounde,
> And to hym rennen thanne his wyves alle.
>
> [3172-83]

The rapid, paratactic movement of this quickly sketched series of actions and attitudes ironically balances the rhetorical windiness of Chauntecleer's lecture on the *somnium coeleste.* But the quickened narrative pace and rapid activity immediately dissipate into the stasis of another rhetorical set-piece. The machinery of words cranks up again, backtracking in hilarious fashion; the lines read almost as if the Nun's Priest were parodying the opening of the *General Prologue:*

> Whan that the month in which the world bigan,
> That highte March, whan God first maked man,
> Was compleet, and passed were also,
> Syn March bigan, thritty dayes and two,
> Bifel that Chauntecleer in al his pryde,
> His sevene wyves walkynge by his syde,
> Caste up his eyen to the brighte sonne,
> That in the signe of Taurus hadde yronne
> Twenty degrees and oon, and somwhat moore,
> And knew by kynde, and by noon oother loore,
> That it was pryme, and crew with blisful stevene.
>
> [3187-97]

This factitious chronology nearly succeeds in making May 3 a day in March—a neat trick to pull off, since it permits analogies with Adam's fall from bliss. The Nun's Priest begins a search for a heroic context large enough to embrace the tragedy of Chauntecleer's fall. He places the event not only by its day (3341), month, and astrological sign, but in relation to the spiritual history of man in the

world. By similar rhetorical magnification he can include the fox in a
notorious group of traitors and murderers:

> O false mordrour, lurkynge in thy den!
> O newe Scariot, newe Genylon,
> False dissymulour, o Greek Synon,
> That broghtest Troye al outrely to sorwe!
>
> [3226-29]

Thus, the simple narrative action repeatedly bogs down, first in the
argument on dream theory, then in heroic and tragic invocations,
and in homiletic digressions on predestination, the treachery of
women, and the insidious working of flattery. Rhetoric attempts to
subordinate the action of the *Tale* to a higher scheme and a nobler
moral.

The Nun's Priest tells us in the end that his fable has a serious
didactic message:

> But ye that holden this tale a folye,
> As of a fox, or of a cok and hen,
> Taketh the moralite, goode men.
> For seint Paul seith that al that writen is,
> To oure doctrine it is ywrite, ywis;
> Taketh the fruyt, and lat the chaf be stille.
>
> [3438-43]

But he undercuts his claim by repeatedly indicating the patent incongruity of the experience that the *Tale* presents with the form
imposed upon it. We are never allowed to forget that the hero is a
rooster. Moreover, by this point in Chaucer's poetry we have been
trained to be suspicious of any supposed fruit-chaff scheme—
especially given the ironic resonances of fruit and chaff, and of corn
and sheaf, in the *Prologue* to the *Legend of Good Women.* Here too
the cortical image is used ironically: the Nun's Priest tells us that he
"ne kan nat bulte . . . to the bren" (3240) the scholastic dispute
about free will and predestination. What, then, are we to call the
"fruit" of the *Nun's Priest's Tale*? That one should not follow his
wife's advice? Chauntecleer in fact does not; he simply disregards his

own.[14] That one should believe in prophetic dreams? The *Tale*
makes this issue irrelevant. Its hero flees as soon as the fox appears,

> For natureelly a beest desireth flee
> Fro his contrarie, if he may it see,
> Though he never erst hadde seyn it with his ye.
>
> [3279-81][15]

That one should beware of flattery? Perhaps—but surely this moral,
like the others, is comically simple-minded after the wonderful
complexity of the *Tale*; and it is impossible to choose which kernel
should be winnowed from what chaff. When rhetoric can make a
case for anything—Chauntecleer as everyman, Chauntecleer as epic
hero, Chauntecleer as rooster—no case is secure.

The *Nun's Priest's Tale* shows that experience is as obscure to us
as our dreams or the books we rely on for knowledge of the past. It
expresses in mature form the vision of the world that Chaucer
adapted from Ovid and used throughout his poetic career. The Nun's
Priest takes off explosively from his drab predecessors, replacing
their narrow limits with a profusion of simultaneously maintained
viewpoints on the simple action he describes. This opposition
between the pilgrims of Fragment Seven is analogous to the contrast
between the attempted objectivity of the *Troilus* narrator and the
bias imposed on the hagiographer of the *Legend of Good Women*.
Yet the real lesson of the *Nun's Priest's Tale* is the same as that of
the *Legend* or of the Monk's boring string of tragedies. Either pose,
objectivity or biased commitment, the vision of a reductionist or
human consciousness and language pushed to their limits, leads to
the same, ultimately comic result. Chaucer creates in us a consciousness of human frailty, as it reveals itself in the confused poet
who tries without much success to put the world in order. In this
respect, it is fitting that when Dante chooses Vergil to be his guide,
he leaves Ovid to Chaucer by default. Vergil and Dante are poets
who speak for fate and the universal, rational order of things: who
recognize the human cost of leaving Dido or of finding one's friends
in Hell, but who then move on to the vision of order and justice that

can supersede, if not entirely quench, an idiosyncratic, emotional view. Chaucer and Ovid, on the other hand, are poets who speak for the comic pathos of human frailty and human pretensions, including those of the poet himself—emphatically human, emphatically limited, unable to rest assured in any earthly truth he discovers.

NOTES

Chapter 1

1 From the Preface to *Fables* (1700); quoted in *Geoffrey Chaucer,* ed. J. A. Burrow (Baltimore: Penguin, 1969), p. 60.

2 From "The Study of Poetry" (1880); quoted in ibid., p. 100. To take another example: Mario Praz argues that Chaucer "really meant *The House of Fame* to be a sort of Dantesque journey through the realm of allegory, and tried to assimilate from the *Commedia* what was accessible to his spirit." *The Flaming Heart* (Garden City: Doubleday, 1958), p. 52.

3 *The Aeneid of Virgil,* ed. T. E. Page (1894; rpt. London: Macmillan, 1964), VI.129.

4 Quotations from Ovid are from the following editions: *Amores; Medicamina Faciei Femineae; Ars Amatoria; Remedia Amores,* ed. E. J. Kenney (Oxford: Clarendon Press, 1961); *Fasti,* ed. Sir James Frazer (1931; rpt. Cambridge, Mass.: Harvard University Press, 1959); *Heroides,* ed. Grant Showerman (Cambridge, Mass.: Harvard University Press, 1914); and *Metamorphoses,* ed. Frank J. Miller, 2 vols. (2d ed., Cambridge, Mass.: Harvard University Press, 1921).

5 See Eleanor Winsor Leach, "Georgic Imagery in the *Ars amatoria,*" *Transactions and Proceedings of the American Philological Association* 95 (1964), 142–54. For examples, see *Ars* I.399ff., II.351–52, II.668, and III.81–82.

6 W. K. Wimsatt, Jr., and Cleanth Brooks, *Literary Criticism: A Short History* (New York: Alfred A. Knopf, 1957), p. 80.

7 Ibid., p. 83. They add: "There is little direct evidence of what Horace thought about this difficult question. His criticism does,

however, offer a good example of the thorough interpenetration of nature and convention in the classical literary tradition."

8 Chapter 5 of Alexander Pope, *Peri Bathous: or of the Art of Sinking in Poetry,* quoted in ibid., p. 96. This ironic treatise could function well as an accurate, if unsympathetic, description of Ovid's poetry: "In the very Manners he will affect the *Marvellous*; he will draw Achilles with the patience of Job; a Prince talking like a Jack-pudding; a Maid of honour selling bargains; a footman speaking like a philosopher; and a fine gentleman like a scholar."

9 Brooks Otis, *Virgil: A Study in Civilized Poetry* (Oxford: Oxford University Press, 1964), pp. 90-95 (see also p. 209 and p. 309). The same point is made by Charles Norris Cochrane, *Christianity and Classical Culture* (1939; rpt. London: Oxford University Press, 1972), p. 69. Cf. Cochrane's discussion of Livy (p. 108).

10 Ibid., p. 391. Wendell Clausen's "Interpretation of the *Aeneid*" discusses the darker side of the poem and Vergil's ambivalence; in *Virgil: A Collection of Critical Essays,* ed. Steele Commager (Englewood Cliffs, N.J.: Prentice-Hall, 1966), pp. 75-88. For a powerful contrast between passages in Vergil and their sources in Homer, see W. R. Johnson, *Darkness Visible: A Study of Vergil's* Aeneid (Berkeley and Los Angeles: University of California Press, 1976).

11 Otis, *Virgil,* p. 154 and pp. 389ff.

12 As Otis says, "if Virgil had not wholly changed the nature and meaning of the Homeric gods and heroes [in the direction of gravity and high seriousness], the basic premise of Ovidian humour would not have existed." *Ovid as an Epic Poet* (Cambridge: Cambridge University Press, 1966), p. 324.

13 W. R. Johnson, "The Problem of the Counter-classical Sensibility and Its Critics," *California Studies in Classical Antiquity* 3 (1970), 123-51, esp. 137-48.

14 Otis, *Ovid,* p. 47.

15 Though some of the pungency of the line is lost, the Loeb edition's reading of *ius* for *dux* does not significantly alter its effect.

16 It may be objected that Alexander Pope, who could not be called

anticlassical, also uses zeugma for ironic purposes. But Pope's handling of the device differs in that he uses it to satirize the lack of proper generic (or moral) discrimination in others. Ovid, on the other hand, emphasizes this failure in "himself" as comic narrator.

17 L. P. Wilkinson, *Ovid Recalled* (Cambridge: Cambridge University Press, 1955), p. 159: "Ovid's method is to take the traditional story and 'play it straight,' to imagine what would, as a matter of fact, have happened in the circumstances, human nature being what it is, and gods and demigods only human in their emotions."

18 Cf. Otis's commentary (*Virgil*, p. 302) on *Aeneid* VI.791ff.

19 Ovid ironically raises love to the status of the traditional Roman pieties (law, war, and agriculture). *Carpe diem* is used as a motive for the comic advocacy of love, war, and agriculture as bustling pursuits (*Ars* II.669-74).

20 Robert Durling, *The Figure of the Poet in Renaissance Epic* (Cambridge, Mass.: Harvard University Press, 1965), p. 35. Durling's account—which I read after writing the first version of this chapter—is an excellent treatment of Ovid's ironic method. Though my conclusions differ from his, I echo several of his analyses of Ovidian technique.

Since 1971, when I published (with minor variations) this discussion of Ovid, several exceptionally interesting essays have appeared on this subject: Eleanor Winsor Leach, "Ekphrasis and the Theme of Artistic Failure in Ovid's *Metamorphoses,*" *Ramus* 3 (1974), 102-42; Richard A. Lanham, "The Fundamental Strategies: Plato and Ovid," in *The Motives of Eloquence* (New Haven: Yale University Press, 1976), pp. 36-64; and Joseph B. Solodow, "Ovid's Ars Amatoria: The Lover as Cultural Ideal," *Wiener Studien,* Neue Folge, Band 11 (1977), 106-27.

21 Durling argues that Ovid has "precisely the attitude of the sophist," that is, "the ability to arm both sides in a struggle—or to do away with the struggle itself—all with equal effectiveness" (*The Figure of the Poet,* p. 40). He errs, I think, by giving too much emphasis to Ovid's sophistication as a raconteur: "to arouse the reader's awareness of the artificiality of conventions,

the contrivance, the pretense, and his admiration of the virtuosity of bold manipulation is the primary intention of these poems" (p. 43).

22 Translated by Sir James Frazer (see note 4 above).

23 E. J. Kenney has noted that the image traditionally characterizes the poet's awareness of a high and holy calling: "Nequitiae Poeta," in *Ovidiana: Recherches sur Ovide,* ed. N. I. Herescu (Paris: Les Belles Lettres, 1958), p. 205. Also Ernst Robert Curtius, *European Literature and the Latin Middle Ages,* trans. Willard R. Trask (Princeton: Princeton University Press, 1953), pp. 128-30.

24 Durling, *The Figure of the Poet,* p. 37.

25 Otis, *Virgil,* p. 161.

26 Ibid., p. 390.

27 Chaucer was probably unacquainted with the *Amores.*

There are several useful studies that catalogue the details of Chaucer's debt to Ovid: Edgar F. Shannon, *Chaucer and the Roman Poets,* Harvard Studies in Comparative Literature, 7 (Cambridge, Mass.: Harvard University Press, 1929); Nancy Dean, "Studies in Chaucer's Use of Ovid in Selected Early Poems" (Ph.D. diss., New York University, 1963); Richard L. Hoffman, *Ovid and the Canterbury Tales* (Philadelphia: University of Pennsylvania Press, 1967); and Richard L. Hoffman, "The Influence of the Classics on Chaucer," in Beryl Rowland, ed., *Companion to Chaucer Studies* (Toronto / New York / London: Oxford University Press, 1968), pp. 162-75.

28 It is explicitly so regarded by Pierre Bersuire, the most influential of the fourteenth-century commentators on Ovid: see Fausto Ghisalberti, "L' 'Ovidius Moralizatus' di Pierre Bersuire," *Studj Romanzi* 23 (Rome, 1933), 25.

29 St. Jerome attacks Ovid's poem because metamorphosis makes divinity look ridiculous: *Commentaria in Jonam,* in *Patrologia Latina (PL)* 25, col. 1132; cited by Simone Viarre, *La Survie d'Ovide dans la Littérature Scientifique des XIIe et XIIIe Siècles* (Université de Poitiers, 1966), p. 25, n. 11. The early twelfth-century Conrad of Hirsau does so because the metamorphoses of men into animals and stones deny God's order, according to which man was created in his image: *Dialogus super Auctores,*

ed. R. B. C. Huygens, Collection Latomus, 17 (Berchem-Brussels, 1955), p. 51. The first medieval commentator of Ovid, Arnulf of Orléans, gives what becomes the standard answer to such charges. "By showing, through the mutation of bodies the changes in spirit which are inseparable from them, he brings us back to God, inviting us to follow reason and to maintain the soul in its original form by keeping it clear of vice": Fausto Ghisalberti, "Mediaeval Biographies of Ovid," *Journal of the Warburg and Courtauld Institutes* 9 (1946), 18.

30 In so doing, he follows the example of Machaut: see A. Thomas, "Guillaume de Machaut et l'*Ovide Moralisé*," *Romania* 41 (1912), 382-400; and C. de Boer, ed., *Ovide Moralisé*, in *Verhandelingen der Koninklijke Nederlandse Akademie*, 15 (1915), 28-43. John L. Lowes describes Chaucer's practice: "Chaucer and the *Ovide Moralisé*," *PMLA* 33 (1918), 302-25.

31 In this, as in his use of the medieval commentaries, his procedure contrasts with Dante's: C. A. Robson, "Dante's Use in the *Divina Commedia* of the Medieval Allegories on Ovid," in *Centenary Essays on Dante,* ed. C. G. Hardie (Oxford: Clarendon Press, 1965), pp. 1-38.

32 The exception proves the rule. The sole appearance of this characteristically Ovidian effect in Chaucer is in one couplet: "The blod out of the wounde as brode sterte / As water, whan the condit broken is" (*Legend of Good Women* 851-52). The lines translate *Metamorphoses* IV.122-24.

33 The appendix of James J. Wilhelm's *The Cruelest Month* (New Haven: Yale University Press, 1965) gives a useful tabulation of medieval instances of Ovidian oxymoron, antithesis, and paradox.

34 H. Kühne and E. Stengel, eds., "Maître Élie's Überarbeitung der Ältesten Französischen Übertragung von Ovid's Ars Amatoria," *Ausgaben und Abhandlungen aus dem Gebiete der Romanischen Philologie*, 47 (Marburg, 1886), vv. 133-42, 167-68.

35   En amor que pouretez blece
            Ne ne puet demener largece,
            Couuient molt savoir de losange.
                                                    [870-72]

[In love he whom poverty injures and who cannot show largesse must know a great deal about flattery.]

He may well have used a commentary such as the one by Arnulf of Orléans, which also shows that the idiom was understood correctly by medieval readers; see Fausto Ghisalberti, "Arnolfo d'Orléans: un cultore di Ovidio nel secolo XII," *Memorie del R. Istituto Lombardo di Scienze e Lettere,* 24, fasc. 4 (1932), 170, on *Remedia Amoris* 34: "*verba* i. deceptiones."

36 A. Baudouin, ed., *Pamphile, ou l'Art d'Être Aimê, Comédie Latine du Xe Siècle* (Paris: Librairie Moderne, 1874). There is a convenient translation by Thomas Jay Garbaty, "*Pamphilus, De Amore:* An Introduction and Translation," *Chaucer Review* 2 (1967), 108-34.

37 Peter Dronke recounts a hilarious example of this situation: *Medieval Latin and the Rise of European Love-Lyric* (Oxford: Clarendon Press, 1965), I, 256.

38 Jean de Meun, *Le Roman de la Rose,* ed. Felix Lécoy, Classiques Français du Moyen Âge (CFMA), 3 vols. (Paris: H. Champion, 1965-70).

39 R. W. Southern, *The Making of the Middle Ages* (New Haven: Yale University Press, 1953), p. 221. Also see Colin Morris, *The Discovery of the Individual 1050-1200* (London: SPCK, 1972). Robert W. Hanning discusses the sophisticated twelfth-century use of Ovid's notion of *ingenium:* "*Engin* in Twelfth-Century Courtly Texts," in *The Individual in Twelfth-Century Romance* (New Haven: Yale University Press, 1977), pp. 105-38.

40 F. J. E. Raby, *A History of Secular Latin Poetry in the Middle Ages* (2d. ed.; Oxford: Clarendon Press, 1957), I, 323.

41 "XLIII," vv. 95-110, in *Les Œuvres Poétiques de Baudri de Bourgueil (1046-1130),* ed. Phyllis Abrahams (Paris: H. Champion, 1926).

42 See William Calin, *A Poet at the Fountain: Essays on the Narrative Verse of Guillaume de Machaut* (Lexington: University Press of Kentucky, 1974).

43 The standard treatment of Chaucer's narrator is E. Talbot Donaldson's "Chaucer the Pilgrim," *PMLA* 69 (1954), 928-36; most recently reprinted in *Speaking of Chaucer* (London: Athlone Press, 1970), pp. 1-12. Although Donaldson compares

Chaucer's narrator with Dante's (*Speaking of Chaucer*, p. 9), he resists making any simple opposition between poet and *persona*: "In this complex structure both the latent moralist and the naive reporter have important positions, but I am not persuaded that in every case it is possible to determine which of them has the last word" (p. 12).

44 Even in the *General Prologue* moral categories operate in a rather hazy fashion. Indeed, according to one interesting recent discussion, we see the "consistent removal of the possibility of moral judgement. In other words, our attention is being drawn to the *illusion*; its occasional dispersal is to demonstrate that it is an illusion, but the illusion itself is made into the focal point of interest." Jill Mann, *Chaucer and Medieval Estates Satire* (Cambridge: Cambridge University Press, 1973), p. 197.

45 *Controversiae* 2.2.12, trans. M. Winterbottom (Cambridge, Mass.: Harvard University Press, 1974), I, 264.

46 Larry D. Benson, among many others, has spoken of "the late Gothic ability to maintain contradicting attitudes and to derive aesthetic pleasure from the tension of unresolved conflicts": "The Alliterative *Morte Arthure* and Medieval Tragedy," *Tennessee Studies in Literature* 11 (1966), 75. See also W. H. Clemen, *Chaucer's Early Poetry*, trans. C. A. M. Sym (London: Methuen, 1963), pp. 16–17. The most influential treatment of this aspect of Chaucer's poetry is Charles Muscatine, *Chaucer and the French Tradition* (Berkeley and Los Angeles: University of California Press, 1957), esp. pp. 167–73.

47 Several recent discussions of Chaucer share my interest in these issues. See especially Peter Elbow, *Oppositions in Chaucer* (Middletown, Conn.: Wesleyan University Press, 1975); and Stewart Justman, "Medieval Monism and Abuse of Authority in Chaucer," *Chaucer Review* 11 (1976), 100: "For our purposes, the important point is that the world of experience, which is the world of multiplicity, brings contradiction with it. It makes trouble for systems. Even great authorities well known to Chaucer—St. Paul, Jerome, Boethius—are compelled at the crucial turn to forego, in fact to forfeit, narrow logical integrity. Inevitably they must compromise their austere monism to accommodate experience."

Chapter 2

1 The fullest exposition of this argument is Robert Jordan's *Chaucer and the Shape of Creation: The Aesthetic Possibilities of Inorganic Structure* (Cambridge, Mass.: Harvard University Press, 1967).

2 F. N. Robinson, ed., *Works*, note to vv. 1 ff., p. 779.

3 To make matters more complicated, the two terms come from different traditions of late antique commentaries on dreams. *Visio* is Macrobius's term; *revelatio* is from Chalcidius's commentary on the *Timaeus*. Chaucer may have used some authority such as the twelfth-century Pascalis Romanus, who keeps Macrobius's list of dream types but identifies his term *oraculum* with Chalcidius's *revelatio: Le* Liber Thesauri Occulti *de Pascalis Romanus*, ed. S: Collin-Roset, in *Archives d'Histoire Doctrinale et Littéraire du Moyen Âge*, 38 (1963), 156-57; the terms are defined on 160.

4 The phrase is Charles Muscatine's: *Chaucer and the French Tradition*, p. 108.

5 John Leyerle, "Chaucer's Windy Eagle," *University of Toronto Quarterly* 40 (1971), 249.

6 *Thebaid* X.112-13, in *Statius*, trans. J. H. Mozley, II (1928; rpt. Cambridge, Mass.: Harvard University Press, 1957). Translation his.

7 *Anticlaudianus*, ed. R. Bossuat (Paris: J. Vrin, 1955). The same phrasing occurs elsewhere in the poem: Fama "soleat uerum corrumpere falso" (VII.87) [is accustomed to corrupt the truth with falsehood]. The idea and the phrasing go back to the *Aeneid* itself (IV.188), and to Ovid's *Metamorphoses* (XII.54).

8 Beryl Smalley, *English Friars and Antiquity in the Early Fourteenth Century* (Oxford: Blackwell, 1970), p. 40.

9 *Le Roman de Troie*, ed. Leopold Constans, Société des Anciens Textes Français (SATF) (Paris: Firmin Didot, 1904), I, 4, Prologue, vv. 109-11 and 51-56.

10 *Historia Destructionis Troiae*, ed. Nathaniel Edward Griffin (Cambridge, Mass.: The Mediaeval Academy of America, 1936), pp. 4, 204, and 276.

11 *Commentum super Sex Libros Eneidos*, ed. G. Riedel (Griefs-

wald: J. Abel, 1924), p. 15, as summarized by Winthrop Wetherbee, *Platonism and Poetry in the Twelfth Century* (Princeton: Princeton University Press, 1972), p. 106. The Latin reads: "Et quoniam sermo quidam verus quidam falsus, ideo in hac narratione per hoc quod veritati historiae falsitas fabulae admiscetur hoc idem figuratur. Est enim historia quod Graeci Troiam deleverunt, quod vero Eneae probitas enarratur fabula est. Narrat enim Dares Frigius Eneam prodidisse civitatem."

12 Wolfgang Clemen, *Chaucer's Early Poetry*, p. 84, gives line references.

13 Richard Rowland, or Verstegan, *Restitution of Decayed Intelligence* (Antwerp, 1605), p. 102; quoted by T. D. Kendrick, *British Antiquity* (London: Methuen, 1950), p. 110.

14 Smalley, *English Friars and Antiquity*, pp. 130-31; the text of Ridevall's comments appears on p. 320.

15 John Taylor, *The* Universal Chronicle *of Ranulf Higden* (Oxford: Clarendon Press, 1966), p. 77. Taylor cites *Polychronicon* i.166 and ii.432.

16 *Litterae Seniles* iv.5; cited by Smalley, *English Friars and Antiquity*, p. 293.

17 *Trionfo della Pudicizia,* 10-12, 154-59, in *Opere,* ed. Emilio Bigi (Milan: Ugo Mursia, 1963), pp. 285, 288. For St. Jerome's views, see *Adversus Jovinianum* I.43, in *PL* 23, col. 273; noted by C. G. Osgood, *Boccaccio on Poetry* (Princeton: Princeton University Press, 1930), p. 173, n. 26.

18 *De Mulieribus Claris,* ed. Vittorio Zaccaria (vol. 10 of *Opere,* ed. Vittore Branca; Milan: Mondadori, 1970), p. 168.

19 *De Genealogia Deorum* XIV.13; in Osgood, *Boccaccio on Poetry,* p. 67. This distinction survives in Sidney's *Defence of Poetry;* in *Miscellaneous Prose of Sir Philip Sidney,* ed. Katherine Duncan-Jones and Jan Van Dorsten (Oxford: Clarendon Press, 1973), p. 88: "For indeed, if the question were whether it were better to have a particular act truly or falsely set down, there is no doubt which is to be chosen. . . .But if the question be for your own use and learning, whether it be better to have it set down as it should be, or as it was, then certainly is more doctrinable the feigned Cyrus in Xenophon than the true Cyrus in Justin, and the feigned Aeneas in Virgil than the right Aeneas in Dares Phrygius. . . ."

20 E. M. Forster, introduction to *Virgil's Aeneid* (London: Dent, 1957), pp. x-xi.

21 J. A. W. Bennett summarizes the changes: *Chaucer's* Book of Fame (Oxford: Oxford University Press, 1968), p. 42.

22 *Commentum super Sex Libros Eneidos,* ed. G. Riedel, p. 9: "dicimus esse carnis concupiscentiam quia omnium fornicationum mater est."

23 *Teseida,* ed. Alberto Limentani (in vol. 2 of *Opere,* ed. Vittore Branca; Milan: Mondadori, 1964), p. 463: "per ciascuno onesto e licito disiderio, sì come è disiderare d'avere moglie per avere figliuoli, e simili a questo"; "è quella per la quale ogni lascivia è disiderata, e che volgarmente è chiamata dea d'amore."

24 B. G. Koonce, *Chaucer and the Tradition of Fame: Symbolism in* The House of Fame (Princeton: Princeton University Press, 1966), p. 106.

25 Koonce, ibid., p. 38, summarizes the poem. Dorothy Bethurum Loomis has an especially useful essay on the two Venuses: "The Venus of Alanus de Insulis and the Venus of Chaucer," in *Philological Essays: Studies in Old and Middle English Language and Literature in Honour of Herbert Dean Meritt,* ed. James L. Rosier (The Hague: Mouton, 1970), pp. 182-95.

26 Clemen, *Chaucer's Early Poetry,* p. 80.

27 So Koonce argues in *Chaucer and the Tradition of Fame:* p. 126.

28 John M. Steadman, "Chaucer's 'Desert of Libye,' Venus, and Jove (*The Hous of Fame,* 486-87)," *MLN* 76 (1961), 196-201.

29 Clemen, *Chaucer's Early Poetry,* p. 89.

30 Bennett, *Chaucer's* Book of Fame, pp. 47-48. See also John Norton-Smith, *Geoffrey Chaucer* (London: Routledge & Kegan Paul, 1974), p. 55.

31 Compare Catullus 7, in *Catullus,* ed. Kenneth Quinn (London: Macmillan, 1970), p. 4. How many kisses from Lesbia would be "satis superque" [enough and more than enough]? More than there are stars, or than the "magnus numerus Libyssae harenae" [great number of the Libyan sands]. Unfortunately for my argument, Chaucer cannot have known this poem. But cf. *Ars Amatoria* I.254.

32 As Bennett, *Chaucer's* Book of Fame, notes (p. 88), line 918

apparently translates Jean de Meun, and understands him to say that Scipio saw Hell as well as Paradise.

33 I have used Charles S. Singleton's edition of *The Divine Comedy* (Princeton: Princeton University Press, 1970-75). The translations are also his.

34 Singleton's *Commentary* on the *Purgatorio*, ibid., p. 798, lists the occurrences of the eagle in Dante and in his sources.

35 *Commentary on the Dream of Scipio*, trans. William Harris Stahl (New York: Columbia University Press, 1952), p. 91.

36 Biblia Vulgata, ed. Colunga-Turrado (Madrid, 1955), trans. Douay-Confraternity.

37 Robert O. Payne, *The Key of Remembrance: A Study of Chaucer's Poetics* (New Haven: Yale University Press, 1963), p. 135.

38 Wetherbee, *Platonism and Poetry*, p. 174. See also Brian Stock, *Myth and Science in the Twelfth Century: A Study of Bernard Silvester* (Princeton: Princeton University Press, 1972), p. 71. It is likely that Chaucer did not know the *Cosmographia,* but its characteristic images strongly influence the works of Alanus, which Chaucer did know.

39 *De Mundi Universitate,* ed. Carl Sigmund Barach and Johann Wrobel (Innsbruck: Verlag der Wagner'schen Universitaets-Buchhandlung, 1876). The translation is by Winthrop Wetherbee, *The* Cosmographia *of Bernardus Silvestris* (New York: Columbia University Press, 1973), p. 97.

40 Leyerle, "Chaucer's Windy Eagle," 252 and 254.

41 Paget Toynbee, trans., *Dantis Alagherii Epistolae: The Letters of Dante* (2d ed., 1920; rpt. Oxford: Clarendon Press, 1966), p. 203. The Latin text appears on p. 180.

42 See Stock, *Myth and Science in the Twelfth Century,* p. 42 n.: "Alan may be the earliest poet of modern Europe to assume this role" "of the poet as a medium." Stock also cites Bruno Nardi's interesting discussion of "Dante Profeta," in Nardi's *Dante e la Cultura Medievale* (Bari: Laterza, 1942), pp. 280-309.

43 Translated by Wetherbee, *The* Cosmographia *of Bernardus Silvestris,* p. 103.

44 Ibid., p. 104. See also *Anticlaudianus* IV.332-40.

45 Joseph Anthony Mazzeo, *Structure and Thought in the* Paradiso

(Ithaca: Cornell University Press, 1958), p. 136.

46 *City of God,* XI.28, trans. Henry Bettenson (Harmondsworth: Penguin, 1972), pp. 462-63. See Mazzeo's eloquent summary of this Aristotelian idea: *Medieval Cultural Tradition in Dante's* Comedy (Ithaca: Cornell University Press, 1960), p. 43. And cf. Dante's *Convivio* III.iii.2-5; quoted and discussed in Singleton's *Commentary* on the *Purgatorio,* p. 391.

47 Cf. St. Thomas Aquinas, *Summa Theologiae* I.a.11.1: "Unde manifestum est quod esse cujuslibet rei constitit in indivisione. Et inde est quod unumquodque sicut custodit suum esse ita custodit suam unitatem" [clearly then everything's existence is grounded in indivision. And this is why things guard their unity as they do their existence]. Trans. Timothy McDermott, O.P. (New York: Blackfriars-McGraw Hill, 1964), 2:156–57.

48 Leyerle, "Chaucer's Windy Eagle," 254-55.

49 There are other, specific allusions to Dante in Book Three: the Invocation, which ends with Chaucer's comic offer to kiss the next laurel tree he sees (1106–08); and line 1908, where he is apparently mistaken for an embodied sound, instead of a living man.

50 Sheila Delany, *Chaucer's* House of Fame: *The Poetics of Skeptical Fideism* (Chicago: The University of Chicago Press, 1972), p. 110. Delany's argument has anticipated mine at several points, though I wrote the first version of this chapter before her book appeared. See esp. p. 111: "This is the depth of Chaucer's skepticism. Experience is no substitute for tradition for it is subject to the same weakness: neither can be relied on for truth."

51 Translated and discussed by W. A. Pantin, *The English Church in the Fourteenth Century* (Cambridge: Cambridge University Press, 1955), p. 213.

52 Translated by Ernest H. Wilkins, *PMLA* 68 (1953), 1247.

Chapter 3

1 Quoted by Elizabeth Armstrong, *Ronsard and the Age of Gold* (Cambridge: Cambridge University Press, 1968), p. 48.

2 *Confessio Amantis* (Prol. 121), in *The English Works of John*

Gower, ed. G. C. Macaulay, EETS, e.s. 81 (1900; rpt. London: Oxford University Press, 1969), I, 7.

3 *Le Paradys d'Amours,* 1-12, in *Œuvres de Froissart: Poésies,* ed. Auguste Scheler (Brussels: V. Devaux, 1870), I, 1.

4 John Gower sums up the paradox in the lovely refrain to his "Balade XXVII": "Mieulx vuill languir qe sanz vous estre sein" [I would rather languish than be healthy without you]. *The Works of John Gower: The French Works,* ed. G. C. Macaulay (Oxford: Oxford University Press, 1899), p. 360.

5 *Le Dit dou Bleu Chevalier,* 1-3, in *Froissart,* ed. Scheler, I, 348. Cf. Chaucer's *Parliament of Fowls,* 90-91.

6 *Paradys d'Amours,* 15-32.

7 "Balade XXXV," 25-30, in *Œuvres Complètes de Eustache Deschamps,* ed. le marquis de Queux de Saint-Hilaire and Gaston Raynaud, SATF (Paris, 1878-1903), I, 118-19.

8 *La Fonteinne Amoureuse,* 699-718, in *Œuvres de Guillaume de Machaut,* ed. Ernest Hœpffner, SATF (Paris, 1908-21), III, 168.

9 *Metamorphoses* XI.410-750. See esp. 445, 544-45, and 740-46.

10 Cf. Petrarch, *Trionfo d'Amore* II.157-59, in *Opere,* ed. Emilio Bigi (Milan: Ugo Mursia, 1963), p. 274:

> que' duo che fece Amor compagni eterni,
> Alcione e Ceice, in riva al mare
> far i lor nidi a' più soavi verni.

[Those two whom Love made eternal companions, Alcyone and Ceyx, on the shore of the sea make their nests in winter's calm.]

See also Gower's "Balade XXXIIII," in *The French Works,* p. 365. Gower uses the metamorphosis to show the truth of his refrain: "U li coers est, le corps falt obeïr" [where the heart is, the body must follow]. The poet wishes that he and his beloved, like Ceyx and Alcyone, could "sanz envie et danger de la gent . . . voler tout francs en nostre esbatement" [without the jealousy and guardedness of our race, fly completely free in our delight].

11 *Metamorphoses* I.610-66.

12 "Lawe of kinde" is so glossed by E. T. Donaldson, *Chaucer's Poetry* (New York: Ronald Press, 1958), p. 425.

I use the term *Golden Age* as the most concise means of defining a complex of conventional attitudes about the relation of love to natural law and the declining world. Many of the traditional features of "The Former Age," which Chaucer's lyric (ed. Robinson, p. 534) copies from Ovid (*Metamorphoses* I.89-112) and Boethius (*De Consolatione Philosophiae* II.m.5), have no relevance to the *Book of the Duchess*: both sorrow and navigation exist in the world of Ceyx and Alcyone. But if their age is not literally the one ruled by Saturn, Chaucer does repeatedly allude to elements of primitivistic myth in order to express the moral superiority of ancient times to modern.

13 For medieval uses of the myth of the Golden Age, see George Boas, *Essays on Primitivism and Related Ideas in the Middle Ages* (Baltimore: The Johns Hopkins University Press, 1948). For the relation of the Golden Age to natural law in medieval political theory, see Sir R. W. Carlyle and A. J. Carlyle, *A History of Mediaeval Political Theory in the West,* 6 vols. (Edinburgh: Blackwood, rpt. 1962), passim, but esp. I, 81ff. and V, 441ff.

14 Cicero, as filtered through the *Roman de la Rose,* may well have influenced Chaucer here. Jean de Meun ties Cicero's claim that the world has witnessed only three or four true friendships (*De Amicitia,* par. 15) to the myth of the Golden Age (*Roman* 5356-62). Once the giants deposed the gods, Amans tells Raison, the kind of love she has been advocating " 'fu si esperdue / qu'el s'en foï, si est perdue' " (5363-64) [was so harassed that it fled and is lost]. This love is Cicero's *amicitia,* the friendship of virtuous men. But Jean's phrasing opens other possibilities; even Cicero could not so exercise his ingenuity

> qu'onc plus de .III. pere ou de .IIII.,
> de touz les siecles trespassez
> puis que cist mond fu conpassez,
> de si fines amors trouvast.

[5378-81]

[that he ever found more than three couples or four with such noble loves, in all the ages that have passed since this world was created.]

"Pere" can include two sexes as easily as one; and "fin amour" is the usual medieval term for "courtly love." Whether or not Chaucer was directly influenced by this passage in the *Roman*, the analogue it offers is an interesting one.

15 *Roman* 8325–8424.

16 *Metamorphoses* II.846–47.

17 See also 9409–12. Chaucer paraphrases 8421–24 in the *Franklin's Tale* (764–66):

> Love wol nat been constreyned by maistrye.
> Whan maistrie comth, the God of Love anon
> Beteth his wynges, and farewel, he is gon!

18 "Balade CX," in *Deschamps*, I, pp. 225–26. Cf. "Balade CCLXXI," "Contre le mariage, bonheur de l'indépendance," in *Deschamps*, II, 116–17. But see esp. "Balade XDI," which begins with the question "Quant revenra le doulx temps amoureux?" [When will the sweet amorous time return?] and has as its refrain "Car meilleur temps fu le temps ancien" [For the ancient age was a better time]: *Deschamps*, III, 315.

The idea that true love has disappeared from the declining world is conventional in medieval romance. See *The Works of Sir Thomas Malory*, ed. Eugène Vinaver (2d ed.; Oxford: Oxford University Press, 1967), III, 1119–20; and the *Yvain* of Chrétien de Troyes, ed. Mario Roques, CFMA (Paris: H. Champion, 1964), 5388–90:

> que la genz n'est mes amoronge
> ne n'ainment mes, si con il suelent,
> que nes oïr parler n'an vuelent.

[for people don't fall in love nowadays, nor do they love as they used to do, so they do not care to hear of it.]

Trans. W. W. Comfort, Chrétien de Troyes, *Arthurian Romances* (1914; rpt. London: Dent, 1970), p. 250.

19 The unstable relationship of love and *seignourie* will of course interest the Wife of Bath, the Clerk, and the Franklin. The Franklin's definition of a happy marriage (761–98) is closely akin to the man in black's portrayal of his life with "White"; its source is Ami's speech in the *Roman*, concerning the boorish jealous husband:

> et se fet seigneur de sa fame,
> qui ne redoit pas estre dame,
> mes sa pareille et sa compaigne,
> si con la loi les acompaigne,
> et il redoit ses compainz estre
> sanz soi fere seigneur ne mestre.
>
> [9395-9400]

[And he makes himself the lord of his wife, who ought not herself to be the lady, but his equal and his companion, as the law joins them, and he ought in turn to be her companion without making himself lord or master.]

The seriousness of Chaucer's egalitarian solution in the *Book of the Duchess* makes one distrust some of the recent attempts to find irony in the *Franklin's Tale.*

20 Cf. Donaldson, *Chaucer's Poetry,* p. 953: "That Nature, like the pagan god Pan, abhors the paralysis of grief and does everything it can to cure it is the underlying and unifying theme of the poem."

21 See the note to line 368 in *Works,* ed. Robinson.

22 Bernard F. Huppé and D. W. Robertson, Jr., argue that "Octovyen" is a pun meaning "Christ is coming": *Fruyt and Chaf: Studies in Chaucer's Allegories* (Princeton: Princeton University Press, 1963), pp. 49-50. Their argument has been echoed by Russell A. Peck, "Theme and Number in Chaucer's *Book of the Duchess,*" in *Silent Poetry,* ed. Alastair Fowler (London: Routledge & Kegan Paul, 1970), p. 100.

23 *Behaingne,* 421, in *Machaut,* I, 73. Machaut's poem is a major source for the *Book of the Duchess*; it no doubt gave Chaucer the idea of comparing the sorrow of two lovers—in *Behaingne,* a lady whose lover had died and a knight betrayed by his lady. John Lawlor emphasizes this correspondence between the two poems: "The Pattern of Consolation in *The Book of the Duchess,*" *Speculum* 31 (1956), 638. Rpt. in *Chaucer Criticism,* ed. Richard J. Schoeck and Jerome Taylor (Notre Dame: Notre Dame University Press, 1961), II, 243.

On the identification of "Octovyen," cf. Howard Rollin

Patch, *On Rereading Chaucer* (1939; rpt. Cambridge, Mass.: Harvard University Press, 1959), p. 199: "Perhaps Octovyen is brought in, not by way of romance at all, but as the emperor of the Golden Age, which, the poet thus implies, obtained during the happy reign of Edward the Third."

24 The association is, of course, Augustan in origin: for example, *Aeneid* VI.791-93. For its medieval history, see E. von Frauenholz, "Imperator Octavianus Augustus in der Geschichte und Sage des Mittelalters," *Historisches Jahrbuch* 46 (Munich, 1926), 86-122. I owe this reference to D. M. Grisdale, ed., *Three Middle English Sermons,* Leeds School of English Language: Texts and Monographs, no. 5 (Kendal: T. Wilson, 1939), p. 82.

25 Benvenuto's commentary on Dante interprets the *prima gente* of *Purgatorio* i.24 to mean the Romans: Charles Singleton, *Dante Studies 2: Journey to Beatrice* (Cambridge, Mass.: Harvard University Press, 1958), pp. 185-86. And Petrarch "sets forth an allegory of the virtues . . . , assigning the cardinal virtues to a first time which is that of the ancients, not of Adam and Eve" (p. 202, n. 7).

26 "Balade CLXXXVIII," in *Deschamps,* II, 15. There is also a ballade, "Plaintes contre le siècle" [Lamentations against the age], with the ironic opening "Je voy le temps Octovien / Que toute paix fut reformée" [I see the Octavian time, in which utter peace was exalted] and the refrain: "Dit il voir? Par ma foy, il ment" [Is he telling the truth? If you ask me, he's lying]. "Balade MCCCXCIV," in *Deschamps*, VII, 251.

27 *Roman* 8376. The source of this description is the "Sedes Naturae" in Alanus's *Anticlaudianus,* ed. R. Bossuat (Paris: J. Vrin, 1955), I.61ff.

28 *Paradys d'Amours,* 903-53. There is a discussion of several poems with love hunts in James Wimsatt, *Chaucer and the French Love Poets,* University of North Carolina Studies in Comparative Literature, no. 43 (Chapel Hill: University of North Carolina Press, 1968), pp. 39-48. The theme is treated exhaustively by Marcelle Thiébaux, *The Stag of Love: The Chase in Medieval Literature* (Ithaca: Cornell University Press, 1974).

29 The pun is noted by Helge Kökeritz, among others: "Rhetorical Word-Play in Chaucer," *PMLA* 69 (1954), 951. It has been most

fully incorporated into a reading of the poem by Joseph E.
Grennen, "*Hert-huntyng* in the *Book of the Duchess*," *MLQ* 25
(1964), 131-39. But also see M. Angela Carson, "Easing of the
'Hert' in the *Book of the Duchess,*" *Chaucer Review* 1 (1966),
157-60.

30 At the end of the *Paradys d'Amours*, Froissart thanks

> . . . Morpheüs le Dieu dormant
> Par lequel tout li vrai amant
> Sont conforté, et c'est raisons,
> En songes et en visions.
>
> [1718-21]

[Morpheus the sleeping god, by whom all true lovers are
comforted, and rightly so, in dreams and in visions.]

31 As Wolfgang Clemen notes, "some of the *topoi* used for the
lament (the theme of Fortune for instance), belong to the
'complaint' as well as to the elegy. A strange state of sus-
pense . . . was induced by this intermingling of the *complainte
d'amour* and the elegy": *Chaucer's Early Poetry*, p. 46.

32 Other critics have also argued that the narrator misunderstands
the knight's lyric: Kemp Malone, *Chapters on Chaucer* (Baltimore: The Johns Hopkins University Press, 1951), p. 38; and
esp. W. H. French, "The Man in Black's Lyric," *JEGP* 56 (1957),
231-41. George Lyman Kittredge's reading has been more widely
adopted: the narrator becomes a subtle confessor who does
understand the lyric but chooses to hide his knowledge in order
to provoke a therapeutic opening of the heart: *Chaucer and His
Poetry* (Cambridge, Mass.: Harvard University Press, 1915), p. 49.
(See also Clemen, *Chaucer's Early Poetry*, and Bertrand H.
Bronson, "*The Book of the Duchess* Re-opened," *PMLA* 67
[1952], 877.) This reading is initially more satisfying than the
other, but it becomes less and less so on reflection. It requires us
either to forget the first half of the poem or to believe that the
narrator, simply by falling asleep, can suddenly become a subtle
amateur psychotherapist. Kittredge's argument depends on the
fact that the knight is at first unaware of the other's presence
(460): there is no point to any pretense if he knows that the
narrator has eavesdropped, and has understood his lyric. But in

fact, after his reverie is interrupted the knight does directly tell
Chaucer the cause of his sorrow: " 'Y wreche, that deth hath
mad al naked / Of al the blysse that ever was maked' " (577-78).
If the narrator had been pretending before, there would be no
excuse to do so any longer. I think we must assume instead that
he misunderstands both these lines and the earlier lyric.

33 W. H. French alone seems to have noticed this glaring mistake:
"The Man in Black's Lyric," 236, n. 15.

34 Bronson, *"The Book of the Duchess* Re-opened," 878-79.

35 The contrast between ancient and modern has its comic side, in
the exaggerated claims the narrator makes for his decidedly
modern dream. He implies that dream-interpreters (283) and for
that matter dreams (288) are not what they once were.

36 See Ovid's tongue-in-cheek description of love in the Golden
Age:

> blanda truces animos fertur mollisse uoluptas:
> constiterant uno femina uirque loco.
> quid facerent, ipsi nullo didicere magistro;
> arte Venus nulla dulce peregit opus.
>
> [*Ars* II.477-80]

[Enticing pleasure is said to have softened savage spirits: a
woman and a man had stood still together in one place.
What they were to do, they learned without a teacher;
without art Venus completed the sweet work.]

The purpose of the *Ars Amatoria* is to teach the stratagems that
a decadent age makes necessary for success in love. The drunk,
we are told, is one of the few modern types in whom simplicity
survives: "tunc aperit mentes aeuo rarissima nostro / simplicitas,
artes excutiente deo" (I.241-42) [then simplicity, most rare in
our age, opens up the mind, when the god drives out strata-
gems]. In Jean de Meun's *Roman,* Ami prefaces his description
of the Golden Age with extensive quotations from Ovid on the
modern need for bribery and deceit (7277-7764).

37 Cf. *Knight's Tale* (1751-52): "Greet pitee was it, as it thoughte
hem alle, / That evere swich a chaunce sholde falle."

38 As editor Félix Lecoy notes, Jean de Meun copies this attack on
the declining world from Walter Map's "Dissuasio Valerii ad

Ruffinum philosophum ne uxorem ducat," in *De Nugis Curialium*, ed. M. R. James, Anecdota Oxoniensia, 14 (Oxford: Clarendon Press, 1914), p. 146: "Vexilla pudicicie tulerunt cum Sabinis Lucrecia et Penolope, et paucissimo comitatu trophea retulerunt. Amice, nulla est Lucrecia, nulla Penolope, nulla Sabina; omnes time." [Lucrece and Penelope, along with the Sabine women, carried the banners of chastity, and with an exceedingly small following brought back trophies. Friend, there is no Lucrece, no Penelope, no Sabine woman around now; fear all women.] See also vv. 129-36 of the *Comoedia Lidiae*, reprinted and translated in Larry D. Benson and Theodore M. Andersson, *The Literary Context of Chaucer's Fabliaux* (Indianapolis and New York: Bobbs-Merrill, 1971), pp. 212-13.

The jealous husband's tirade (some of which the Wife of Bath quotes in her *Prologue*) both describes and illustrates the degeneracy of modern love. It immediately follows Ami's discourse on the Golden Age, from which Chaucer translates directly his description of the *locus amoenus* (410-15). Chaucer clearly had this part of the *Roman* very much in mind when he wrote the *Book of the Duchess*; and his close attention to Jean's extended discussion of the Golden Age and declining world is the most convincing corroboration for my reading of the poem.

39 Cf. the sinister Diomede, whose artful sophistication as a lover contrasts with Troilus's innocence: "This Diomede, as he that koude his good" (*Troilus and Criseyde* V.106; also V.89).

40 D.S. Brewer lists this and other allusions to the *Commedia* in his edition of *The Parlement of Foulys* (London: Nelson, 1960), pp. 45-46.

41 The subtlety of the narrator's position is most evident in the second stanza of the poem, especially in the variety of readings editors have made of the phrase "his strokes been so sore" (13). Should the line read "I dar nat seyn 'His strokes been so sore,' " as Brewer prints it? That is to say: "I dare not utter these words because I am not a lover." Or is its meaning, as Robinson and Donaldson imply, and as seems to me more likely: "I dare not say, because his strokes are so sore, anything but 'God save swich a lord!' "? That is, that love, as the paradoxes of the first stanza made apparent, is as terrifying as it is attractive; and that Cupid delights in punishing his detractors (e.g., Troilus).

42 Critics have too readily made her choice for her. For a more restrained statement than some, see Brewer, ed., *Parlement of Foulys,* pp. 11-12: "But the first suitor is obviously preferable. He is the most noble, eloquent, dignified. Granted the premises of the whole concept of love in the *demandes d'amour*, he is obviously and eminently preferable. In contrast with the usual *demande d'amour* . . . no-one could be puzzled whom to choose."

43 Robert W. Frank, Jr., makes this point: "Structure and Meaning in the *Parlement of Foules,*" *PMLA* 71 (1956), 538.

44 He changes Cicero's "Know, therefore, that you are a god" (trans. Brewer, p. 137) to "Know thyself first immortal" (73); and he de-emphasizes "commune profyt" as a political virtue.

45 Clemen, p. 136 n.

46 Arthur Piaget, *Oton de Grandson: Sa Vie et Ses Poésies,* Société d'Histoire de la Suisse Romande: Mémoires et Documents, ser. 3, 1 (Lausanne: Librairie Payot, 1941), p. 197:

> Le dieu d'Amours a fait une maison
> Comme un chastel auprés de son manoir,
> Et si a fait deux huis en son dongon,
> Dont l'un a nom Joye et l'autre Douloir.
> Et si vous di, se la l'alez veoir,
> Par Joye fault que dedens vous entrez
> Et par Douloir fault que vous en partez.

[The god of love has made a building like a castle, next to his manor, and also has built two doors in its donjon, of which one has the name Joy and the other Dolor. And thus I tell you, if you go to see it there, by Joy you will have to enter within and by Dolor you will have to depart.]

47 The usual form of this mistake is a too close identification of Venus's temple with love's hell and of Nature's garden with its heaven. See Brewer, ed., *Parlement of Foulys,* p. 41. Also S. S. Hussey, "The Minor Poems and the Prose," in *The Middle Ages,* ed. W. F. Bolton (Sphere History of Literature in the English Language, 1; London: Sphere Books, 1970), pp. 245-46: "The first gate leads the way to 'all good fortune,' 'the heart's delight' and 'green and pleasant May,' a love which is not specifically

'courtly.' The inscription above the second gate seems to show an extreme courtly love . . . as an unattractive, indeed arid occupation."

48 Bertrand H. Bronson, *In Appreciation of Chaucer's* Parlement of Foules (University of California Publications in English, 3, No. 5; Berkeley, 1935), p. 203: "Heaven and Hell are now one; and the gates invite and threaten at the same time." Also Clemen, *Chaucer's Early Poetry*, p. 140: "For he is not concerned with two gates or paths of which one has to be selected, but with *one* entrance bearing *two* inscriptions. No 'choice' then is possible; whoever goes through the gateway accepts both possibilities."

49 Charles O. McDonald, "An Interpretation of Chaucer's *Parlement of Foules*," rpt. in *Chaucer: Modern Essays in Criticism*, ed. Edward Wagenknecht (New York: Oxford University Press, 1959), pp. 312-13. Also Brewer, ed., *Parlement of Foulys*, p. 41. Such an interpretation is analogous to the frequent effort to find Scipio's "commune profyt" at work in Nature's parliament.

50 This Chartrian myth is another version of the Ovidian theme that Chaucer develops in the *Book of the Duchess*: Nature and Venus define more emphatically, by their timeless relationship, the tonal difference between an artless, innocent past and the self-conscious, deceitful present.

51 *De Planctu Naturae*, ed. Thomas Wright, in *Anglo-Latin Satirical Poets and Epigrammatists of the Twelfth Century*, Rolls Series (London, 1872), 2: 470. Translated by Douglas M. Moffat, Yale Studies in English, 36 (New Haven, 1908), 45. See also *Roman de la Rose* 19305-11.

52 Clemen, *Chaucer's Early Poetry*, p. 146. J. A. W. Bennett also makes this point: "Yet between Chaucer's park and his temple precincts there is . . . no clear division. Nature's glade is not precisely located, Cupid's well seems to be under one of the sempiternal trees. . . ." *The Parlement of Foules: An Interpretation* (Oxford: Clarendon Press, 1957), p. 115.

53 Clemen, *Chaucer's Early Poetry*, p. 147. Also Dorothy Bethurum Loomis, "The Venus of Alanus de Insulis and the Venus of Chaucer," in *Philological Essays: Studies in Old and Middle English Language and Literature in Honour of Herbert Dean Meritt*, ed. James L. Rosier (The Hague: Mouton, 1970), p. 192:

"I think she is still the handmaiden of Nature, who presides as beneficently over this poem as she did over Alanus' *De Planctu*, and I do not find quite the contrast between the Temple of Venus and the Garden that Professor Bennett finds. To be sure, Venus is here sexual desire in a rather pure form, but I do not see it as necessarily evil or corrupt. Intense it is, and it is its intensity that Chaucer emphasizes, and its singlemindedness." She adds, on p. 193: "The principal reason why I cannot see the love of the Garden outside the Temple as good and that within as evil is simply that there are too many dubious characters in the Garden. Rape, for example, is not in the Temple but outside in the open air, and no distance at all from 'Curteysie,' 'Delyt,' and 'Gentilesse.' "

54 For example, the *City of God* XII.4, trans. Henry Bettenson (Harmondsworth: Penguin, 1972), p. 475: "As for those defects, in things of this earth, which are neither voluntary nor punishable; if we observe them closely we shall find that . . . they attest the goodness of the natures themselves, every one of which has God as its sole author and creator."

55 "Balade XXV," 22-25, in *The French Works*, ed. Macaulay, p. 366. Also see John Lydgate's St. Valentine's Day poem, "The Flour of Curtesye," in *Chaucerian and Other Pieces*, ed. W. W. Skeat (Oxford: Clarendon Press, 1897), pp. 266ff.

56 Ed. Piaget, *Oton de Grandson*, pp. 309-23. For a full summary of the poem, see Brewer, ed., *Parlement of Foulys*, p. 131.

57 H. M. Leicester, Jr., "The Harmony of Chaucer's *Parlement*: A Dissonant Voice," *Chaucer Review* 9 (1974), 25. The phrase is his, but not the argument carried to its extreme.

58 *City of God* XII.1 (p. 472): "Yet the other things in the created universe are not in a better condition because they are incapable of misery; for the other members of our body are not to be called better than our eyes, just because they cannot be blind. A sentient nature, when suffering, is better than a stone which is quite incapable of suffering; and in the same way the rational nature, even in wretchedness, is superior to the nature which is bereft both of reason and sense and therefore cannot be the victim of misery."

Chapter 4

1 He was also, in this regard, probably influenced by Machaut's
Jugement dou Roy de Navarre. James Wimsatt gives a convenient
summary of the poem: *Chaucer and the French Love Poets,*
University of North Carolina Studies in Comparative Literature,
no. 43 (Chapel Hill: University of North Carolina Press, 1968),
pp. 93-102. See also William Calin, *A Poet at the Fountain*
(Lexington: University Press of Kentucky, 1974), pp. 110-29.

2 Elsewhere, the high-toned Man of Law praises Chaucer for not
writing

> "Of thilke wikke ensample of Canacee,
> That loved hir owene brother synfully;
> (Of swiche cursed stories I sey fy!)."

                                                                    [II.78-80]

3 Eleanor Winsor Leach, "A Study in the Sources and Rhetoric of
Chaucer's *Legend of Good Women* and Ovid's *Heroides*" (Ph.D.
diss., Yale University, 1963). I arrived at this reading of the
legends independently, and discovered her excellent dissertation
halfway through writing this chapter of my own. Her work is the
fullest available description of Chaucer's ironic use of his sources.

4 *De Mulieribus Claris,* ed. Vittorio Zaccaria (vol. 10 of *Opere,* ed.
Vittore Branca; Milan: Mondadori, 1970), p. 344. I have used the
translations of Guido A. Guarino, *Concerning Famous Women*
(New Brunswick, N.J.: Rutgers University Press, 1963). Chaucer
may not have known this work, though as Robinson notes, it
seems to be the source for the tragedy of Zenobia in the *Monk's
Tale* (*Works,* p. 746). In any case, it usefully sums up medieval
attitudes toward Chaucer's "good women."

5 "Regina vero ad pedes Augusti provoluta temptavit eius oculos,
sed spreta ab eo desperavit" [the queen in fact, having thrown
herself down at the feet of Augustus, tried to tempt his eyes, but
spurned by him she despaired]. Quoted by Pauline Aiken,
"Chaucer's *Legend of Cleopatra* and the *Speculum Historiale,*"
Speculum 13 (1938), 232-33.

6 *De Mulieribus Claris,* ed. Zaccaria, p. 354.

7 With a great deal of reluctance I exclude Cleopatra's most

notorious ship, the golden barge on which she sailed up the Cydnus to meet Antony. It is described, so far as I have been able to discover, only by Plutarch's *Life of Antony*, which Chaucer could not have known. But there are several other over-loaded ships associated with Cleopatra, in the medieval accounts of her life and in the Latin classics available to a medieval reader. One was the cause of Ptolemy's death: "fugam scapha temptaret et plurium irruentium pressa pondere mergeretur" (*De Mulieribus Claris*, ed. Zaccaria, p. 346) [when he attempted to flee in a boat, it sank, weighted down by the great number of men in it] (Guarino, *Concerning Famous Women*, p. 193). This detail comes from Orosius's *Historiae adversum Paganos*, ed. C. Zangemeister (Leipzig: Teubner, 1889), VI.16.2; a few lines before, Caesar himself is nearly done in by a *scapha* overloaded with other men (VI.15.34; p. 216), but he escapes by swimming.

There is also Boccaccio's description in *De Casibus Illustrium Virorum* of the fleet of Antony and Cleopatra just prior to the battle of Actium; *A Facsimile Reproduction of the Paris Edition of 1520*, ed. Louis B. Hall (Gainesville, Fla.: Scholars' Facsimiles & Reprints, 1962), p. 164: "Parataque classe in qua potius Sabaeorum Arabum Syrorum aliorumque odores purpuras et insignia Regum quam hostilia armi gestari arbitrareris" [with an equipped fleet in which you would have thought were carried Sabaean, Arabian, Syrian, and other perfumes, purple cloths, and the insignia of kings instead of hostile arms]. Florus's *Epitome* blames the clumsy bulk of their ships for their defeat; trans. Edward Seymour Forster (1929; rpt. Cambridge, Mass.: Harvard University Press, 1960), II.xxi.5-6: "non sine gemitu maris et labore ventorum ferebantur; quae quidem ipsa moles exitio fuit" [they made the sea groan and the wind labour as they moved along. Their very size, indeed, was fatal to them]. The sea is littered after the battle by "Arabumque et Sabaeorum et mille Asiae gentium spolia purpura auroque inlita" (II.xxi.7) [the purple and gold-bespangled spoils of the Arabians and Sabaeans and a thousand other Asiatic peoples].

8 Robert Worth Frank, Jr., *Chaucer and* The Legend of Good Women (Cambridge, Mass.: Harvard University Press, 1972), p. 42.

9 Quoted by Aiken, "Chaucer's *Legend of Cleopatra,*" 232.
10 *De Mulieribus Claris,* ed. Zaccaria, p. 350. Guarino, *Concerning Famous Women,* p. 194.
11 The detail appears in the *Metamorphoses* and the *Ovide Moralisé;* see Sanford B. Meech, "Chaucer and the *Ovide Moralisé—*A Further Study," *PMLA* 46 (1931), 187.
12 *De Mulieribus Claris,* ed. Zaccaria, p. 80. Guarino, *Concerning Famous Women,* p. 33.
13 Meech, "Chaucer and the *Ovide Moralisé,*" 197-98. Also Leach, "Chaucer's *Legend of Good Women,*" p. 190.
14 Guido delle Colonne, *Historia Destructionis Troiae,* ed. Nathaniel Edward Griffin (Cambridge, Mass.: The Mediaeval Academy of America, 1936), p. 17.
15 Ibid., p. 25.
16 The Man of Law accuses

"The crueltee of the, queene Medea,
Thy litel children hangynge by the hals,
For thy Jason, that was of love so fals!"
[II. 72-74]

17 To be sure, Jason's deceit against the two heroines is punished in the *Inferno* (xviii.86-97).
18 Frank, *Chaucer and* The Legend of Good Women, p. 68. Also Robinson's note to 1114ff., in *Works,* p. 849.
19 Valerius Flaccus, *Argonautica* II.369-92; quoted and discussed by Leach, "Chaucer's *Legend of Good Women,*" p. 173.
20 Cf. the extreme view of Boccaccio, in *De Mulieribus Claris,* where the good woman is essentially a man.
21 Donaldson, "The Ending of 'Troilus,' " in *Speaking of Chaucer,* p. 94.
22 Leach, "Chaucer's *Legend of Good Women,*" p. 200.
23 For Chaucer's continuing interest in this issue, see Robert O. Payne, *The Key of Remembrance.* It also appears in Guido delle Colonne's account of the Trojan War (ed. Griffin, p. 3), and in the fifteenth-century English translations of his work, Lydgate's *Troy Book* and the *Destruction of Troy.* See Paul Strohm, "*Storie, Spelle, Geste, Romaunce, Tragedie*: Generic Distinctions in the Middle English Troy Narratives," *Speculum* 46 (1971), esp. 348-52.

24 Translated by C. G. Osgood, *Boccaccio on Poetry* (Princeton: Princeton University Press, 1930), pp. 10-11.

25 Quoted by Aage Brusendorff, *The Chaucer Tradition* (London: Oxford University Press, 1925), p. 35.

26 D. S. Brewer notes in the *Sphere History: The Middle Ages,* ed. W. F. Bolton, p. 205, that "this," in *Troilus,* is "usually a distancing, even half-mocking qualifier." But cf. Margaret Schlauch, "Chaucer's Narrative Art," in *Chaucer and Chaucerians,* ed. D. S. Brewer (University, Ala.: University of Alabama Press, 1966), pp. 134-35.

27 See E. Bagby Atwood, "Two Alterations of Virgil in Chaucer's *Dido,"* Speculum 13 (1938), 454-57.

28 *Works,* p. 849, note to 1232-37.

29 See Louis B. Hall, "Chaucer and the Dido-and-Aeneas Story," *Mediaeval Studies* 25 (1963), 158.

An amusing epilogue to this controversy appears in Gavin Douglas's translation of the *Aeneid*: see Priscilla Bawcutt, *Gavin Douglas* (Edinburgh: Edinburgh University Press, 1976), pp. 83-84. Douglas, after mounting "a respectful attack on Chaucer"— "My mastir Chauser gretly Virgill offendit"—" . . . then defends Aeneas in terms of his destiny and his duty to obey the will of the gods. . . . That such an approach was new and uncongenial to some at least of Douglas's Scottish readers can be seen" in one of the marginal notes: "This argument excusis nocht the tratory of Eneas na his maynsweryng. . . . He falit than gretly to the sueit Dydo, quhilk falt reprefit nocht the goddes diuinite, for thai had na diuinite, as said is befoir."

30 Cf. Boccaccio's remarks on the laziness of scribes (*librariorum desidia*): *De Mulieribus Claris,* p. 394. Trans. Guarino, *Concerning Famous Women,* p. 220.

31 Jorge Luis Borges, "Pierre Menard, Author of the *Quixote,"* trans. James E. Irby, in *Labyrinths* (New York: New Directions, 1964).

32 Roger Ascham's *Scolemaster* lists as one of the ways by which a poet may imitate a classical model: "This and that he leaueth out, which he doth wittelie to this end and purpose." Quoted by Alice S. Miskimin, *The Renaissance Chaucer* (New Haven: Yale University Press, 1975), p. 45.

33 See John L. Lowes, "The Prologue to the *Legend of Good*

Women as related to the French Marguerite Poems, and the *Filostrato,*" *PMLA* 19 (1904), 593-683; and James I. Wimsatt, *The Marguerite Poetry of Guillaume de Machaut,* University of North Carolina Studies in the Romance Languages and Literatures, no. 87 (1970).

34 *Froissart,* ed. Scheler, II (1871), p. 33, vv. 1106-09.

35 Ibid., I, 187; vv. 3380-83. See B. J. Whiting, "Froissart as Poet," *Mediaeval Studies* 8 (1946), 189-216; esp. 197, 203.

36 Bernardus Silvestris, *De Mundi Universitate,* ed. Carl Sigmund Barach and Johann Wrobel (Innsbruck: Verlag der Wagner'schen Universitaets-Buchhandlung, 1876), I.iii.375-76; trans. Winthrop Wetherbee, p. 84.

37 Wimsatt, ed., *The Marguerite Poetry,* p. 22.

38 *Froissart,* II, p. 211. Froissart also invents a myth about the origin of the daisy (65-79); it also appears in *Pastourelle* XVII, 57-66 (p. 345). He may well have given Chaucer the idea for doing so.

39 "Balade DXXXIX," in *Deschamps,* III, p. 380.

40 For whatever reason, the G version of the *Prologue*—usually considered to be the later of the two—tones down or deletes a good deal of this religious imagery. Because of its greater clarity, I quote from the F version, except when otherwise noted.

41 Described by C. S. Lewis, *The Allegory of Love* (Oxford: Clarendon Press, 1936), p. 20. Also see his essay "What Chaucer Really Did to *Il Filostrato,*" rpt. *Chaucer Criticism,* ed. Richard J. Schoeck and Jerome Taylor (Notre Dame: Notre Dame University Press, 1961), II, 26.

42 Cf. the opening of the *Filostrato* (I.2), trans. Nathaniel E. Griffin and Arthur B. Myrick (Philadelphia: University of Pennsylvania Press, 1929), pp. 132-33:

> Tu donna se' la luce chiara e bella,
> Per cui nel tenebroso mondo accorto
> Vivo. . . .

> [Thou, lady, art the clear and beautiful light under whose guidance I live in this world of shadows.]

43 Cf. Dante's mention, and Charles Singleton's interesting discussion of the "blackbird's days," in *Purgatorio* xiii. 123.

44 See D. A. Pearsall, ed., *The Floure and the Leafe and The Assembly of Ladies* (London and Edinburgh: Nelson, 1962).

45 G. L. Marsh, "Sources and Analogues of 'The Flower and the Leaf,' " *MP* 4 (1906-07), 128.

46 *De Mulieribus Claris,* ed. Zaccaria, p. 20. Guarino, *Concerning Famous Women,* p. xxxiv.

Chapter 5

1 *The Book of Theseus,* trans. Bernadette Marie McCoy (New York: Medieval Text Association, 1974), p. 336. The Italian text appears in *Teseida,* ed. Limentani, pp. 246-47: "sotto il nome dell'uno de' due amanti e della giovane amata si conta essere stato, ricordandovi bene, e io a voi di me e voi a me di voi, se non mentiste, potreste conoscere essere stato detto e fatto in parte: quale de' due si sia non discuopro, ché so che ve ne avvedrete."

Machaut uses the surrogate relationship in much the same way, as William Calin shows in his discussion of the *Fonteinne Amoureuse.* "The Narrator and the Lover are spiritual twins. They both suffer from insomnia and melancholia. They are both unhappy lovers. They both write poetry. . . . The Lover is, to some extent, the Narrator's double, an alter ego on whom he has projected his own frustration. By rendering the Lover even more miserable than himself and by placing him in a situation more hopeless than his own, the Narrator renders his own burdens lighter." *A Poet at the Fountain: Essays on the Narrative Verse of Guillaume de Machaut* (Lexington: University Press of Kentucky, 1974), p. 157; also see pp. 47-48 and 87.

2 See Robert K. Root's note to *Troilus* I.161: Root ed., p. 413.

3 *Filostrato,* trans. Nathaniel E. Griffin and Arthur B. Myrick, pp. 124-27: "E il modo fu questo, di dovere in persona di alcuno passionato, siccome io era e sono, cantando narrare i miei martirii. Meco adunque con sollecita cura cominciai a rivolgere l'antiche storie, per trovare cui potessi verisimilmente fare scudo del mio segreto e amoroso dolore. Nè altro più atto nella mente mi venne a tal bisogno, che il valoroso giovane Troilo. . . ."

It is interesting, though not directly relevant to my argument, that "in the margin of the Laurentian autograph, Boccaccio has designed a conventional hand directing attention to his comment on the innate feminine vanity of Emilia." Also, "Boccaccio's description of the anguish of the lovers, Palemone and Arcita, ... is glossed ... with the words *che sono io*" [McCoy, trans., *The Book of Theseus,* p. 95: "I am that man"]. Robert A. Pratt, "Chaucer's Use of the *Teseida,*" *PMLA* 62 (1947), 601, n. 9.

4 This is as good a place as any to forestall two possible objections from biographical criticism—namely, that Chaucer does not identify himself with Troilus or the two lovers of the *Knight's Tale* simply because he was in his forties when he wrote the two poems; and that one cannot talk about the Knight as a narrator because Chaucer wrote "Palamon and Arcite" before he began the *Canterbury Tales.* We in fact have no idea how much Chaucer revised this earlier poem to make it the *Knight's Tale*; and I will argue that, in its present form, it serves to characterize the Knight. No doubt Chaucer would inevitably have changed Boccaccio's decidedly youthful and passionate narrator, unless an unaltered *Teseida* were to become, say, the *Squire's Tale.* But whatever the historical genesis of the change, this chapter argues for its carefully worked out detail and complex poetic effect.

5 "Palamon and Arcite" is named as one of Chaucer's works in the *Prologue* to the *Legend of Good Women* (F 420); Chaucer adapts Arcite's apotheosis at the end of the *Teseida* for use at the end of *Troilus.* W. W. Skeat lists a number of phrases in the *Knight's Tale* which he believes have been copied from *Troilus* in *The Complete Works of Geoffrey Chaucer* (Oxford: Clarendon Press, 1894-97), III, 394.

6 For example: John L. Lowes, *Geoffrey Chaucer and the Development of His Genius* (Boston: Houghton Mifflin, 1934), p. 144.

   There has been increasing attention to the parallel roles of Pandarus and the narrator as artists. See, for example, Gerry Brenner, "Narrative Structure in Chaucer's *Troilus and Criseyde,*" *Annuale Mediaevale* 6 (1965), 10; and Donald W. Rowe, *O Love O Charite! Contraries Harmonized in Chaucer's* Troilus (Carbondale: Southern Illinois University Press, 1976), p. 153. Indeed, much of my argument has been made, in adumbrated form. See note 10 to Morton Bloomfield, "Distance and Predestination in *Troilus and Criseyde*," *PMLA* 72 (1957), 14-26; Robert W. Hanning, "The Theme of Art and Life in Chaucer's Poetry," in *Geoffrey Chaucer*, ed. George D. Economou (New York: McGraw-Hill, 1975), p. 19; and Donald R. Howard, intro. to *Troilus and Criseyde*, ed. Donald R. Howard and James Dean (New York: Signet, 1976), p. xxiv.

7 *Filostrato* I.2, in Griffin and Myrick, pp. 132-33.

8 Pandaro's lack of success, in contrast, is his own fault: he has violated the lover's vow of secrecy, and thus deserves his lady's disdain. *Filostrato* II.11.

9 Cf. the *Knight's Tale* (1530-31), where Arcite falls "into a studie," "As doon thise loveres in hir queynte geres."

10 In the *Filostrato*, these lines are addressed to the "bella donna" who is Boccaccio's muse: "Tuo sia l' onore, e mio si sia l'affanno, / Se i detti alcuna laude acquisteranno" (I.5, pp. 134-35) [Thine be the honor and mine be the labor, if these words shall acquire any praise].

11 See Robinson's note to I.1065ff. in *Works*, p. 818.

12 Noted by Root's edition, p. 430. This part of my argument is implicit in note 10 to Morton W. Bloomfield's important essay "Distance and Predestination in *Troilus and Criseyde*," rpt. *Chaucer Criticism*, ed. Richard J. Schoeck and Jerome Taylor (Notre Dame: Notre Dame University Press, 1961), II, 210.

13 John J. O'Connor, "The Astronomical Dating of Chaucer's *Troilus*," *JEGP* 55 (1956), 556-62.

14 E. T. Donaldson has an interesting discussion of this issue: *Chaucer's Poetry*, pp. 972-73.

15 Bloomfield, "Distance and Predestination," pp. 202ff.

16 He makes the same joke in the *House of Fame* by referring to the "lytel laste bok" of the poem, which is in fact as long as the first two books combined (1093).

17 Payne, *The Key of Remembrance*, pp. 210-11.

18 He does so, in each work, by giving an undue weight to predestination and the workings of blind fate. For an example, see *Knight's Tale* 1303ff. In the speeches Chaucer adapts from Boethius, Troilus's soliloquy on predestination (IV.998ff.) and Theseus's discourse on the First Mover (2987ff.), he omits the

more optimistic, consolatory parts of Boethius's argument.

19 The most important essay on this aspect of the *Tale* remains Charles Muscatine's "Form, Texture, and Meaning in Chaucer's *Knight's Tale*," *PMLA* 65 (1950), 911-29; included in a revised form in *Chaucer and the French Tradition*. A recent discussion of the issue is Ronald B. Herzman's "The Paradox of Form: *The Knight's Tale* and Chaucerian Aesthetics," *PLL* 10 (1974), 339-52.

20 There is some attention paid to this doubling, though a very different interpretation of its meaning, in Alastair Fowler and Douglas Brooks, "The Meaning of Chaucer's 'Knight's Tale,' " *Medium Ævum* 39 (1970), 141.

21 The process of their estrangement is much more drawn out in the *Teseida*. The two lovers comfort each other after their first sight of Emilia (III.26). Palemone's response when Arcita is released from prison is much more restrained than that of Chaucer's Palamon: "quasi prese nova gelosia / di ciò ch'ancor non aveva in balia" (III.60) [a new jealousy, which did not yet have him in its power, almost took hold of him] (trans. McCoy, *The Book of Theseus*, p. 88). But they part as friends and embrace each other warmly (III.81).

22 Boccaccio describes the rites in detail (VII.72-76).

23 Robinson notes: "These lines, which are omitted in the best MSS., seem to be by Chaucer, though he may have intended to cancel them." *Works*, p. 681.

24 To name two instances among several: Joseph Westlund, "The *Knight's Tale* as an Impetus for Pilgrimage," *PQ* 43 (1964), 526-37; Jeffrey Helterman, "The Dehumanizing Metamorphoses of *The Knight's Tale*," *ELH* 38 (1971), 493-511.

25 Translated by McCoy, *The Book of Theseus*, p. 72.

26 I am indebted to William R. Crawford for this point. K. B. McFarlane retells a macabre anecdote, which reveals in an interesting fashion the typical fourteenth-century expectations about ransom. *The Nobility of Later Medieval England* (Oxford: Clarendon Press, 1973), p. 19: "I am reminded of an incident described by the Oxfordshire chronicler, Geoffrey le Baker of Swinbrook. It was in October 1338 and at Southampton, when the town had been surprised and occupied one Sunday morning

during Mass by a fleet of French privateers. Among these latter was a young knight, the King of Sicily's son, and when next day the townsmen, with the help of their country neighbours, quickly turned the tables on the invaders, he was clubbed to the ground by a rustic. Prostrate, he cried for quarter: 'Rancon' (i.e., 'ransom'). But, 'Yes, I know you're a Francon,' the man replied and killed him; for, says Baker, 'he did not understand the other's lingo (*idioma*), nor had he been taught to hold gentlemen prisoners for their ransom.' "

27 Teseo gives a similar speech in the *Teseida* (VII.8-12), but its tone and context are entirely different.

28 Saturn, its deviser in the *Knight's Tale,* does not appear in the *Teseida.*

29 Walter Clyde Curry, *Chaucer and the Mediaeval Sciences* (1926; rpt. New York: Barnes & Noble, 1960), pp. 130ff.

30 Cf. the portrait of Envy in the *Romaunt of the Rose*, which the Monk in this respect embodies:

> And by that ymage, nygh ynough,
> Was peynted Envye, that never lough,
> Nor never wel in hir herte ferde,
> But if she outher saugh or herde
> Som gret myschaunce or gret disese.
> Nothyng may so moch hir plese
> As myschef and mysaventure;
> Or whan she seeth discomfiture
> Upon ony worthy man falle,
> Than likith hir wel withalle.
> She is ful glad in hir corage,
> If she se any gret lynage
> Be brought to nought in shamful wise.
> And if a man in honour rise,
> Or by his wit or by his prowesse,
> Of that hath she gret hevynesse.
> For, trustith wel, she goth nygh wod
> Whan any chaunce happith god.

[247-64]

Chapter 6

1 The recent work of Donald R. Howard on this topic is very useful: *The Idea of the Canterbury Tales* (Berkeley: University of California Press, 1976).

2 Howard emphasizes this aspect of the shift: "In this sequence of tales, Knight-Miller-Reeve-Cook, there is a degenerative movement. We begin with something magnificent and end with something gross . . ." (ibid., p. 245).

3 Cf. Jill Mann, *Chaucer and Medieval Estates Satire* (Cambridge: Cambridge University Press, 1973), p. 200. She argues that "the centre of interest in the *Prologue* is not in any depiction of human character, in actuality for its own sake; it is in our relationship with the actual, the way in which we perceive it and the attitudes we adopt to it, and the narrator stands here for the ambiguities and complexities that characterise this relationship."

4 Much of this paragraph rehearses critical commonplaces. See, for example, Kemp Malone's discussion of the *Prologue* in *Chapters on Chaucer*, pp. 144-67. Also see Mann, *Chaucer and Medieval Estates Satire*, p. 174, on the Manciple's "sette hir aller cappe" (586) and the Shipman's "by water he sente hem hoom" (400). These phrases reveal "the euphemistic way in which the perpetrator of an action represents it *to himself.* Such specialist, elusive idioms represent a refusal to apply absolute values to the practice of one's profession."

5 See D. S. Brewer's interesting essay "Class Distinction in Chaucer," *Speculum* 43 (1968), 290-305.

6 See William Frost, "An Interpretation of Chaucer's Knight's Tale," *RES* 25 (1949), 303; and W. C. Stokoe, "Structure and Intention in the First Fragment of the *Canterbury Tales,*" *University of Toronto Quarterly* 21 (1952), 120-27.

7 Donaldson, *Chaucer's Poetry,* p. 948.

8 Richard Hazelton's essays are useful: "The *Manciple's Tale*: Parody and Critique," *JEGP* 62 (1963), 1-31; and especially "Chaucer and Cato," *Speculum* 35 (1960), 357-80.

9 The temptation to quote Hamlet is irresistible here; and I find that Donald Howard has anticipated me in doing so: "The Manciple's Tale lets language itself fall beneath corrupt human

nature. The rest, or at least the end, is silence" (*The Idea of the Canterbury Tales*, p. 304).

10 Alan T. Gaylord has argued that the subject of Fragment VII is "the art of storytelling": "*Sentence* and *Solaas* in Fragment VII of the *Canterbury Tales*: Harry Bailly as Horseback Editor," *PMLA* 82 (1967), 226.

11 A point made by Edmund Reiss, in his review of Beryl Rowland's *Blind Beasts*: in *Speculum* 49 (1974), 152.

12 J. Leslie Hotson, "Colfox *vs.* Chauntecleer," rpt. on *Chaucer*, ed. Edward Wagenknecht (New York: Oxford University Press, 1959), pp. 108-09. The essay originally appeared in *PMLA* 39 (1924), 762-81.

13 Cf. *Le Roman de Renart*, where the dream apparition is fragmentary and mysterious:

> Et tenoit un ros pelicon
> Dont les goles estoient d'os.
> Si li metoit par force el dos.
>
> (140-42]

[It wore a red fur coat, the neck of which was of bone, and forced it on Chauntecleer's back.]

Trans. James R. Hulbert, in *Sources and Analogues of Chaucer's Canterbury Tales*, ed. W. F. Bryan and Germaine Dempster (1941; rpt. New York: Humanities Press, 1958), p. 650.

14 In the *Renart* Pinte (i.e., Pertelote) interprets the dream correctly and warns Chantecler; the foolish rooster disregards her good counsel (ibid., pp. 652-53). Chaucer's Chauntecleer wins the argument, at least to his own satisfaction; but he forgets the victory because of his amorous desires (3157-71), and falls prey to the fox's flattery.

15 There is a similar irony in the *Speculum Stultorum*: Brunellus spends seven years at the University of Paris, but all he knows how to do afterward is to say "hee-haw," which he knew how to do naturally. See Jill Mann's interesting remarks on this work in "The *Speculum Stultorum* and the *Nun's Priest's Tale*," *Chaucer Review* 9 (1975), 262-82.

BIBLIOGRAPHY

Bennett, J. A. W. *The Parlement of Foules: An Interpretation.* Oxford: Clarendon Press, 1957.

Bethurum, Dorothy. "Chaucer's Point of View as Narrator in the Love Poems." *PMLA* 74 (1959), 511-20.

Bloomfield, Morton W. "Distance and Predestination in *Troilus and Criseyde,*" *PMLA* 72 (1957), 14-26.

Brewer, Derek S. *Chaucer in His Time.* London: Nelson, 1963.

Bronson, Bertrand H. *In Appreciation of Chaucer's* Parlement of Foules. *University of California Publications in English*, 3, no. 5 (Berkeley, 1935), 193-223.

Clemen, Wolfgang. *Chaucer's Early Poetry,* trans. C. A. M. Sym. London: Methuen, 1963.

Delany, Sheila. *Chaucer's* House of Fame: *The Poetics of Skeptical Fideism.* Chicago: The University of Chicago Press, 1972.

Donaldson, E. Talbot. *Speaking of Chaucer.* London: Athlone Press, 1970.

Donaldson, E. T., ed. *Chaucer's Poetry: An Anthology for the Modern Reader.* New York: Ronald Press, 1958; 2d. ed., 1975.

Elbow, Peter. *Oppositions in Chaucer.* Middletown, Conn.: Wesleyan University Press, 1975.

Eldredge, Laurence. "Chaucer's *Hous of Fame* and the *Via Moderna.*" *Neuphilologische Mitteilungen* 71 (1970), 105-19.

Frank, Robert W., Jr. "Structure and Meaning in the *Parlement of Foules.*" PMLA 71 (1956), 530-39.

Hanning, Robert W. "The Theme of Art and Life in Chaucer's Poetry." *Geoffrey Chaucer,* ed. George D. Economou (New York: McGraw-Hill, 1975), pp. 15-36.

Howard, Donald R. *The Idea of the Canterbury Tales.* Berkeley and Los Angeles: University of California Press, 1976.

Kittredge, George L. *Chaucer and His Poetry.* Cambridge, Mass.; Harvard University Press, 1915.

Koonce, B. G. *Chaucer and the Tradition of Fame: Symbolism in The House of Fame*. Princeton: Princeton University Press, 1966.

Lanham, Richard A. *The Motives of Eloquence: Literary Rhetoric in the Renaissance*. New Haven: Yale University Press, 1976.

Lawlor, John. "The Pattern of Consolation in *The Book of the Duchess.*" *Speculum* 31 (1956), 626–48.

Leach, Eleanor Winsor. "A Study in the Sources and Rhetoric of Chaucer's *Legend of Good Women* and Ovid's *Heroides.*" Ph.D. dissertation, Yale University, 1963.

Leyerle, John. "Chaucer's Windy Eagle." *University of Toronto Quarterly* 40 (1971), 247-65.

Lowes, John L. *Geoffrey Chaucer and the Development of His Genius*. Boston: Houghton Mifflin, 1934.

Lowes, John L. "Is Chaucer's *Legend of Good Women* a Travesty?" *JEGP* 8 (1909), 513-69.

Lowes, John L. "The Prologue to the *Legend of Good Women* as related to the French Marguerite Poems, and the *Filostrato.*" *PMLA* 19 (1904), 593-683.

Malone, Kemp. *Chapters on Chaucer*. Baltimore: The Johns Hopkins University Press, 1951.

Murtaugh, Daniel. "Women and Geoffrey Chaucer." *ELH* 38 (1971), 473-92.

Muscatine, Charles. *Chaucer and the French Tradition*. Berkeley and Los Angeles: University of California Press, 1957.

Owen, Charles A., Jr. "The Problem of Free Will in Chaucer's Narratives." *PQ* 46 (1967), 433-56.

Patch, Howard R. *On Rereading Chaucer*. Cambridge, Mass.: Harvard University Press, 1939.

Payne, Robert O. *The Key of Remembrance: A Study of Chaucer's Poetics*. New Haven: Yale University Press, 1963.

Pratt, Robert A. "Chaucer and the Hand That Fed Him." *Speculum* 41 (1966), 619-42.

Robertson, D. W., Jr. *A Preface to Chaucer: Studies in Medieval Perspectives*. Princeton: Princeton University Press, 1963.

Smyser, H. M. "The Domestic Background of *Troilus and Criseyde.*" *Speculum* 31 (1956), 297-315.

Wetherbee, Winthrop. *Platonism and Poetry in the Twelfth Century*. Princeton: Princeton University Press, 1972.

INDEX

203